DAG HAMMARSKJÖLD REVISITED

United Nations

Dag Hammarskjöld photographed in his private apartment on the 38th floor of the Secretariat building at United Nations Headquarters in New York. He is standing in front of "Woman Combing Her Hair," a painting by Fernand Leger, lent to the United Nations by New York's Museum of Modern Art.

Dag Hammarskjöld Revisited

The UN Secretary-General as a Force in World Politics

EDITED BY Robert S. Jordan

International Relations Series Number 8
Institute of International Studies
University of South Carolina

Carolina Academic Press

Durham, North Carolina

© 1983 by the University of South Carolina
All rights reserved.
ISBN 0-89089-233-4
LCC 81-70434
Printed in the United States of America.

Carolina Academic Press
Post Office Box 8795
Durham, North Carolina 27707

THIS BOOK IS DEDICATED TO

Dr. Joseph E. Black
Former Director, Social Sciences
The Rockefeller Foundation

As a Director in the Foundation, he shared with Dag Hammarskjöld an abiding commitment to help the new states of the international community through their birth pangs so that they could achieve political, economic, and social self-development.

Peter Steiner, whose original sketches are contained in this book, has a Ph.D. in German Literature from the University of Pittsburgh. He taught German at Dickinson College in Pennsylvania from 1969 until 1977 when he resigned his position as Associate Professor to work as an artist. His drawings appear in *The New Yorker*, *The Nation*, *The Christian Science Monitor*, *Worldview*, and a variety of other publications.

Contents

Acknowledgements   IX

Introduction   XI
   James B. Holderman
      President, The University of South Carolina

Preface   XV
   Richard L. Walker
      James F. Byrnes Professor of International Relations and former Director, Institute of International Studies, University of South Carolina

Prologue: The Legacy Which Dag Hammarskjöld Inherited and His Imprint On It   3
   Robert S. Jordan, Professor of Political Science and Dean of the Graduate School, University of New Orleans, former Dag Hammarskjöld Professor of International Relations, University of South Carolina

One: Dag Hammarskjöld and the Office of United Nations Secretary-General   15
   Kurt Waldheim
      Former Secretary-General of the United Nations

Two: The Importance of Secretaries-General of the United Nations   25
   James Barros
      Department of Political Economy, University of Toronto

Three: The International Civil Servant: Neutrality
and Responsibility 39
Oscar Schachter
> Hamilton Fish Professor of International Law and Diplomacy, School of Law, Columbia University, and a former legal adviser to Secretaries-General Lie, Hammarskjöld, and Thant

Four: An Informal Retrospection on Dag Hammarskjöld's
Commitment to Economic and Social Development 65
Philippe de Seynes
> Director, Program of Future Studies United Nations Institute for Training and Research, and former U.N. Under-Secretary-General for Economic and Social Affairs

Five: Hammarskjöld and Peacekeeping 77
Indar Jit Rikhye
> President, International Peace Academy, and former Military Adviser to the Secretary-General of the United Nations

Six: Hammarskjöld's Conception of the United Nations' Role in
World Politics 111
Mark W. Zacher
> Professor of Political Science and Director, Institute of International Relations, University of British Columbia

Seven: Dag Hammarskjöld: The Private Person in a Very
Public Office 133
Brian Urquhart
> Under-Secretary-General for Special Political Affairs, United Nations

Eight: A Bibliographic Essay on Dag Hammarskjöld 149
Larry Trachtenberg
> Department of International Relations, London School of Economics and Political Science

Bibliography 179

Index 195

Acknowledgements

The idea for this book was conceived while I was serving as the first Dag Hammarskjöld Professor of International Relations at the University of South Carolina. Each of the contributors either possesses personal knowledge of Mr. Hammarskjöld, or has written authoritatively about him or about the office which he held. The book, therefore, is intended to be in keeping with the tradition of a *Festschrift*, a set of personalized essays that capture various aspects of the career of Dag Hammarskjöld as Secretary-General, in commemoration of the twentieth anniversary of his unfortunate death.

I am grateful to many persons for their interest and support in this project, not the least of which is Dr. Richard L. Walker, who as Director of the Institute of International Studies at the University of South Carolina, was both a mentor and a valued colleague, and Dr. James B. Holderman, President of the University of South Carolina, who first took the initiative to create the Dag Hammarskjöld Chair on the occasion of awarding an honorary degree to the former Secretary-General, Dr. Kurt Waldheim. Among those who have made specific suggestions or given support in other ways, in addition to the contributors, are Elizabeth Ann Brown, Margaret Croke, Devin Ehrlich, Geoffrey Goodwin, Leon Gordenker, Matthew Gordon, Rosalyn Higgins, John Holmes, Alan James, James Kuhlman, William C. Powell, John P. Renninger, Dean Rusk, Ruth Russell, Herbert W. Sanborn, George Sherry, Susan Strange, James Sutterlin, and Richard Swift.

I am indebted also to Dr. Donald Weatherbee and Dr. Morris Blachman, in their capacities at different times as Acting Director, and Acting Associate Director, respectively, of the Institute of International Studies at the University of South Carolina, for negotiating the contract for the book and for providing budgetary support. Barbara Anderson of the Institute, and Jonnell Burgess, Gwendolyn Chaney, Judy Ladner and Carolyn Mangiaracina of the Graduate School of the University of New Orleans, provided help in manuscript preparation; Judith Wilkinson and Charles Duffy, graduate students at the University of New Orleans, assisted in the preparation of the Prologue, and Ms. Wilkinson also assisted in the compiling of the bibliography. Mr. Keith Sipe of Carolina Academic Press was a pleasant and effective collaborator as the manuscript was brought to publication, and Mr. Peter Steiner gave generously of his talent in providing original graphic and art work, and in supplying advice on the overall layout of the book.

Special thanks must go to the American-Swedish Foundation (New York), the Swedish Institute (Stockholm), the Swedish Institute of International Affairs, and the Central Research Fund (London University) for their support to Mr. Trachtenberg while he was researching the bibliographic essay.

Robert S. Jordan
New Orleans, August 1981

Introduction

The University of South Carolina and the State of South Carolina have maintained a special relationship with the United Nations throughout its development as a symbol of world peace and international development. Our own distinguished statesman and leader James F. Byrnes addressed the first session of the UN General Assembly in his capacity as United States Secretary of State. Decades later Secretary-General Kurt Waldheim inaugurated a series of public appearances by world leaders at the James F. Byrnes International Center of the University of South Carolina. In his comments before a State-wide audience on April 18, 1979, the former Secretary-General emphasized the cautious reception that world opinion gave to the new Organization in those early post-War years by quoting from Secretary Byrnes that we should, ". . . not expect a feat of magic overnight from the institutions we have created. . . Let us avoid casting excessive burdens upon the institutions of the United Nations, especially in their infancy."

Despite such admonition, certainly the people of all nations have come to expect almost impossible progress toward permanent peace and almost unattainable heights of development and prosperity out of the United Nations and its many organs. Most certainly it has been the primary accomplishment of men such as Secretary-General Hammarskjöld then and Secretary-General Waldheim later to sustain these hopes and beliefs in the face of nearly insurmountable odds.

It is with these thoughts and history in mind that we at South Carolina take privilege and pleasure in playing a small but sincere part in bringing this book before the global public. *Dag Hammarskjöld Revisited* underlines a theme in the history of humankind itself, namely that man does indeed make history and yet inevitably becomes part of the historical process itself. Hammarskjöld, Waldheim and indeed the institution of the Secretary-Generalship itself have come to embody the Organization of the United Nations. Their values and energies have determined the degree of success in the mission of the United Nations, and at the same time have guaranteed the continued faith in that Organization over and above the realities of hunger, conflict and hatred in the daily existence of men, women and children on this planet.

In any volume dedicated to the philosophy and practice of the Secretaries-General of the United Nations, it is necessary to state again the actual achievements, successes too often ignored in our attention to the events of the day. First and foremost the United Nations and the indispensable figures who have served us as its Secretary-General have brought the world to a new level of awareness and understanding of the nature of our socio-economic condition and the necessity for a new order in those economic and social affairs of all nations. Closely tied to this achievement is the fact that human rights as a universal concept first reached heightened concern and organizational action within the framework of the United Nations.

Both at the level of the unthinkable and the level of the inescapable, the United Nations and its leaders from Hammarskjöld to Waldheim have concentrated their efforts on freeing humankind from the most inhuman of outcomes, nuclear war and conventional regional conflicts. The United Nations still remains as the most hopeful of all institutions for the realization of disarmament and the halting of reckless experimentation in the quest for military superiority of one nation over another. Some six separate UN peacekeeping operations with participation by thousands of soldiers from twenty-seven nations are on watch nearly everywhere in the world for new outbreaks which threaten a precarious peace.

This world-wide monitoring by the United Nations is not confined to the military sphere of international relations, but also is sensitive to the development mission of the Organization. Energy, environment, health, and law, among other crucial concerns of the peoples on our planet are reviewed, reassessed and in many ways revitalized by the activities of the Secretary-General and the United Nations on a continuing basis. Secretary-General Hammarskjöld and all who have followed him have made great gains for the process of multilateral diplomacy, a first step in the direction of an ultimate goal to create a world community. As noted by Kurt Waldheim in his address at the University of South Carolina, "Our aim today, as it was in 1946, is nothing less than world community." While it is this bringing the world together that signifies the men and institutions about which we write in these pages, another important contribution has been made by the international civil servants and the programs of the United Nations, that of the movement for independence.

A constant theme underlies these men and their institution in their own writing and work. It is a principle that allows nations to come together with trust in the United Nations, and the people of the world to come together with pride in their nations. The United Nations represents the achievement of independence to hundreds of millions of people and to more than a hundred and fifty of their nations, clearly "the greatest independence movement in history." That fact has been institutionalized in the United Nations and has been personified from Dag Hammarskjöld to Kurt Waldheim. The scholars and practitioners in this volume who work in their name have provided us with an important statement on how human dedication can assure the achievement of independence for all of humankind.

On behalf of the University of South Carolina, its State, its Institute of International Studies, and its James F. Byrnes International Center, and in particular on behalf of the closeness with which this Carolina community feels to the development of the ideals and principles of the United Nations and the great leaders who have guided it in the critical decades since World War Two, I want to express my appreciation to the editor, authors and contributors of *Dag Hammarskjöld Revisited*. As Kurt Waldheim allowed us to revisit personally that spirit of world peace and human security by his presence and participation at the University of South Carolina, so we wish this book might in a modest way allow the world to share in that inspiration.

James B. Holderman, President
The University of South Carolina

Preface

The tragic death of United Nations Secretary-General Dag Hammarskjöld on September 17, 1961 marked the beginning of a period of doubts about the vitality and utility of the United Nations itself, particularly in the United States. Aspects of what was referred to as a "crisis of confidence" for the world organization were explored in a volume published by the Institute of International Studies of the University of South Carolina under the title *The United Nations Reconsidered*, edited by Professor Raymond A. Moore. While many of the problems explored in that volume have continued to trouble the United Nations—budgetary limitations, overloading the Secretary-General with problems which should belong with the members, expansion of peace-keeping missions, and excessive expectations from UN bodies—we are now, perhaps, sufficiently experienced to understand just what the United Nations is and what it is not. The United Nations is now accepted as a permanent fact of international life. There is certainly a clearer understanding now of its role and its limitations than two decades ago.

The UN Secretary-General has evolved into a very formidable institution in world politics. The office now has its own distinct role and style. Much of the present role of the office can be traced to developments which came under Hammarskjöld. It is fitting, therefore, that we examine Hammarskjöld's contributions and his performance in office now that there has been sufficient interval to put them in perspective.

The Editor of this volume, Professor Robert S. Jordan, served as the Dag Hammarskjöld Professor of International Relations and was an Associate of the Institute of International Studies during the academic year 1980-1981. It was he who developed the project which led to a Conference at the United Nations in May 1981 and was sponsored by the Institute. We believe that the Conference papers presented here make a significant contribution to understanding not only Hammarskjöld and his role, but to a more scholarly presentation of the office of the Secretary-General of the United

Nations, its powers and limitations. Members of the Institute of International Studies at the University of South Carolina are grateful to Professor Jordan for his energy and initiative. I believe the result is an important contribution to a scholarly understanding of the evolving institutions centered at the United Nations.

Richard L. Walker
James F. Byrnes Professor of International Relations

DAG
HAMMARSKJÖLD
REVISITED

Prologue:
The Legacy which Dag Hammarskjöld Inherited and his Imprint on it

Robert S. Jordan

Robert S. Jordan, Professor of Political Science and Dean of the Graduate School at the University of New Orleans, received his Ph.D. from Princeton and his D. Phil. from Oxford, where he was a member of St. Antony's College. His field of expertise is international relations, with a special emphasis in international organization, international administration, and West African politics. Immediately preceding his move to New Orleans in 1981, Professor Jordan served as the first Dag Hammarskjöld Professor of International Relations at the University of South Carolina. In addition to his academic positions, which includes an appointment as the Lucius N. Littauer Visiting Professor of Political Science and International Politics at the University of Sierra Leone, he has held a variety of administrative positions, most recently being Director of Research at the United Nations Institute for Training and Research (UNITAR). He has also served as a consultant to the U.S. National Aeronautics and Space Administration, the Ford Foundation, the U.S. Department of State, the U.S. Department of Education, and various professional organizations. His more recent books are *The World Food Conference and Global Problem-Solving* (with T. G. Weiss), *Political Leadership in NATO: A Study in Multinational Diplomacy;* and *The International Civil Service: Changing Role and Concepts* (with N. Graham).

One of the most memorable events in the history of the United Nations occurred when Nikita Krushchev called for Dag Hammarskjöld's resignation as Secretary-General to make way for a *troika*. This event was significant for at least two reasons. First, the failure of the call for resignation illustrated how firmly established was the notion that there should be a politically independent officer at the top of the United Nations structure, supported by an international secretariat modelled after the British civil service tradition. But at the same time, the attack on the office was a harbinger of what today has become a very open debate as to whether the original conceptions of the office and of the supporting staff can survive the political, social, and cultural pluralism of the membership itself. For example, the principles of the parliamentary process, while allowing for free expression from large and small countries alike, has not yet achieved the institutional restructuring which the non-Western membership of the Organization has encouraged. The expansion of the membership, due to the influx of Third World states over the past twenty years, has generated pressures for altering the Organization's typically Western bureaucratic construct to make it more accommodating to non-Western needs and values (bureaucratic as well as political).

The question as to the appropriate character of the United Nations had already surfaced before Dag Hammarskjöld's career as Secretary-General.[1] Thus, it is necessary to recall the founding concepts of the United Nations in order to place in proper context an understanding of the legacy which Hammarskjöld inherited and of his imprint upon this legacy.

In 1904, the concept of a disinterested secretariat was put into practice with the creation of such a staff to support the British Committee of Imperial Defense (CID), which was a permanent sub-committee of the Cabinet. This "bureaucratic cadre of non-political officials who would serve whatever 'government of the day' the sovereign empowered to rule,"[2] became the core of civil servants whose experience was applied during World War I to the problems of inter-Allied coordination. By the time of the Paris Peace talks, following the end of the protracted conflict, the influence of the British Cabinet model led to the incorporation into the Covenant of the League of Nations of a provision for a Secretary-General whose mission would be to serve all the member-states.

Even though no specific mandate was given to form a truly international secretariat composed of persons whose careers were tied to the Organization, the first Secretary-General, Sir Eric Drummond, proceeded to create such a secretariat. This meant introducing the concept of a career service, with a set of bureaucratic values sharply different from those tied to the nationalistic impulse. Despite the many other shortcomings of the League System, the creation of such an international secretariat was considered to be a desirable precedent by those who met together to create the United Nations as a means of ensuring the peace after World War II. And in fact, both the office of Secretary-General and the role of the secretariat, were strengthened in the Charter.[3] As one observer noted: ". . .

1. Philippe de Seynes, in his chapter in this book, alludes to this point.
2. Robert S. Jordan, "The Influence of the British Secretariat Tradition on the Formation of the League of Nations," in Robert S. Jordan (ed.), *International Administration: Its Evolution and Contemporary Applications* (New York: Oxford University Press, 1971) p. 29. Sidney Bailey, in his book, *The Secretariat of the United Nations* (New York: Carnegie Endowment for International Peace, 1962), places the first discussion of the idea of an international secretariat in 1693, in an essay by William Penn. (p. 17).
3. See Dag Hammarksjöld, *The International Civil Servant in Law and in Fact*, Part III. This is a lecture delivered to Congregation, University of Oxford, 30 May 1961, and reprinted in Jordan, *op. cit.*, pp. 245-271.

what had happened was the transference to an international environment of an essentially British concept of the disinterested official."[4] This is the concept that Trygve Lie inherited when he became the first Secretary-General of the United Nations in 1946.

Lie, Secretary-General from 1946 to 1953, was primarily concerned with the peacekeeping function of the United Nations. He viewed the United Nations as "the chief force that holds the world together against all the conflicting strains and stresses that are pulling it apart."[5] In contrast to Sir Eric Drummond, who was a great believer in "behind-the-scenes" diplomacy, Lie took a very public approach to the political activities of the Secretary-General. He also embraced the notion of implied powers—as derived from the American constitutional tradition—that whatever was not specifically forbidden to the office was, by implication, permissible. His successors carried the notion even further than did Lie in justifying initiatives, some of which became very controversial indeed. As Lie put it as early as 1946:

> Just a few words to make clear my own position as Secretary-General and the rights of this office under the Charter. Should the proposal of the United States representative not be carried, I hope that the Council will understand that the Secretary-General must reserve his right to make such enquiries or investigations as he may think necessary, in order to determine whether or not he should consider bringing any aspect of this matter up to the attention of the Council under the provisions of the Charter.[6]

The right to bring matters to the attention of the main political organs—the Security Council and the General Assembly—on his own initiative led to the assertion that the Secretary-General had the right by implication, under Article 99, to carry out independent investigations of situations which either could lead to a threat to the peace, or were clearly such.

As is well known, Lie encountered in the Korean crisis a situation that led to a sustained attack by the Soviet Union and its allies on the office which he held. The crisis, therefore, although described officially as a "police action" legitimized by the Security Council and sustained, through the Uniting for Peace Resolution, by the General Assembly, was in fact a civil war in the United Nations. The Secretary-General, as a consequence,

---

4. Robert Rhodes James, "The Concept of an International Civil Service," in Jordan, *Ibid.*, p. 57. This concept had its challengers, of course. See, for example, James Barros, *Betrayal from Within: Joseph Avenol, Secretary-General of the League of Nations, 1933-1940*, (New Haven: Yale University Press, 1969). For a more recent appraisal of the concept, see Robert S. Jordan, "What Has Happened to our International Civil Service? The Case of the United Nations," in *Public Administration Review*, March/April 1981.

5. Lie liked the phrase, "force for peace." See, for example, the quotation in Arthur W. Rovine, *The First Fifty Years: The Secretary-General in World Politics, 1920-1970*, (Leyden: A.W. Sitjthoff, 1970), pp. 212-213.

6. *Ibid.*, p. 258.

became a partisan presence, considered pro-Western. In the opinion of some observers, not necessarily pro-Soviet (or pro-Chinese) in political orientation, Trygve Lie deepened the split between the protagonist superpowers and prolonged a situation of open hostility that perhaps could have been ameliorated. Whatever one's view, the fact remains that Lie found himself unable to act as the spokesman for the Organization as a whole, and therefore he could not fulfill his own mandate of being "responsible to the collectivity of the Member States." Any "collective judgment of world opinion" (to use his phrase) would be hard to find as the Korean crisis evolved into a war of attrition, with one of the major parties to the conflict not even a member of the United Nations. It was doubtless scant solace, as he contemplated the prospect of an abbreviated second term, for Lie to recall his own words:

> I have been criticized by some people who are good friends of the United Nations for not intervening often enough in political issues before the United Nations. I have been criticized by others, who are equally good friends, I am sure, for intervening at all. Between these two extremes I have tried to take a common-sense middle course, conscious always of my responsibility to stand only for the interests of the United Nations as a whole.[7]

Dag Hammarskjöld was elected to succeed Lie partly in the expectation that he would concentrate on restoring the morale and self-confidence of the secretariat, which had been shaken as the superpowers waged their Cold War within the United Nations as well as elsewhere. The public, highly political, role of his predecessor was one that appeared excessive to the capacities of the office. Hammarskjöld's previous career and his personality gave credence, furthermore, to the expectation. And in fact he often avoided, in his early years, public pronouncements and other ceremonial activities, even though he did enjoy public life and unquestionably considered his election to this very visible post a great honor. Mr. Lie, conforming to the general opinion of the time, was not happy with Hammarskjöld's election precisely because Lie wanted the incumbent to carry on in a forthright, openly declarative mode. Whatever the evolution of Hammarskjöld's role might have been perceived, he himself remained uncomfortable with the ceremonial aspect of the position and did not initially view the Secretary-General as the spokesman for world public opinion. He told the Security Council in 1956, for example, that: ". . . the Secretary-General has the duty to maintain his usefulness by avoiding public stands on conflicts between Member Nations unless and until such an action might help to resolve the conflict."[8]

In his first years as Secretary-General, then, Hammarskjöld seemed

7. *Ibid.*, pp. 259-260.
8. As quoted in Leon Gordenker, *The UN Secretary-General and the Maintenance of Peace* (New York: Columbia University Press, 1967), p. 74.

prepared to remain a quiet, relatively non-controversial international civil servant, much in the Drummond tradition. But he also held cherished views about the need to hold to what would appear to be the "right" course of action, and for him this meant not only mediating between the superpowers, but also looking out for the interests of the smaller and weaker member states. Eventually, almost inevitably, he became a spokesman for the larger interests of the "world community" and not just for the "Organization." Events have a way of transforming perceptions and official behavior. In this respect, he was the obverse of his predecessor, who had started out advocating a universal concept of international political leadership, and later on was forced to justify an interventionist role viewed by a considerable minority of members to be divisive. In 1954, Lie had written:

> Should [Hammarskjöld's] conception be the same as mine, he will find it impossible to avoid the displeasure of one or more of the greater or smaller states during the years to come. He will be the target of criticism from right, left, and center.[9]

Hammarskjöld's tendency to prefer "private diplomacy" helped to resolve successfully his first major political challenge after taking office. In December, 1954, the General Assembly, after condemning the People's Republic of China for having shot down in 1953 a United Nations aircraft carrying eleven Americans, called upon the Secretary-General to seek their release through "appropriate means." In response, Hammarskjöld developed the "Peking Formula," which he based on his general authority as Secretary-General under the Charter, rather than, more narrowly, on the resolution passed by the Assembly. By doing this, Hammarskjöld believed that he had provided himself with more discretion as he negotiated with Chou En-lai for their release, which came in August. Through this experience, he also illustrated his unusual quality to form friendships with important leaders, as well as to carry on private diplomacy in a mediatory fashion.

Through this episode, not only was some good accomplished for the Organization as well as for one of the leading members, but an important precedent had been established that would enable Hammarskjöld, in the future, to base his actions on a mandate derived from the office itself under the general terms as provided in the Charter, rather than being confined to the limits of a specific resolution.[10] As time would tell, resolutions could reflect only too frequently either a shifting consensus, or a vanishing consensus.

In any event, whatever the form of consensus or non-consensus that

---

9. As quoted in Rovine, *op. cit.*, p. 269.
10. Dr. Waldheim, in his chapter in this book, refers to the Secretary-General as the "custodian of the idea of world community which is set forth in the United Nations Charter." (p. 21).

might obtain in a threat to the peace, the Secretary-General had inevitably to be involved with the Security Council or the General Assembly, although in the earlier years of the Organization a distinction in the respective roles clearly existed. Gradually, however, the Secretary-General had come to play a greater role in the Council, rather than standing back and carefully preserving a Drummond-like "servant-to-the-political masters" posture.[11]

By 1956, Hammarskjöld had taken the power of the office to its highest point yet when the General Assembly overwhelmingly approved his plan for a United Nations Emergency Force (UNEF) to resolve the Suez crisis. His handling of the crisis in such a fashion was important because it marked the first use of what Hammarskjöld came to term "preventive diplomacy"—i.e., using the United Nations to intervene in order to forestall or preclude intervention by the major world powers, and in particular the two superpowers. Perhaps more important in practical political terms, the Secretary-General had delegated to him discretionary power to organize and administer an international military force. He became a commander-in-chief of his own army—a role which Sir Eric Drummond would never have hoped for, or for that matter, wanted. This elevated Hammarskjöld's office to a leading place in international politics. No longer could the office be compared to the Pope's as consisting of moral authority, but without the terrestrial means to change the course of history.[12] Both occupants of these very high and very visible political offices must, of course, be constantly aware of the limitations of their positions as well as of the institutional sources of their power. But the Secretary-General, perhaps, must be more sensitive of the need to conduct his office so that he will not create prejudices against the office in the future.[13]

There are some observers who feel that Dag Hammarskjöld indeed left such a prejudicial legacy to his successor. The over-reaching of his authority by pursuing the "outer limits" of a resolution, in the view of some qualified

11. The tendency to intertwine the political activities of the Secretary-General with those of the Security Council has continued into the present, and has led to the growing practice of private consultations, with the public sessions given over to formal debate. Some observers have feared that the Secretary-General would become too powerful behind-the-scenes. One result, paradoxically, has been a greater involvement of the President of the Security Council in the implementation of Council decisions. (See Davidson Nicol, *Paths to Peace: The UN Security Council and Its Presidency* (New York: Pergamon Press, 1981).)

12. See J. David Murphy, "The Papacy and the Secretary-Generalship: A Study of the Role of the Exceptionally-Situated Individual Actor in the International System," *Coexistence*, Vol. 7, 1970. Hammarskjöld once referred to his office as the "representative of a secular church of ideals and principles in international affairs."

13. Professor Barros, in his chapter in this book, claims that ". . . Hammarskjöld's adroit use of the office was exceptional and does not reflect the norm." (p. oo). This observation reflects Professor Barros' predilection for private diplomacy over the public—even publicity-making or -seeking—role that, for example, both Dr. Waldheim and Mr. Urquhart view as essential.

observers, left U Thant no choice but to proceed with such a sense of caution that the office threatened to decline in world influence. For example, how readily could U Thant act according to this dictum, without incurring widespread criticism?

> It is in keeping with the philosophy of the Charter that the Secretary-General should be expected to act also without such guidance [the Charter or a decision of a major organ], should this appear to him necessary in order to help in filling any vacuum that may appear in the system which the Charter and traditional diplomacy provided for the safeguarding of peace and security.[14]

Hammarskjöld's success in promoting, through Suez, the notion that the United Nations must be capable of acting independent of the major world powers came to haunt him when he tried to do this in the Congo crisis. Even if the veto in the Security Council could be neutralized by a majority vote of the General Assembly, in practical power terms the victory could be less in the long run than it would appear in the short run.

However, the quick resolution of the Lebanese crisis of 1958, which occurred shortly after his re-election to a second term of office whose completion was denied by fate, tended to belie this observation. The United Nations Observation Group (UNOGIL), formed of personnel from countries neutral to the crisis, transformed a very sensitive conflict situation into a triumph of United Nations peace-keeping. Throughout a four-month period, Hammarskjöld's office was the central point of reference for all the parties while a compromise was worked out. An imaginative and willing third party was needed, and Hammarskjöld, both in his person and in his office, provided it. Also, the presence of UNOGIL became a symbolic reminder that there was an alternative to endless and inevitable superpower rivalry, especially in the emerging Third World.

As to Congo, which erupted in June 1960, according to Hammarskjöld the United Nations Congo Force (ONUC) was to be organized along the same lines as UNEF. The Secretary-General was to have exclusive command of the force, and the troops composing it would not be drawn from either of the superpowers, or from the other major Western powers. Furthermore, almost contradictorily, the force was to remain neutral in internal Congolese political rivalries, but would have free movement throughout the country. This was truly intervention in the old-fashioned sense. At its height, the United Nations force came to number 20,000.

The *de facto* isolation of Premier Patrice Lumumba by the United Nations, in his Soviet-supported power struggle with President Joseph Kasavubu, and then the ultimate seizure of power by Joseph Mobutu, resulted in what appeared to be an alignment of Hammarskjöld with the West—and especially the United States—against the Socialist states—and

14. Murphy *op. cit.*, p. 167. In a discussion of this point, see Professor Zacher's chapter in this book.

especially the Soviet Union.[15] Inevitably, the whole thing spilled over into the major political organs of the United Nations with the Soviet Union delivering its harshest criticism of the Secretary-General on September 1960, during the now-famous Fifteenth Session of the General Assembly. Nikita Khrushchev put it thus:

> We consider it advisable to set up, in the place of a Secretary-General who is at present the interpreter and executor of the decisions of the General Assembly and the Security Council, a collective executive organ of the United Nations consisting of three persons each of whom would represent a certain group of States. That would provide a definite guarantee that the work of the United Nations executive organ would not be carried on to the detriment of any one of these groups of States. The United Nations executive organ would then be a genuinely democratic organ; it would really guard the interests of all States Members of the United Nations. . . .[16]

Even though the Secretary-General received strong support in the General Assembly that cut across conventional ideological lines, his prestige had undoubtedly been damaged. Hammarskjöld was put in the position of defending his office as well as his conduct of the office. In this respect, his dilemma was greater than that of his predecessor Lie.

One of the reasons for this obviously strong concern of the Soviet Union over a United Nations peace-keeping operation that, in their view, had gone off the rails, was that there was no clearly-established procedure in United Nations practice to halt such an operation once authorized, except by explicit resolution. The Congo crisis had become, through Uniting for Peace, the province of the General Assembly, and the Soviet Union was apparently unable to put through a resolution to have ONUC withdrawn. In the General Assembly, although an operation can be launched by a two-thirds majority of those member states present and voting (or can be blocked by one-third plus one), an operation, once underway, can be halted only by an express decision of a two-thirds majority.[17]

One of the criticisms of Hammarskjöld's conduct of the Congo crisis was that he had not integrated the new Afro-Asian states into the

---

15. For a recent article on this highly conspiratorial period of United Nations history, see Madeleine G. Kalb, "The C.I.A. and Lumumba," *The New York Times Magazine*, 2 August 1981, pp. 32-56. General Rikhye, in his chapter in this book, describes fully the Congo crisis and Hammarskjöld's role in it.

16. Delivered at the Fifteenth Session of the General Assembly, 23 September 1960. This attack, it is noted, came before Lumumba's assassination, so that any assumption that the Soviet position was a response to this set-back for them is not well-founded.

17. That is, unless the operation is established for a limited period, in which case a one-third minority can stop it from continuing. Professor Zacher, in his chapter in this book, makes a special point of the dilemma of how to stop an operation whose political support has eroded badly. In a letter to R. Jordan of 7th July 1981, Professor Zacher put it thus: "I think that it is necessary to give a great power (or at least a superpower) or a major segment of the UN membership *or* [his emphasis] the host state the power to terminate a force within a relatively short period after it has become 'disenchanted' with it. I do not think that the continuation of operations in the absence of a fairly broad consensus is realistic or is helpful to the future of international organizations."

Prologue

institutional structure of the United Nations. While this may or may not be valid, it did pose an irony in that Hammarskjöld viewed himself as enlightened when it came to decolonization and its political, social and economic ramifications. In fact, his concept of preventive diplomacy arose out of his concern that the *de jure* independence claimed for the new member states should be *de facto* as well.

Even though most of his time while in office was consumed by political issues, he retained a strong commitment to economic and social issues as well, which might have grown out of his time with the Central Bank of Sweden and in the Monetary Committee of the Organization for European Economic Cooperation (OEEC). Furthermore his personal knowledge of the effects of the depression of the 1930's on Western industrial society probably motivated him to ensure that the United Nations, under his leadership, did not neglect the consequences of poverty and unemployment for political stability.[18]

Within the secretariat, a notable change in the economic field was Hammarskjöld's gearing of research to operations. A wide range of political-economic problems were approached on the basis of technical modes of analysis that allowed the preparation of such widely-respected economic studies as the *World Economic Survey*.[19] Economic forecasting became of great interest to the secretariat during this period. Another example of Hammarskjöld's leadership in this respect was his frequent travels to Third World countries—especially in 1957 and 1958—to learn more about technical co-operation and of the work of the United Nations' regional economic commissions.

Hammarskjöld envisioned that, while the United Nations could intervene in political conflicts in ways that could only have temporary effects, in economic and social matters the United Nations' contribution could be lasting in the construction of a new type of international society, or, in current terminology, of a new international economic order.

The growth of the responsibilities placed upon both the Secretary-General and the secretariat since Dag Hammarskjöld's death has been remarkable. Although some of the increase in personnel has been criticized as being unnecessary and even counterproductive, it is a direct consequence of the rapid growth in the overall membership.[20] A virtual doubling of the membership has shifted not only the political balance of the Organization, it has altered fundamentally the nature of the political dialogue. Even though to many observers, the new international economic order—the

18. From 1930 to 1934, Hammarskjöld was Secretary of the Swedish Royal Commission on Unemployment, and later served as Under-Secretary in the Ministry of Finance and Chairman of the Board of Governors of the Bank of Sweden. He thus, during the depression years, had ample opportunity to learn about its consequences.

19. Philippe de Seynes, in his chapter in this book, discusses this point more fully.

20. For a recent discussion of the state of affairs in the secretariat, see Norman A. Graham and Robert S. Jordan (eds.), *The International Civil Service: Changing Role and Concepts* (New York: Pergamon Press, 1980).

phrase used to describe the demands of the Third World for a greater share and control over the world's resources—appeared at the outset of the 1970's to have burst with dramatic suddenness onto the international agenda, it was in fact ignited by a slow fuse which had been burning since the Hammarskjöld era.

The developing states have consistently sought to use the United Nations as a means for the promotion of their economic and social development.[21] In doing so, they have taken their cue from the industrial states' lesson of the depression, and have stressed the importance of economic factors in promoting political stability. This was captured in the phrase "development is a new name for peace." The growth of the regional economic commissions, which interested Hammarskjöld very much, stand as a good example of the developing states' efforts to gain a greater measure of control over United Nations development programs and funds. But Hammarskjöld's successors, U Thant and especially Kurt Waldheim, were confronted with a much more determined and organized "lobby" for the Third World. As one observer put it:

> The change in power relations in the world became evident in 1974. The action of the OPEC countries was a shock to the tradition of international relations and reflected a crisis in the world economy.[22]

Paradoxically, however, the growth of responsibilities and of institutions within the United Nations as a result of the expansion of the membership, has been accompanied by a diminished role for the secretariat as the governments have tended to rely less on it. This is definitely true in the political arena, where neither the Security Council nor the General Assembly is prepared to give the Secretary-General and the secretariat the sort of blank check which they gave Hammarskjöld in his earlier days. Not only is this attitude a result of what appeared to be the delegation of too much power to the Secretary-General and hence to the secretariat, over whom he had executive authority, but also because of the nature of the political policy process, which has not kept pace with the economic policy process. As a widely respected senior member of the secretariat put it:

> There are, however, clearly . . . reasons for the backward state of the political work of an international Secretariat. One reason is that no technique of analysis for political problems has been built up which corresponds to the widely accepted techniques of economic analysis. Some would deny that any such agreed technique, which might offer some possibility of translating at least some aspects of political controversy into

---

21. For a review of the evolution of the components of the new international economic order, see Robert S. Jordan, "Why an NIEO? The View from the Third World," in Harold K. Jacobson and Dusan Sidjanski (eds.), *The Emerging International Economic Order: Dynamic Processes, Constraints and Opportunities* (Beverly Hills, Calif.: Sage Publications, 1982).

22. Jelica Minic, "Third World Challenge," a World Press Report in the *World Press Review*, March 1981, p. 35.

technical discussion, is at all feasible. For the Secretariat, the development of agreed methods for the analysis of political problems by citizens of diverse nationalities is essential . . . the Secretariat must work out for itself its own approach, derived from the objectives of the United Nations, which affords some definition of the range of necessary and legitimate interest and a scale of evaluation among the multifarious aspects of international politics. The mere juxtaposition of national interests, interpreted in a so-called objective manner, is no solution of this problem.[23]

In the economic field, the developing states have been openly distrustful of the secretariat, and have established their own international institutions as well as acting aggressively to "de-Westernize" existing institutions. Whether Dag Hammarskjöld would have felt comfortable with this institutional pluralism, or whether he could have accepted in practice the sharp shifts in power assessments that are going on in such areas as food, oil, nuclear power and weapons, and the other subjects of global conferences, can only be conjectured. But it is not unrealistic to assert that the ideas represented by these global problems, and the development of global institutions charged with managing these problems, would have appealed to him greatly.[24]

Hammarskjöld's singular contributions, however, were his thoughtful innovations and efforts to building and keeping peace. He believed that ways of diplomacy can be improved through multilateral institutions and through a flexible use of these institutions. The manner in which he conducted the instrumentality of the United Nations was like a player with a large keyboard which included, among others, semi-arbitrating groups, conciliation groups, high-level emissaries, and all the potentialities of multilateral diplomacy. In the solution of immediate conflicts and the preservation of peace through situations which remain precarious, multilateral diplomacy has historically had a watchdog function which he utilized. His contribution to international politics, therefore, has stood well the test of time in that his successors have continued to pursue his precedent of innovating ways of dealing with intractable diplomatic problems.

---

23. Quoted from an unpublished memorandum by the late William Jordan, dated 28 May 1962.

24. Oscar Schachter presents a challenging view, writing in 1970 (and discussed further in his chapter in this book):

[In the fields of development and modernization of the less developed countries, of environmental deterioration, and the sea-bed and the regime of the oceans] . . . the emphasis has moved dramatically from specialized professional techniques to interrelationships and comprehensive planning . . . the global character of the problems and their interdependencies are strong reasons for turning to an international mechanism. That is not to say that the present international staffing is sufficient, only that there is a need and consequently an opportunity for the international secretariats to play a central role in the formulation of the required strategies. ("Some Reflections on International Officialdom," in Fawcett and Higgins, (eds.), *International Organization: Law in Movement, etc.* (London: Oxford University Press, 1974), p. 62.)

A portrait of Dag Hammarskjöld

1

Dag Hammarskjöld and the Office of United Nations Secretary-General

Kurt Waldheim

Kurt Waldheim was born in Austria in 1918. He graduated from the Vienna Consular Academy and took a doctorate in law at the University of Vienna. He joined the Austrian diplomatic service in 1945 and his first assignment included serving on the negotiating delegation for the Austrian State Treaty. In 1947 he was posted to the Austrian Legation in Paris and, when Austria regained its sovereignty in 1955, Dr. Waldheim became his country's Permanent Observer to the United Nations. During these years he had a number of personal contacts with Hammarskjöld and learned to appreciate his outstanding qualities. He has held a number of positions at home and abroad, including Ambassador to Canada and Director General for Political Affairs in the Austrian Foreign Ministry. He was appointed Austria's Permanent Representative to the United Nations in 1964 and a few months later was elected Chairman of the United Nations Outer Space Committee. In early 1968 he became Minister for Foreign Affairs of Austria and, after a change of Government, returned to New York in 1970. Dr. Waldheim held office as Secretary-General of the United Nations from 1972 through 1981, having been unanimously reappointed for a second five-year term commencing in 1977.

We look back to the time of Dag Hammarskjöld's Secretary-Generalship with nostalgia for a simpler world now gone forever. Since that period of long vanished statesmen—Eisenhower, Krushchev, de Gaulle, Chou En-lai, Nehru, Tito, Eden, Nasser, Ben-Gurion, Nkrumah, to name only a few—the world and the United Nations have changed radically. When Hammarskjöld became Secretary-General the United Nations had sixty members and, when he died, one hundred. The People's Republic of China was not then represented in the World Organization, and the phrase "The Third World" had yet to be coined. The estimated world population was about 2 1/2 billion as opposed to nearly 4 1/2 billion in 1980.

Hammarskjöld unquestionably played a key role in the development of the Secretary-Generalship. He developed the political capacity of the office in a number of directions through quiet diplomacy, preventive action and peace-keeping. He constantly championed the standards of the Charter as guiding practical principles in the affairs of nations. He made heroic efforts, not always with success, to prevent volatile regional conflicts becoming involved in the East-West rivalries of the cold war. He struggled hard to develop the international civil service as an independent and objective body of officials.

Hammarskjöld did not, I think, regard the Secretary-General primarily as a "force" in world politics but rather as an honest broker, a catalyst, and someone to whom governments could go for help in critical situations. During his term of office the Secretary-Generalship became an important political resource of the international community in times of crisis, and it has remained so. This was certainly due in part to Hammarskjöld's exceptional qualities and personality, but also to the inexorable facts of the international situation as it had developed since 1945 and to the way in which the Charter had been formulated.

The United Nations Charter was very much a product of World War II and of the disastrous decade that had preceded it. Thus its main focus was on the prevention of conventional aggression, if necessary by force, and the very core of the membership of the Security Council was the victorious wartime alliance represented by the permanent members, without whose concurrence or at least acquiescence serious political or military action by the Council was impossible.

It was clear from the first that in critical situations the unanimity of the permanent members might prove to be more of an exception than a rule. Moreover the introduction of nuclear weapons vastly altered the willingness of great powers to engage in ventures which might end in nuclear confrontation. At the same time the international political situation had developed in such a way that the Security Council would find it impossible in most cases to agree on a clear-cut identification of aggression.

For all these reasons the early years of the United Nations were marked by disappointment and frustration. The Charter which had emerged triumphantly after the war seemed more and more difficult to put into practical action. Evidently new approaches, or at least different uses of the machinery set up by the Charter, were required to deal with most of the post-war situations affecting international peace and security. It is perhaps for this reason that, of all the main organs of the United Nations, the office of the Secretary-General has been developed and tested more than any other in the first thirty-five years of the Organization's history.

The Charter was heavily influenced by the Covenant of the League of Nations in which the Secretary-General was primarily the Chief Administrative officer. This is also the first function of the Secretary-General in the United Nations Charter. But the Charter also gave political functions to the Secretary-General under Articles 98 and 99. The first of these provides for the Secretary-General to be assigned "other" functions by the main organs, while Article 99 gives him political initiative in his own right by authorizing him to bring to the attention of the Security Council situations which in his opinion constitute threats to international peace and security. This implies a watching brief on the whole range of international relations and an obligation to keep in constant touch with governments and events having a bearing on international peace and security.

These Articles are the constitutional basis for the political role of the Secretary-General, a role which has constantly developed since the early 1950's until it now dominates the working life of the Secretary-General. But the emergence of this political role is also due to the necessity, in many situations, for an objective third party responsible to the United Nations as a whole but subject to the authority or influence of no single member or group of member States. It was in filling this need that the political role of the Secretary-General took firm root in the early days of Dag Hammarskjöld's Secretary-Generalship and has flourished and grown ever since. Starting with the highly charged case of the seventeen American prisoners in China in 1954, Hammarskjöld succeeded in building the Secretary-Generalship into an important device for maintaining a peaceful balance in the world by defusing situations which contained the seeds of potentially fatal confrontations. Suez, Lebanon in 1958, the ominous development in Laos leading to war in Indo-China, and the crisis which attended the independence of the Congo were only a few examples of this phenomenon. At the same time the Secretary-General became the world's favorite repository—and sometimes scapegoat—for insoluble major international problems, especially those involving the great powers.

Paradoxically, one of the main factors in the Secretary-General's usefulness in critical situations is that he is not, in any normal sense, a "force" in world politics and is therefore acceptable in situations where others are not.

What is the true nature of the Secretary-General's role? What are its strengths and its weaknesses? First of all, the Secretary-General should be regarded by all States as being uncommitted to any particular nation, group or interest and as acting for the United Nations and in the general interest alone. The Secretary-General can never act, nor be seen to act, as the representative of a particular government or interest, nor can his role be that of an emissary of any particular group. This essential characteristic of his job also imposes certain limitations, but the impartiality of the Secretary-General gives him, in delicate situations, possibilities denied to virtually all national governments or other agencies.

The Secretary-General can say or suggest many things to governments in confidence which, coming from any other source, would be likely to be misunderstood. He therefore has unique possibilities for exploring options through quiet diplomacy and suggesting face-saving devices through which governments may change their positions without losing face either at home or abroad. In controversial situations, governments can come to the

Dag Hammarskjöld making a statement to the Security Council on a trip to Tunisia in connection with a Tunisian complaint against France, July 1961.

common ground of the United Nations, and particularly to the Secretary-General, who is the servant of *all* the member states, without appearing to show weakness or make politically damaging concessions. In a conflict situation it is much easier, for example, to accept a cease-fire called for by the Secretary-General or by the United Nations than one suggested from any other source.

In being able to talk to any party concerned in a conflict in a way from which governments are often precluded, the Secretary-General can provide a unique channel of communication between combatants who refuse to meet or to recognise each other. In this way dangerous misunderstandings and confusions have been defused, as for example on the cease-fire lines in the Middle East or Kashmir.

The development of peace-keeping forces has latterly provided occasions when the Secretary-General disposes of limited practical means to influence a situation. Although these forces are under the overall supervision of the Security Council, responsibility for their day-to-day direction and control inevitably falls upon the Secretary-General. Peace-keeping forces are control mechanisms rather than operational military forces in the conventional sense, and they cannot be used to promote initiatives outside their approved terms of reference. They are, however, an essential element in keeping a sensitive situation from developing into a full-scale conflict and threat to the peace. Their success depends on vigilance and careful day-to-day direction by the Secretary-General as much as on the performance of the members of the peace-keeping force itself.

Finally, and perhaps most important, the Secretary-General must be prepared, in situations which in his view are potential threats to international peace and security, to take the initiative if governments, for various reasons, are reluctant to do so. In the last year I have seen fit to move in this way in the matter of the American hostages in Iran and over the war between Iran and Iraq, and I have done so in a number of previous situations, for example in Cyprus and Lebanon. I have also taken the initiative in a series of major humanitarian tragedies, for example in regard to the problems of refugees especially in Africa and the afflicted populations of Indo-China. Even then the power to take decisive action must rest ultimately with governments, especially those most closely involved, and with the Security Council. The Secretary-General, however, serves to mobilise international interest and support for positive action and to present various options to the parties concerned.

The resort to the Secretary-General in political matters has traditionally been a last resort when other means have failed. As Hammarskjöld once put it,

> The Secretary-General's initiative . . . is, in principle, a supplementary one. When governments reach a deadlock, he may be the person to help them — and help them with their complete acceptance — out of the deadlock . . . If governments are seized of a matter, if there is no deadlock, if discussions are going on and if contacts have been established . . . the Secretary-General — no matter how concerned he may be — should keep back . . . He has no reason to jump on the stage and take over the part of any responsible government.

There seems to be no shortage of situations where governments do require the Secretary-General's assistance and this fact has certain implications. Problems usually come to the Secretary-General — and indeed to the United Nations — when other means of solving them have failed; in other words they are particularly obstinate problems. Secondly, governments may have very different ideas of how the Secretary-General should approach them and their mutual difficulties, and much time and effort may be required to evolve a generally acceptable approach.

The basic demands on the Secretary-General, although greater in quantity and scope, have not changed much since Hammarskjöld's time. The Secretary-General is the world's ranking international civil servant with theoretically unlimited responsibilities in relation to international peace and security but very little real power and no sovereign authority—or even readily available resources—at all. His capacity for independent action is in fact extremely limited, since in the end he can work effectively only with and through governments. If their co-operation or good will is withheld, he can in practice do little. He has of course considerable moral authority. He is expected to act and to take a position in matters of human rights. He can, and does, speak out for principle, for the Charter and for the general interest and conscience, but in an expedient world results and positive reactions inevitably take time. Moreover, if he is to preserve his usefulness he can rarely point the finger of judgement. Real authority tends to be vested in him only when things have reached a stage so dangerous and so confused that his intervention is the last remaining hope and his prospects of success correspondingly small.

Dag Hammarskjöld died at the height of a crisis over the nature and principles of peace-keeping operations particularly as regards the authority of the Secretary-General. His successor, U Thant, was well suited both by temperament and by his third-world standing, to moderate that crisis and to bring the United Nations back to a more pragmatic course in the world. For all the studied calm of U Thant's public performance, his courage and vision should not be forgotten. The world stands in his debt for his activity as the author of the face-saving procedure in the Cuban missile crisis, for the setting up, at the height of the peace-keeping crisis, of a new peace-keeping operation in Cyprus and for his courageous personal efforts to put an end to the war in Viet Nam.

The United Nations has changed and grown since Hammarskjöld died twenty years ago. It is less polarised by the East-West struggle and, with the emergence of the non-aligned Third World, more oriented to the relationship between the developed and developing world—the so-called North-South dialogue. The developing world is a new constituency in which the United Nations and the Secretary-General have an important role to play, especially in the evolution of long-term measures and strategies such as the new international economic order, or the assault on the new generation of global problems—population, food, water resources and energy, to name a few. This has added another dimension—and a variety of new activities—to the role of the Secretary-General.

On the political side, I believe that the twenty years of experience and practice since 1961 have created a closer and more positive relationship between the Secretary-General and the Security Council. It has, for example, proved possible, after the great peace-keeping controversy of the early '60s, to develop a practical consensus on the running of peace-keeping operations.

The growing habit of private consultations by the Council has also given the Secretary-General a means of keeping the Council informed and consulting it on delicate situations affecting international peace and security and of enlisting the support and understanding of the Council in his day-to-day efforts on such problems.

But real authority or power to act effectively is still notably missing from the United Nations, and in its absence the Secretary-General must improvise and make do with what influence and support he can muster and with his own powers of negotiation and persuasion. I am convinced that the Secretary-General must do two basic things. In day-to-day international life, he must keep touch as closely as possible with all of the main constituents of the world scene. He must be informed of their problems and be ready whenever required—which is surprisingly often—to lend a hand in resolving those problems. He must be responsive to the apprehensions, aspirations and sensitivities of all the member states and must do what he can to harmonise their policies and to provide them with a reasonable means to get out of the dilemmas in which many sovereign states often find themselves.

The Secretary-General is also the custodian of the idea of world community which is set forth in the United Nations Charter. On a day-to-day basis, it is sometimes very hard to see what progress is being made towards this distant but essential goal, but I believe that we can only expect very gradual progress and that we must store up and value every small advance that is made on all the many fronts of United Nations activity. Working in the United Nations, especially for the Secretary-General, would be hard to bear if one did not believe that steady, if slow, progress is in fact being made towards the realisation of this essential concept. The world has become technologically, industrially and economically interdependent long before it is politically ready for it. The United Nations at the moment represents the only possible forum in which the global political arrangements can be developed which may eventually enable us to catch up. I believe that we have made some progress along this road in thirty-five years, and for me it is the most compelling challenge of all.

The Secretary-General is not a sovereign force in world politics. I believe, however, that in the torturous and complicated development of human affairs he can provide something perhaps in the long run more valuable, a quiet centre for finding solutions, an honest go-between who can bear signals to anyone in the world even from their worst enemies and still maintain their confidence, and a caretaker of the delicate but essential idea of world community.

The Secretary-Generalship is in a constant state of evolution. This is one of the factors that makes the job as fascinating as it can, on occasion, be frustrating. Each year adds new facets and new possibilities to this office,

An informal picture of Dag Hammarskjöld, taken at a press conference in August 1954.

while often underlining the limitations of an official who is the servant of 154 sovereign nations but who commands no element of sovereign authority.

Dag Hammarskjöld, through his skill, imagination, leadership and personality, made an extraordinary contribution to this evolution. In facing our own problems we often revert for guidance to his experiences and his precepts. We are still very much in the early stages of building the institutions and traditions of world order. At this uncertain stage the effort must, inevitably to some extent, be a continuous act of faith. Hammarskjöld well described the spirit of the office when he said:

> Working at the edge of the development of human society is to work on the brink of the unknown. Much of what is done will one day prove to have been of little avail. This is no excuse for the failure to act in accordance with our best understanding, in recognition of its limits but with faith in the ultimate result of the creative evolution in which it is our privilege to co-operate.

Leo Rosenthal

A farewell toast on board ship to Trygve Lie, in May 1953, by his successor, Dag Hammarskjöld, and colleagues.

2
The Importance of Secretaries-General of the United Nations

James Barros

James Barros holds the rank of Professor in the Department of Political Economy at the University of Toronto. Previously he had served on the faculties of Barnard College, Columbia University (where he earned his doctorate), and Dartmouth College. He is the author of several studies of the office of Secretary-General, including *Betrayal from Within: Joseph Avenol, Secretary-General of the League of Nations, 1933-1940; Office Without Power: Secretary-General Sir Eric Drummond, 1919-1933*; and is working on *The Cold War's Secretary-General: Trygve Lie, 1946-1953*.

Some Secretaries-General are more important than others largely because of the way they executed their high international office. Indeed, the way the office is discharged must be the bench mark against which one compares and evaluates the performances of various Secretaries-General of the League of Nations or of the United Nations. The differences in their individual performances is especially important in view of the fact that the office is intrinsically political, and because of the power and influence that its holder can wield as the hub of the multinational secretariat's administrative wheel.

As the director of a large multinational staff whose first task is the continual surveillance of world politics, a Secretary-General, almost inevitably and regardless of whether one does or does not think his actions appropriate as the chief administrative officer of the world organization, either willingly or unwillingly must partake in secret or public discussions with states either in or out of the organization involving the use of the organization's political procedures, its facilities, or its staff. How the Secretary-General reacts to the request, the attitude he assumes, and the resources of the organization or its organs he makes available, draw him immediately, like it or not, into a political vortex where the choices he makes further the political drives and desires of one supplicant state over another. Though the Secretary-General may perhaps rationalize his choices on legal or administrative grounds he is nevertheless involved in what are essentially political acts. The very nature of the Secretary-General's office is unavoidably political.[1] The political importance of the office and the Secretary-General's power and influence are mirrored in the memoirs of those who have held the office,[2] and in any serious studies of its holders during the last sixty years.[3]

Because of the actions of the Secretaries-General of the United Nations, especially Dag Hammarskjöld, the idea has developed, particularly in some academic circles and among well-meaning people, that the most important and desirable use of the office is manifested through public political activities,[4] even beyond those public activities intrinsically associated with the office and permitted the Secretary-General under the Charter.[5] Among some this idea of public political activities has been shrilly argued. Any attempt to avoid such public activity, for example, by the present incumbent in the human rights field, is viewed as a sort of snivelling retreat from virtue,[6] though the present Secretary-General may be quite active in this field by his private initiatives. This view about public political activities by the Secretary-General appears to take precedence over his administrative duties and responsibilities which as the organization's chief administrative officer are not unimportant. Underemphasized and perhaps unappreciated, these administrative duties and responsibilities have been allowed to flounder and accordingly administrative efficiency has not been an overabundant commodity among most Secretaries-General of the United Nations.

This public political activity is certainly perceived as more important than the less flashy and hence newsy but perhaps most difficult and important political activity that the Secretary-General can be involved in

---

1. James Barros, *Office without Power: Secretary-General Sir Eric Drummond, 1919-1933* (Oxford: The Clarendon Press, 1979), p. 385; James Barros, *Betrayal from Within: Joseph Avenol, Secretary-General of the League of Nations, 1933-1940* (New Haven: Yale University Press, 1969), p. 262.

2. Trygve Lie, *In the Cause of Peace* (New York: Macmillan Co., 1954) and U Thant, *View from the UN* (New York: Doubleday & Co., 1978), passim.

3. Barros, *Office without Power*; Barros, *Betrayal from Within*; Brian Urquhart, *Hammarskjöld* (New York: Knopf, 1972); Arthur W. Rovine, *The First Fifty Years: The Secretary-General in World Politics 1920-1970* (Leyden: Sijthoff, 1970).

4. For example see Rovine, pp. 415-463; Arthur W. Rovine, "A More Powerful Secretary-General for the United Nations?", *American Journal of International Law (Proceedings of the American Society of International Law)*, Vol. 66, No. 4 (September 1972), pp. 78-81 ff.

5. For these activities see the thoughtful study by Leon Gordenker, *The UN Secretary-General and the Maintenance of Peace* (New York: Columbia University Press, 1967), passim.

6. Shirley Hazzard, "The League of Frightened Men," *The New Republic*, January 19, 1980, pp. 17-20.

behind the scenes. The Secretary-General's private political activity, which can be both frustrating and tedious, involves attempts to use whatever power and influence he has to assist in hammering out solutions to international problems. Imperfect as these proferred solutions, contributed to directly or indirectly by the Secretary-General, may appear to one side or the other, they may be more palatable than other possible solutions in an imperfect world governed by imperfect men.

The perceived public political role for the Secretary-General is popular because it is dramatic, and since the organization is in a sense a political theater with much of the drama, but not all of it, played out in the open one needs a leading character, as does all theater, and who is better fitted for that role than the Secretary-General?[7] Some of the assumptions made about this public political use of the office are questionable, if not actually dangerous. The notion that somehow a Secretary-General is impartial or neutral in world affairs falls under these two rubrics.[8]

No Secretary-General is impartial or neutral. When someone is recommended by the Security Council and appointed by the General Assembly as Secretary-General he is already mature in years. He has long since passed his formative years of development when one's political values and attitudes are shaped. Khrushchev was closer to the truth than those who espouse the notion of the impartial or neutral Secretary-General when in April 1961, following his confrontation with Hammarskjöld at the fifteenth session of the General Assembly and the defeat of his "troika" proposal, he told Walter Lippmann that "while there [were] neutral countries, there [were] no neutral men."[9] Indeed, if he had been versed in international law, which he was not, he could have supported his assertion by pointing out that under international law nationals of neutral countries are not restrained in dealing with warring factions, despite their state's neutrality, except if prohibited from doing so by municipal law.

In fact, the empirical evidence clearly shows that governments both democratic and non-democratic have tacitly admitted to the inevitable partiality and non-neutrality of Secretaries-General, but not in any public debate. Lord Robert Cecil's whole idea of the League's "Chancellor," that all-powerful figure who was to run the League and be politically influential on the world scene, was based almost solely on giving the post to someone whose political attitudes and general orientation would dovetail with those of the United Kingdom. No impartiality here. Cecil's decision, supported by others, was that the role envisaged for the Chancellor could best be played by the charismatic and Anglophile Greek Prime Minister Eleftherios

---

7. See Conor Cruise O'Brien, *The United Nations: Sacred Drama* (New York: Simon and Schuster, 1968).
8. Rovine, p. 416ff.
9. *New York Herald Tribune*, April 17, 1961.

Venizelos, who had the added advantage of being able to mesmerize President Wilson, a not unimportant consideration keeping in mind the long shadow that Wilson cast in the period immediately after the war. Frustrated in this search for the "right" Chancellor, but cognizant of the intrinsic political importance of the office and the man who would hold it, and despite the fact that in the subsequent negotiations at Paris the post was seemingly de-politicized, Cecil sought and pressed only British candidates. He was fortunate that in so unstructured a selection process he was able to choose and convince Sir Eric Drummond, a longtime Foreign Office official, to take the post.[10]

When Drummond resigned in 1933, the British, despite the oral agreement that they had made at Paris in 1919 that Drummond would be succeeded by his French deputy, hoped that another Englishman could follow Drummond, but the French no less than the British were aware of the political importance of the office and of the fact that no Secretary-General could ever be truly impartial or neutral. No doubt they hoped that a French Secretary-General, like Joseph Avenol, would mirror French political values and attitudes, or to twist the old quip about the Monroe Doctrine, Avenol would be a French cheesebox floating in the wake of a French man-of-war. Unfortunately, they miscalculated with Avenol who was more at home with Pierre Laval and the French Right, than with Édouard Herriot and Léon Blum and the French Center or Socialist Left.[11] Avenol's Right-wing orientation and lack of political acumen propelled him to play a role during the inter-war period which tended to hasten the upsurge of the anti-status quo and anti-democratic powers and the demise of the world organization he served.

The problem was no more different in 1946 when the permanent members of the United Nations Security Council met in London to recommend the first Secretary-General of the United Nations. Trygve Lie was Russia's man. Radicalized in his youth during World War I, Lie was a longtime member of the leftist faction of the Norwegian Labor Party—one of the most leftist oriented of the European labor parties. Moscow, based on these considerations and on its prior dealings with him, thought it had the measure of the man.

To have Lie recommended as Secretary-General Russia played its cards with the skill of a Talleyrand. It succeeded, thanks to western bungling and ineptness, and Lie assumed the post, though he was held in low esteem and considered a poor candidate by Dean Acheson and Philip Noel-Baker, the British Minister of State, as well as by Noel-Baker's academic assistant, Charles K. Webster.

By no stretch of the imagination were the Russians disappointed in

10. Barros, *Office without Power*, pp. 1-19.
11. Barros, *Betrayal from Within*, pp. 1-22 and passim.

their choice of Lie, or in his machinations as Secretary-General, at least up to the inception of the Korean War. Lie's memoir, if carefully examined and juxtaposed against the archival evidence and private papers now available, presents a lamentable picture of Lie as Secretary-General. His partiality, prejudices, and political interventions both public and private, particularly against the western powers when a plunging thermometer gave us the Cold War, can be largely traced to his youthful and strong Marxist orientation that with time evolved into an ambivalent attitude toward Soviet Russia compounded by feelings of fear and awe.[12]

Even from the limited evidence that is now available we know that the question of the prospective Secretary-General's potential propinquity to public political activities as well as his possible partiality or non-neutrality were important considerations in the selection of Lie's successors. In Hammarskjöld's case there is evidence to show that Sir Gladwyn Jebb, in proposing him and the permanent members of the Security Council in accepting him, thought that they had chosen for the office an administrative technocrat who unlike Lie would concentrate on administrative problems and eschew any public involvement in political questions.[13] At the same time Washington and London suspected that Hammarskjöld, unlike his predecessor, was fully in the western camp, and it would not be unfair to say in the long run they were not disappointed.[14] Similar considerations were raised during Thant's as well as Waldheim's appointments, if one can read between the murky lines of Thant's recollections.[15]

In addition, the assumption made about the public political use of the office and the Secretary-General's impartiality or neutrality subsumes that the holder of the office is committed to the values and ideals of the world organization he serves. This surely was not the case of the Right-wing oriented Avenol who steered the League during the rise of Nazi Germany and the Rome-Berlin-Tokyo Axis to the German military breakthrough and the fall of France in the summer of 1940. No political activities by Avenol either public, which were few, or private, which were substantial especially during the Italian-Ethiopian crisis, contributed to the survival of

12. James Barros, "Pearson or Lie: The Politics of the Secretary-General's Selection, 1946," *Canadian Journal of Political Science*, X, No. 1 (March 1977), pp. 65-92; James Barros, "Trygve Lie: De Mortuis nil nisi bonum," *International Journal*, XXV, No. 2 (Spring 1970), pp. 405-413; James Barros, *The Cold War's Secretary-General: Trygve Lie, 1946-1953* (forthcoming).

13. Lord Gladwyn, *The Memoirs of Lord Gladwyn* (London: Weidenfeld and Nicolson, 1972), p. 257; Joseph P. Lash, *Dag Hammarskjöld Custodian of the Bushfire Peace* (New York: Doubleday, 1961), pp. 7-15; Urquhart, pp. 11-15, 27.

14. United States Department of State, *Foreign Relations of the United States 1952-1954* (Washington, D.C.: Government Printing Office, 1979), III, pp. 448-449.

15. Thant, pp. 3-19, 437-438. See also Stephen M. Schwebel's articles "Selecting a New Secretary-General for the U.N." and "The Choice of a New U.N. Secretary-General," *The Washington Post*, September 13 and December 23, 1971.

Dag Hammarskjöld, as Secretary-General Designate, arriving in New York in April 1953, being greeted by Secretary-General Trygve Lie.

the League, or to the defense of the status quo instituted by the peace settlements of 1919-1920.[16]

In an ever changing international arena there can be no guarantee that another Avenol-type personality might not be appointed as Secretary-General. The possiblity is there and though the probability is remote, it is not nil, especially in view of the fact that any recommendation of a candidate is not based on his intelligence or experience, but on political expediency and the momentary consensus that can be hammered out by the permanent members of the Security Council. We must never forget that selecting a Secretary-General is not based on a competitive civil service examination akin to that required of persons who wish to enter the administrative class of the British civil service.

The rapid growth in the United Nations membership has complicated the procedure, for the so-called Third World states now have at their disposal more than enough votes to block appointment by a one-third vote of any candidate recommended to the General Assembly who fails to satisfy the Afro-Asian world. Though this has never occurred, it would be legal within the terms of the Charter, and under the right conditions politically feasible, adding a future complicating factor to an already complicated procedure and thus contributing to the vagaries of the selection process and the person chosen.

One can cogently argue that any opinions as to whether the private or public political activities of the Secretaries-General are partial or impartial, stem almost exclusively from what a nation perceives to be its national interests. As one knowledgeable observer has succinctly noted: one's views toward a Secretary-General depend "on whether one agrees with the policies of the man on the job."[17] Though most have conveniently forgotten Lie's early political initiatives, both public and private, which did not amuse the western powers, these very activities by mid-1949 had triggered western discussions as to who might replace Lie when his contractual tour of duty terminated in February 1951. The political orientation of any prospective candidate was the important consideration, and the possible candidature of Sweden's Gunnar Myrdal or Australia's Herbert V. Evatt, Dean Rusk explained to the Canadians, gave the State Department "cold shivers."[18] In view of Myrdal's and Evatt's dubious political activities both public and private, as perceived from a western point of view, the State Department's sentiments can be well appreciated.

16. Barros, *Betrayal from Within*, passim, and Rovine, pp. 105-172.

17. See Leo Gross' comments in "A More Powerful Secretary-General for the United Nations," *American Journal of International Law (Proceedings of the American Society of International Law)*, Vol. 66, No. 4 (September 1972), p. 88.

18. J[ohn] W. Holmes, Memorandum for the Deputy Under-Secretary of State for External Affairs, July 26, 1949, File 5475-1-40, Archives Division, Department of External Affairs, Ottawa.

Conversely, the Russians held that only Lie could replace himself,[19] a supportive attitude that quickly vanished when Lie publicly committed himself to the Security Council's recommendation that the membership of the United Nations come to the assistance of South Korea. As to Hammarskjöld, his actions especially in the Congo, in the end dovetailed with western interests and this largely explains why in western academic and layman's literature he looms so large. One would be hard pressed to find him enshrined in what passes for similar literature in the peoples' democracies.

What has been said about Lie's and Hammarskjöld's public activities also applies to Thant's. The first non-western Secretary-General perceived his role with colonialism in mind. Thant viewed the office and the world organization from the vantage point of the Third World, an approach which reflected his understandable resentment that he was born a British subject in a part of the British Empire and accordingly had once carried the "white man's burden." Moreover he had absorbed, like many fellow Asians, what can be fairly described as a simplistic quasi-Marxist view that western domination—or western capitalism, take your pick—of colonial areas had been predicated on the metropolitan's atavistic commercial and fiscal policies and those of its nationals. This had left the colonial domains merely primary producers, and industrially undeveloped. The end result was western induced poverty that led to the need for post independence economic development which had to be a principal concern of the United Nations. Simultaneously, he commendably held that it was his task to "build bridges between peoples, governments, and states," and to execute this task he wisely contended that a quiet tack which avoided public confrontation might often hold some hope of success.

This said, he argued that he was more than an administrator and his political role was justified under Article 99 of the Charter. The important difference, of course, is that his "quiet approach" can never be squared with the "public approach" seemingly justified under Article 99. The use of Article 99 throws him into a public political vortex and goes far to erode whatever influence he might have behind the scenes or whatever bridge building he might attempt between the disputing parties. Each public political intervention whether or not justified under Article 99 will incrementally erode his position, for states whose perceived interests have been undercut or jeopardized by his actions are not likely to trust, confide, or cooperate with him at some future point. Once bitten, twice shy. Interestingly, no doubts appear to have been raised in Thant's mind about the wisdom of the public approach though he admitted that he lacked the range of first-hand information upon which governments based their policies. Thant wanted to have it both ways, but once you enter the public

---

19. Lie, p. 368.

Acting President U Thant of the 14th Session of the General Assembly, and Dag Hammarskjöld.

arena you will soon be branded by one side or the other as partial. Keeping in mind Thant's life experiences, it would not be unfair to say that he had a disguised aversion to the West partially mirrored in his gratuitous comments about American leadership—Adlai Stevenson excluded—whether it be John McCloy, President Johnson, or Dean Acheson, whom Thant considered as "one of the most overrated diplomats of his time." This hostility could not have gone unrecognized in Washington, London, or Paris, and might in part explain his thwarted political initiatives in many of the acute political questions that developed during his tenure as Secretary-General.[20]

In line with the above observations I would venture to suggest that the bench mark that differentiates some Secretaries-General as more important than others is to be found in their tact and discretion, and particularly in their ability to maintain the trust and confidence of the world organization's membership, and especially the trust and confidence of the Great Powers.

20. Thant, pp. 27, 175, and passim.

Public political activities do not contribute toward that end and indeed seriously detract from it. The notion that a single individual devoid of real power and merely directing the multinational staff of an international organization can significantly influence world events by his public interventions because of the high international position he holds is an escape from reality. It is an attempt to avoid the harsh fact that the politics of the world community, as mirrored in the politics of the world organization, are the politics of sovereign states, and especially the politics of the Great Powers. Equally important, the notion that a Secretary-General has special rights or political wisdom that permits him to go beyond the legal and even more important the practical political limits imposed on his office expresses *hubris*.

Of course those who argue the case for public political activities by the Secretary-General hold that these activities are necessary and indeed desirable in order to further world peace. But as noted previously what to some appears to further world peace can be considered as the frustration or denial of another's political right. Public political activities, especially unsolicited ones by the Secretaries-General, can never really substitute for accommodation among the powers themselves. Indeed, such activities may contribute toward continuing world tensions. One side may feel that using the world organization against its opponents, in conjunction with other political advantages that it may have, and with the Secretary-General's support, makes it unnecessary to search for an accommodation with the opposing side. Yet peace in the world community, which in practical terms can never be absolute, is only achievable by great power accommodation. The fault or misperception, call it what you will, lies not so much in what was drafted into the Charter at San Francisco as much as in an unrestrained idealism that outraces what can be achieved by an individual actor in a world organization that recognizes the power of state sovereignty. The end result is essentially an exaggeration of the real power of the office and a fascination with what is desirable over what is possible in world affairs. This attitude does little to give us a more balanced and realistic view of this important international position.

Much of this attitude emphasizing the public use of the office can be traced to what I like to call the "Hammarskjöld model" of Secretary-General. But Hammarskjöld's adroit use of the office was exceptional and does not reflect the norm. If Hammarskjöld were compared with others who have held the office it would soon become obvious that he was an unusual Secretary-General, as he was an unusual person. I do not wish to infer that Hammarskjöld was all-perfect or that his decisions and actions are above criticism—he certainly did not put up with fools gladly, and Patrice Lumumba is a case in point. But the personal qualities that made Hammarskjöld an unusual Secretary-General are not likely to be repeated in most people selected for the office. As I have tried to show in my previous comments the office has been held by good and well-meaning men as well as by fools and knaves. In fact, Hammarskjöld's interpretation of his office might be traced in part to his prior training and longtime service as a senior Swedish civil servant.

Interestingly, the Swedish constitutional system maintains that "undersecretaries are the highest officials in each department immediately under the minister, and the law itself defines their function as 'political.'"[21] Keeping in mind that Hammarskjöld before his appointment as Secretary-General had served as undersecretary in the Finance Ministry and undersecretary as well as Secretary-General in the Foreign Ministry, is it just possible that his later public political activities might in part be traced to this peculiar aspect of the Swedish constitutional system and its civil service? Of course, to admit to this might undermine the image that Hammarskjöld quickly developed during his second contract period, when he claimed during the Congo crisis that he had certain implied powers under the Charter and accordingly could undertake certain political initiatives, in the same way that the President of the United States has certain implied powers under the United States constitution, especially in the conduct of foreign relations.

However, aside from the Hammarskjöld model other models can be conjured up and I would suggest that Sir Eric Drummond's activities as Secretary-General offer an alternate model as valid, if not more valid and politically more practicable: a Secretary-General who acts quietly behind the scenes and whose behavior is epitomized by the two nouns, tact and discretion.[22] This non-public role requires that the Secretary-General be an endless source of ideas, advice, recommendations, proposals, schemes, and formulas, not merely to the attendant delegations, but in many questions directly to the concerned governments, or to those governments not concerned, but interested in peacefully solving the question at issue. To have the maximum impact these initiatives must be behind the scenes, and perhaps transmitted through third parties, to further remove the Secretary-General from the disputing factions. The basic advantage of this non-public approach is that if the Secretary-General's proposal is unacceptable to either of the parties it does not exclude amendment or subsequent proposals. It does not drag the Secretary-General into the public arena and thus it allows him to continue his endeavors which public failure or public comments, particularly of the concerned parties, might quickly compromise or under-

21. Dankwart A. Rustow, *The Politics of Compromise: A Study of Parties and Cabinet Government in Sweden* (Princeton: Princeton University Press, 1955), p. 176. See also Neil C. M. Elder, *Government in Sweden* (Oxford: Pergamon Press, 1970), pp. 81-87.

22. For some of the comments that follow see Barros, *Office without Power*, pp. 397ff., and James Barros, "A More Powerful Secretary-General for the United Nations?", *American Journal of International Law (Proceedings of the American Society of International Law)*, Vol. 66, No. 4 (September 1972), pp. 81-84ff.

cut. In addition, this behind-the-scenes approach shields the Secretary-General, for being human he is open to making mistakes of omission or commission which if exposed to public view would damage his own image and the office's prestige.

One can argue that this private approach is too timid and that a more positive and thus public assertion by the Secretary-General might be in order. The assumption of course is that public political activity is more effective political activity in the sense that it is capable of influencing, affecting, or having an impact on other actors in the world community. This assumes of course that the Secretary-General has a public constituency to which he can appeal. If he feels that he has such a constituency he will have to weigh the advantages of a public stance against the disadvantages that might accrue not only in the question at issue but in his long-term relations with the states involved.

But all that said, what would be the possibilities, one can ask, of a Secretary-General convincing someone by public moves when he could not convince him by private advice and conversations? Is this not true when dealing with permanent members of the Security Council? Indeed, what real power does the Secretary-General have (power defined as the ability physically or psychically to control other actors in the world community) beyond the weak reed of world public opinion, the appeal to world morality, the tenets of international law that he might be able to invoke to buttress his position, or the political support that he might be able to muster from some but not all states of the organization?

In fact, as has already been noted, if experience teaches us anything it is that United Nations Secretaries-General have very often by their public political initiatives undermined whatever political usefulness they had in the world community. In the case of Lie and Hammarskjöld they became politically impotent once they crossed swords with Soviet Russia: Lie because of his actions and attitude following the North Korean invasion of South Korea, and Hammarskjöld because of his initiatives and attitude during the Congo crisis. With Thant though the clash was not as blatant as it was for his predecessors, it was Washington rather than Moscow that was annoyed, largely because of Thant's attitude toward the American involvement in Vietnam. One would be hard pressed to show how the public activities and initiatives of these men in any of these questions hastened a peaceful settlement which justified the political and personal sacrifices that they made. Their actions may have been dramatic, but in the long run and certainly in the short run, they were far less useful and practical than might appear on the surface. These Secretaries-General had by their actions exposed themselves to public view, appeared to show favor, and once drawn in, their credibility and usefulness as an impartial bridge between the contending parties was destroyed.

The difficulty in appreciating the private over the public involvement of a Secretary-General lies in the fact that it is so undramatic. Tedious yes, self-effacing yes, but dramatic it certainly is not. It is a style that demands self-control, discretion, endless imagination, tireless energy, and a grasp of international relations as well as knowledge of the subject under discussion second to none of the secretariat's technical experts. The problem is that this method does not appeal to many investigators of the Secretary-General's office who are moved by dramatic public acts. Nevertheless, I would suggest that it is the only approach that would make it possible for a Secretary-General to develop some influence and increase the chances that his admonitions and advice would be listened to and perhaps even followed by the membership on various political questions. This is certainly not likely to occur if Secretaries-General take public stands on important issues which can only aggravate one side or the other and in turn strain or compromise their relations with the involved states.

Keeping in mind the bench mark suggested which should differentiate some Secretaries-General as more important than others, I do not think it would be unfair to say that none can compare with Sir Eric Drummond who when he left the League was still very much trusted and admired by all the organization's member states, despite his immense behind-the-scenes political activities throughout his tenure as Secretary-General. Indeed, none of Drummond's successors could make a similar claim, including Hammarskjöld. If Hammarskjöld stands high in everyone's esteem in the West it is largely due to the fact that his actions and initiatives in the end dovetailed, whether consciously or not, with Western interests and desires. As someone committed to these values and ideas, I share that image of the man but that image is not likely to be shared by those behind the Iron Curtain. Lie runs a bad third, his counterbalancing indulgences amassed in the period following the commencement of the Korean War, an admittedly Western view no different from the one rendered about Hammarskjöld. Thant runs a very poor fourth compounded by a disguised anti-western orientation which surfaces even in his sanitized memoirs. Avenol will be defended by no one, while Sean Lester was *sui generis* keeping the wartime ship just barely afloat to evolve from League to United Nations. What has been offered here is not the established view and is open to severe criticism, but not if you always keep to the fore the fact that Secretaries-General are but flesh and blood and like the rest of us have no monopoly on political wisdom.

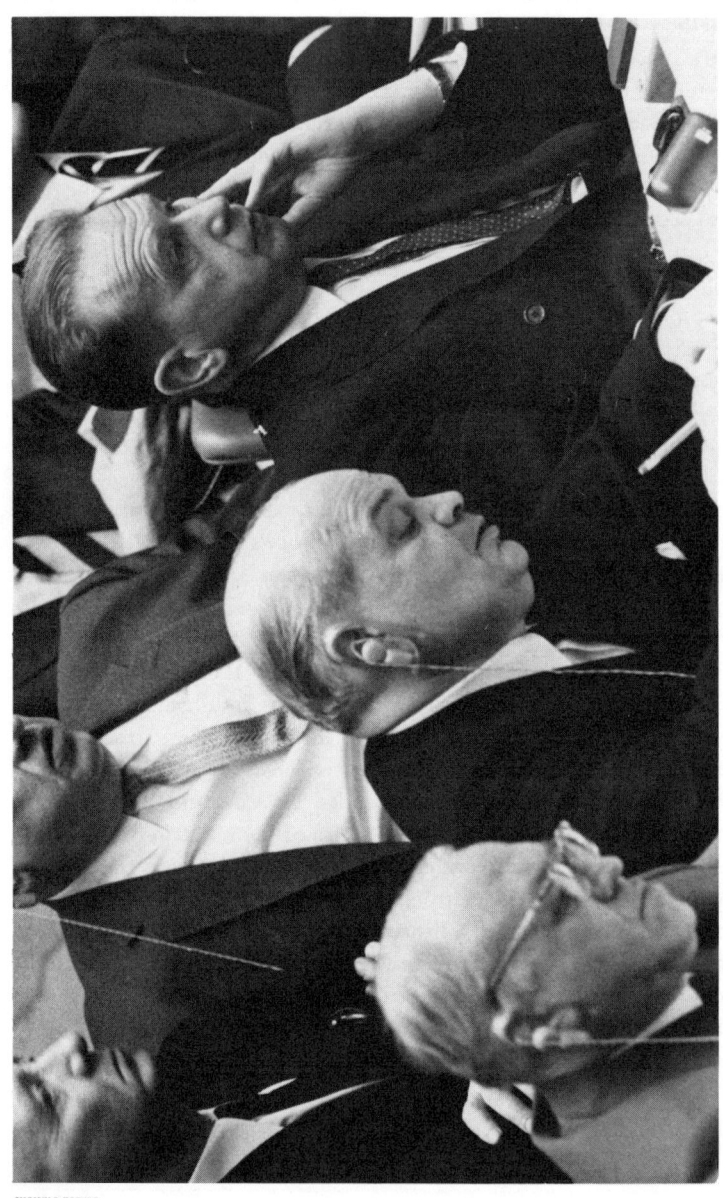

The Security Council meeting on the Congo situation in February 1961. From left: Ambassador V. A. Zorin (USSR), Ambassador Omar Loutfi (UAR), and Dag Hammarskjöld.

3

The International Civil Servant: Neutrality and Responsibility

Oscar Schachter

Oscar Schachter is at present the Hamilton Fish Professor of International Law and Diplomacy at Columbia University. He is a native New Yorker who, soon after receiving his law degree at Columbia, began a career in international affairs, first in the U.S. government and then in international organizations. He was a legal advisor to Herbert Lehman and Fiorello LaGuardia when they headed UNRRA, the post-war international relief organization. From 1946-1966 he served as a legal advisor to UN Secretaries-General Trygve Lie, Dag Hammarskjöld and U Thant. Later he organized research and seminars for the UN Institute for Training and Research (UNITAR) until his appointment at Columbia Law School in 1975. In addition to being on the faculty of the Law School, Professor Schachter is a professor in the Political Science Department of the Graduate Faculty and in the School of International Affairs.

Professor Schachter has written extensively on international law and institutions. He was a pioneer in developing the law of outer space; his article "Who Owns the Universe," written in 1951, advanced ideas which have since become law. A more recent work, *Sharing the World's Resources,* deals with issues of equity and entitlement raised by demands for a new international economic order. Many of his articles deal with international conflict settlement and peacekeeping. He has also written on and been actively involved in promoting international human rights and economic development.

Professor Schachter is at present co-editor-in-chief of the *American Journal of International Law.* He is a past President of the American Society of International Law and has been a member of the Institut de droit international since 1965. In 1981 he was awarded the Manley Hudson Gold Medal for pre-eminent scholarship and achievement in international law.

Dag Hammarskjöld began his 1961 Oxford lecture on the International Civil Servant by referring to an interview of Walter Lippmann with Nikita Krushchev, then head of the Soviet government. In that interview, Chairman Krushchev stated "while there are neutral countries, there are no neutral men." Lippmann drew the conclusion that it is the view of the

Soviet government that "there can be no such thing as an impartial civil servant in this deeply divided world and that the kind of political celibacy which the British theory of the civil servant calls for is in international affairs a fiction."[1]

It is likely that this view of the Soviet government is widely shared across the globe both by the general public and by the political scientists and other experts in international relations. To Hammarskjöld, however, it was a view that challenged a basic tenet of the United Nations, an essential condition of that "experiment" in international cooperation which represents an "advance beyond traditional conference diplomacy."

> Were it to be considered that the experience shows that this radical innovation [i.e., a neutral civil service used for "executive purposes" on behalf of all member states] rests on a false assumption, because 'no man can be neutral,' then we would be thrown back to 1919 and a searching re-appraisal would become necessary.[2]

In the Oxford lecture Hammarskjöld sought to analyze and defend the conception of a neutral civil service, "in law and in fact," to explore its philosophical and political assumptions and to consider its practical value in a sharply divided world. That lecture was not a purely theoretical exercise. It was given at a time when Hammarskjöld was under severe attack by the Soviet Union for an alleged lack of neutrality in his handling of the Congo crisis and for other positions he had taken. Underlying the carefully worded analysis of history and ideas in the Oxford lecture was a poignant personal drama. Hammarskjöld who saw himself as exclusively guided by the ideals and principles of the United Nations and who had been almost universally lauded for his dedication and brilliance in pursuing those ends was then under vehement attack for bias and personal ambition. There was no doubt that he was deeply affected, and that he perceived the criticism as an attack on his personal integrity. But, characteristically, he also saw the issues as transcending his personal position. They were part of the larger drama in which power and ideals clashed and the fragile "organism" based on the common interest of a divided humanity was placed in jeopardy. They were also, as he saw it, manifestations of a historical evolution, fitfully leading to an uncertain world order in which "we, like our ancestors, can only press against the receding wall which hides the future."[3] The questions raised were perhaps most difficult in their

---

1. Dag Hammarskjöld, *The International Civil Servant in Law and in Fact* (Oxford: Clarendon Press, 1961), p. 1. Lecture is also in Wilder Foote (ed.), *Dag Hammarskjöld, Servant of Peace: A Selection of Speeches and Statements* (New York: Harper & Row 1962), p. 329.

2. *Ibid.* For background to the Oxford lecture, see Brian Urquhart, *Hammarskjöld* (New York: Knopf 1972), p. 527.

3. Dag Hammarskjöld, "The Development of a Constitutional Framework for International Cooperation" in Foote, *Hammarskjöld,* p. 252 (address at University of Chicago Law School, May 1, 1960).

philosophical and psychological aspects. Is "objectivity" possible in applying political principles? Is personal integrity adequate to reconcile deep differences in perspective and values? Is legitimacy grounded in consensus or in transcendent principles? Can any individual be entrusted to rise above personal and social conditioning? All of these questions—political, historical, philosophical and psychological—were implicitly raised by the Soviet assault on Hammarskjöld and by his response. The Oxford lecture was the opportunity—and tragically the last opportunity—to reflect on them. In its defense of personal integrity against the claims of power, and its invocation of reason and history, the lecture carries a powerful appeal even today. That appeal is not lessened by the aura of Hammarskjöld's personality and by his sudden death in the performance of duty. But the questions raised have not been put to rest by the lecture or by the two decades of experience that followed it. They remain perplexing and troubling issues; they still merit thoughtful consideration.

The Various Meanings of Neutrality

The term "neutrality" in this context is not expressly used in the UN Charter or other constituent instruments of international organizations. However, Article 100 of the Charter provides one of its meanings. It stipulates that the Secretary-General and staff shall not seek or receive instructions from any government or from any other authority external to the Organization. It also declares that each Member state shall respect the "exclusively international character of the Secretary-General and the staff." Hammarskjöld considered these mutual obligations as the legal expression of the basic tenet of a neutral civil service. The meaning on the surface is plain. Officials do not carry out the orders of their own or any other government. Their responsibilities and instructions must emanate from international authority. Clear and obvious as these principles appear, they leave open a number of questions that have arisen in practice and were of concern to Hammarskjöld. Foremost among them is the question of the source of international authority in the event of conflicting positions. If member states have different views on what should be done and the competent political organ has taken no decision, or none that is entirely clear, is the Secretary-General entitled to take a stand when his duties require him to act? Suppose he is asked to bring about a settlement or to help maintain order, does that international responsibility entitle him to disregard or subordinate a position taken by a political organ of Member States which appears to impede his function? What if Member States differ and no authoritative decision is taken by a competent organ, may the Secretary-General rely on his Charter authority and Charter principles to take action? Suppose he considers that the decision of a political organ is contrary to the Charter, may he then disregard that decision and follow the "higher law" of the Charter? Must he refrain from taking stands on disputes between Member States even though he considers that one or the other of the disputants is violating the Charter? These questions are not wholly answered by Article 100. They require a fuller examination of the idea of impartiality and of the authority of the Secretary-General under the Charter in relation to the positions of political organs and individual Member States. I shall come back to these issues and to Hammarskjöld's views about them.

The idea of a neutral civil service has other connotations than those related to authority. Krushchev presumably had in mind the pervasive role of ideology, as seen by a Marxist. Soviet Foreign Minister Litvinov had remarked much earlier that only an angel could be neutral in issues between the communist and non-communist countries. This notion has at least two distinct meanings. One relates to conscious motivation. It assumes that most, if not all, persons (and especially officials) are on one side or the other of the conflict between the two ideologies (whether for intellectual or political reasons) and that their conduct as international officials will be governed in some measure by their position on that issue. There is a widespread belief grounded in experience that officials from the communist countries act in accordance with that assumption. Similar behavior has been perceived on the other side though many of the noncommunist officials consciously avoid the kind of partisan positions that they believe incompatible with their exclusively international responsibilities.

The second meaning of "non-neutrality" relates to the conditioning of everyone by social and psychological factors of his particular environment. Social values are internalized and individuals brought up and educated within the same national society will share many such values. Insofar as social conditioning is a significant influence on the perceptions and values of international officials, they cannot be said to be free from predispositions which affect their actions. The principles and practices of international bodies implicitly recognize the likelihood of that kind of bias by their requirements of diversity of national representation in "neutral" bodies. The International Court of Justice is a good example. Its members, the judges, are expected to be impartial and objective in applying law. Yet it is an explicit requirement—and one honored in practice—"that in the body as a whole the representation of the main forms of civilization and of the principal legal systems of the world should be assured."[4] The Secretariat is subject to a less exigent standard of "due regard" to the importance of recruitment on "as wide a geographical basis as possible."[5] Though this requirement is subordinated in the Charter to the "necessity of securing the highest standards of efficiency, competence and integrity,"[6] geographical representation has come to play a more important role in practice than the Charter language envisages. This importance obviously results from the

4. Statute of the International Court of Justice, article 9.
5. United Nations Charter, Article 101 (3).
6. *Ibid.*

pressures of governments for posts for their nationals but it also reflects the belief (and is defended on the ground) that a more diversified representation is necessary to avoid the bias of an "unrepresentative" group of "advanced" countries.

The underlying premise here has obvious implications for the Secretary-General. As an individual with almost plenary power over the Secretariat, the question of his bias, conscious or unconscious, could not be avoided. This was of course, perceived from the very outset in San Francisco. The problem emerged sharply during the term of the first Secretary-General leading to a crisis in respect of his re-election and continued tenure.[7] It was even more dramatically evident in the last two years of the Hammarskjöld period especially (though not solely) in connection with his role in the Congo operation. What was clear from the beginning was the view that the possibility of bias was to be dealt with through institutional means and not merely by normative injunctions. The two crucial means were, first, the requirement of the Charter that the appointment of the Secretary-General must be "recommended" by the Security Council thus involving the application of the veto by the major powers and second, the decision that the Secretary-General have a limited term of office (five years) subject to reelection through the same procedure as the original election.[8]

In addition, the General Assembly adopted regulations relating to personnel and other administrative matters that reinforced the idea that the Secretary-General was subject to the authority of the Assembly (and where appropriate to the Security Council). The principal effect of these regulations and other resolutions relating to the functions of the Secretary-General was to underline his ministerial role and in doing that to reduce, more subtly, the sphere of independent political judgment. Yet it was sensed from the earliest days and emphasized later that the Secretary-General could not be a mere subordinate of the political organs. Article 99, for one thing, gave him an independent constitutional right to bring any matter to the attention of the Security Council that in his opinion may threaten international peace and security. This right in itself was soon perceived as authority for independent fact-finding and judgment.[9] Moreover, the very complexity of the matters dealt with by the political organs required information, analysis and execution by an executive organ that could not in the nature of things be given detailed instructions by a multipartisan deliberative organ. Fully aware of this, the leading governments sought in the first instance to select as a Secretary-General a person

---

7. A. W. Rovine, *The First Fifty Years: The Secretary-General in World Politics 1920-1970* (Leyden: Sijthoff 1970), pp. 264-269.

8. *Ibid.*, p 206.

9. S. Schwebel, "Origin and Development of Article 99 of the Charter," 28 *British Yearbook of International Law* (1951) pp. 371-382.

on whom they could rely for the kind of "neutrality" they desired. They did this in large part by a selection of persons from countries seen to be neutral in the East-West conflict. They also sought an individual who could be relied upon to avoid actions in disregard of Member States positions. The most striking—and as it turned out ironic manifestation of that policy—was the selection of Hammarskjöld. He was seen not merely as a citizen of a neutral State but as a true civil servant, essentially a technician, who had served Swedish governments of different political persuasion. He was, in that sense, thought to be a safe choice.

But even with the protection of the veto and the criteria of selection to ensure neutrality, Member governments pressed for other safeguards to assure themselves that the Secretary-General would not be biased, at least not against them. One such device was an agreement reached at the Preparatory Commission and approved by the first General Assembly that the Secretary-General would have as his most senior assistants (each then designated Assistant Secretary-General) eight persons representative of the different political and regional groupings who were regarded as "political" officials rather than as career civil servants.[10] Implicit in this was the idea of a cabinet that would advise the Secretary-General on all important matters, virtually as if it were a representative political body. It seemed to be accepted that these Assistant Secretaries-General would be nominated by the major powers and regional groups and that they would be expected to present the views of their particular government or group in their consultation with the Secretary-General. It would not be unfair to add that it was also assumed as a corollary that they would inform their governments of internal secretariat matters and of the views of the Secretary-General and their colleagues. That this arrangement involved a departure from the obligations of Article 100 prescribing the exclusively international character of their responsibilities was conveniently ignored during the first period of the organization. The question was, however, thrust into the forefront when Hammarskjöld proposed a reorganization of the upper echelon of the Secretariat in 1953.[11] His premise was that the Secretary-General was the only political officer of the Secretariat and that he could not share his political responsibilities with an "international cabinet." As a practical matter, he noted that the development of permanent missions of Member governments made it unnecessary to have the kind of secretariat political liaison officers envisaged by the Preparatory Commission. He then proposed abolishing the title of Assistant Secretary-General and creating a new and very much larger group of "Under-Secretaries" to include both the old Assistant Secretaries-General and the more numerous "principal directors." By thus bringing into the top echelon many who were not appointed as "political"

10. Rovine, *First Fifty Years*, pp. 211-212.
11. Urquhart, *Hammarskjöld*, pp. 71-72.

officials, he sought to eliminate the political role and significance of the Secretariat upper echelon. The proposal received wide support but it was opposed by the U.S.S.R. and its allies who charged a betrayal of the 1946 gentleman's agreement reached in London. It was then evident that the Soviet Union placed importance on a more collegial secretariat as a means of avoiding undue independence of the Secretary-General or, as they might have stated, a Secretary-General who would tend, perhaps unconsciously, toward partisan actions. This point of view emerged emphatically in 1960 when Chairman Krushchev called for the replacement of the Secretary-General by three persons, representing the Western states, the communist bloc and the Third World.[12] The proposal was quickly designated as the "troika." Hammarskjöld responded by charging that the troika idea was an attempt to extend the veto into the Secretariat. He noted in his address to the General Assembly that the proposal involved an attack on "strict impartiality" which (he said) "might become an obstacle for those who work for certain political aims which would be better served or more easily achieved if the Secretary-General compromised with this attitude. But if he did, how gravely he would then betray the trust of all for whom the strict maintenance of such an attitude is their best protection in the world-wide fight for power and influence."[13]

It was apparent to Hammarskjöld, as to others involved, that at the heart of the confrontation with the Soviet Union was the question of "who decides what and how." The defense of impartiality rested on the premise that decisions were properly and legitimately made by the Secretary-General on the basis of the Charter and the resolutions of the competent UN organs. On the other side, the contention was that the Secretary-General had misused and exceeded his authority by his independent interpretation of the Charter and resolutions and that his actions lacked the support of a significant section of the UN Member states. Hammarskjöld recognized that this issue (or cluster of issues) could not be settled simply by an affirmation of his neutrality or (as he once remarked) by a "jeu de mots" on the concept of neutrality.[14] He conceded that no one with ideas and ideals was truly neutral and he asserted that he was not neutral as regards the Charter. But he sought to explain how his "neutrality in relation to [national] interests" was given practical application in his decisions and conduct of his office. That explanation (most fully expressed in the Oxford lecture) linked neutrality to a conception of responsibility that had a tripartite character.

---

12. U.N. General Assembly. *Official Records:* 15th Session 869th, 882d and 904th Plenary Mtgs. (1960).
13. Hammarskjöld, in Foote, *Hammarskjöld, p.* 316.
14. *Ibid.*, p. 351.

Dag Hammarskjöld with Mr. and Mrs. Nikita S. Khrushchev, at an official dinner given by Dag Hammarskjöld, September 1959.

—— First is the responsibility to adhere to the principles and law of the Charter. That this could be achieved despite conflicting views of governments was the burden of a major part of the Oxford lecture (I shall discuss this aspect in greater detail in the next section.)

—— Second is the responsibility of personal integrity, particularly the duty to be aware of personal sympathies and antipathies and "meticulously check himself so that they are not permitted to influence his actions. This is nothing unique. Is not every judge professionally under the same obligation."

—— Third is the responsibility to reduce the element of purely personal judgment (when law and principle do not suffice to settle the question) by seeking the "representative opinion" of Member governments. The Secretary-General is not "a kind of delphic oracle who alone speaks for the international community." There must be a "link between the judgment of the executive and the consensus of the political bodies."

These three broadly stated conceptions of responsibility formed the core of Hammarskjöld's analysis of neutrality and impartiality in the conduct of his office. Stated in general terms, they are highly persuasive, indeed unexceptionable if one accepts the premise that the Secretary-General has a measure of independence under the Charter and is not merely an administrative officer reduced to impotence when governments differ. But persuasive as they appear to be as general propositions, their specific application in the political maelstrom of the United Nations can be highly uncertain and controversial. This hardly needs demonstration in the light of the almost continuous flow of controversy about the action or non-action of the various Secretaries-General. It may be useful, however, to reflect further on the application of the conception of neutrality and responsibility as formulated by Hammarskjöld. I propose to do this under three headings:

1) Law and Principle in Multilateral Diplomacy
2) Circumspection and Restraint
3) Ideas and Action

Law and Principle in Multilateral Diplomacy[15]

As we have seen Hammarskjöld maintained that the obligation of impartiality required in the first instance adherence to the principles of the Charter "which are the fundamental law accepted by and binding on all States." Though these principles are general and abstract, they are, in his words "specific enough to have application in concrete cases." They are, moreover, supplemented by rules and precedents that furnish guidance when the Secretary-General is faced with the duty of applying a general mandate in circumstances that had not been envisaged by the resolution.

Hammarskjöld did not mean that the Secretary-General could override or disregard resolutions and other decisions of the political organs. He had in mind essentially those cases in which the Secretary-General had been entrusted with a task and the terms of the resolution did not resolve the concrete issue presented at the later time. To be sure, he could go back to the organ for instructions. But the real problems arise because it is so often not possible for the organ to resolve the controversial issue faced by the Secretary-General. Over and over again, political bodies have found themselves unable or unwilling to decide the issue at hand by their vote. Hammarskjöld observed that in these cases there was a temptation for the Secretary-General to refuse to act until the organs themselves settle the matter. But this "easy refuge" may be incompatible with his responsibility especially in a matter affecting peace and security. The Secretary-General, he declared, cannot lay aside his responsibilities merely because the execution of decisions is likely to be politically controversial. In acting he

15. This section draws on my article "Dag Hammarskjöld and the Relation of Law to Politics," 56 *American Journal of International Law* 1 (1962).

must, however, seek guidance in principle and law. Only through principled behavior could he fulfill his obligation of impartiality and avoid the risks of partisan pleading.

It should be understood that Hammarskjöld viewed law—and especially the Charter—not solely as a set of technical rules and procedures but as the authoritative expression of principles that determine the goals and direction of collective action. This did not mean of course that he considered that legal precepts alone expressed the aims of states or that they necessarily governed the decisions of international bodies irrespective of other considerations. But while acknowledging the influence of other factors, he laid stress on the binding character of law and consequently on the high priority it should receive. He took that view not merely in deference to formal conceptions but on the premise that the law of the Charter embodied deeply held values of the great majority of the globe and therefore constituted imperatives of international life.

It may be asked whether an emphasis on principles and legal concepts is not incompatible with the flexibility and adroitness that characterized much of Hammarskjöld's political activity. His technique of fusing those opposing elements—rule and flexibility—into workable solutions is not easily described. It is more art than science. Certainly, an essential feature lay in the nature of the general rules. They were, in the main, principles derived from Articles 1 and 2 of the Charter; on that basis, they already commanded, in a psychological and political sense, high priority among the values formally accepted by the governments of the world. They were flexible in that they did not impose specific procedural patterns or detailed machinery for action; they left room for adaptation to the particular needs and the resources available for given undertaking.

A good example is seen in the guiding principles which Hammarskjöld derived from the experience of the United Nations Emergency Force in Gaza, and which he summarized in a report to the General Assembly.[16] He cautioned against a mechanical repetition of the UNEF formula, and indicated the factors which might require a different pattern in the future. However, he also considered that, by distilling the UNEF experience, it was possible to arrive at fundamental criteria which would provide standards and guidelines for future undertakings and consequently facilitate their adoption by the United Nations organs. It was not long before this was tested in the Security Council proceedings dealing with the request for military assistance in the Congo. The precise UNEF arrangement did not fit the Congo, but the guiding principles derived from the experience were advanced by the Secretary General and accepted by the governments as the constitutional basis of the United Nations operation in the Congo. The

---

16. U.N. General Assembly *Official Records:* 13th Session Annexes Agenda Item 65 (1958).

principles included that of nonintervention in internal political conflicts, the exclusion of the major military Powers from the Force, the international character and status of the Force, the independence of the United Nations in the selection of such troops, and the concept of good faith in the interpretation of the purposes of the Force. The fact that these principles had been formulated in advance enabled the Secretary-General at the outset to clarify the legal and practical basis of the Force for the Congo and provided a strengthened foundation for action by the governments. General as these principles might appear to be when stated in the abstract, the experience in the Congo demonstrated that they could have effect in projecting specific policies to be followed and in restraining ill-considered measures.[17]

It is also of significance in evaluating Hammarskjöld's flexibility that he characteristically expressed basic principles in terms of opposing tendencies (applying, one might say, the philosophic concept of polarity or dialectical opposition). He never lost sight of the fact that a principle, such as that of observance of human rights, was balanced by the concept of non-intervention, or that the notion of equality of states had to be considered in a context which included the special responsibilities of the great Powers. The fact that such precepts had contradictory implications meant that they could not provide automatic answers to particular problems, but rather that they served as criteria which had to be weighed and balanced in order to achieve a rational solution of the particular problem.[18] While this theme was not explicitly formulated by Hammarskjöld, it runs through his statements and his actions. He recognized that there was inevitably a tension between principles and concrete needs; his actions showed that, by taking account both, he sought to achieve "that combination of steadfastness of purpose and flexibility of approach which alone can guarantee that the possibilities which we are exploring will have been tested in the full."[19]

Hammarskjöld conceived of his office primarily in terms of diplomacy, a "quiet" diplomacy which he conducted, as Walter Lippmann observed, with "a finesse and courtliness in the great traditions of Europe."[20] But the setting and purposes of that diplomacy were far from the traditional. In Lippmann's eloquent appraisal: "Never before and perhaps never again has any man used the intense art of diplomacy for such unconventional and

---

17. See Schachter, "The Uses of Law in International Peace-keeping," 50 *Virginia Law Rev.* 1096 (1964); Schachter, "The Relation of Law, Politics and Action in the United Nations," 109 *Hague Academy Recueil des Cours* 171 (1963).
18. For a similar approach to the "abstractions" in American constitutional law, see Paul Freund in 69 *Harvard Law Review* 803 (1956).
19. Hammarskjöld in Foote, *Hammarskjöld*, p. 316.
20. Walter Lippman, *New York Herald-Tribune*, Sept. 21, 1961.

novel experiments."[21] Whether unconventional or traditional, diplomacy is normally regarded as separate from—indeed, some would say opposed to—the processes of law, and many have warned against mingling the two. Yet the experience of Hammarskjöld indicates that this is an oversimplified view, and that a properly balanced combination of law and diplomacy may be an advantage, even at times a necessity.

The advantage of a legal basis is perhaps most evident when one considers the initial stage of a conciliation or good offices effort. It is apparent that a third party cannot enter the delicate terrain of inter-state controversy without having a locus standi acceptable to the parties directly concerned. Sometimes this is simply satisfied by the willingness of the parties to accept a friendly third-party intermediary; far more frequently, there are objections to any conciliation efforts, and influential groups within the states concerned (or perhaps external forces) may make it difficult for the governments to agree to a third-party "volunteer." However, when the third party is buttressed by firm legal authority—that is, when his locus standi rests on the rules and procedures to which that state has formally committed itself, that in itself becomes a cogent factor in overcoming resistance. Diplomatic intervention may then be viewed as part of generally accepted procedures agreed to by all states, and consequently involving no invidious connotation for the party to the dispute. Hammarskjöld had a profound appreciation of this aspect of peaceful settlement, and he therefore attached considerable importance to the grant of authority enabling him to enter into private discussions. He recognized in this respect the legal significance of the Security Council's responsibilities under the Charter, and he laid stress on the importance of a mandate by that organ in situations involving threats to the peace.[22] In point of fact, most of his diplomatic activities, notably in the Middle East, Africa and Southeast Asia, were undertaken on the basis of a mandate of the Security Council, bolstered in several cases by agreements of the parties themselves. Only rarely did he offer his good offices without a Security Council or General Assembly mandate, and these instances were limited to situations in which both sides desired his participation in preliminary discussions.[23]

There is another, no less important, aspect of the relation between law and diplomacy which can be discerned in Hammarskjöld's diplomatic technique. An examination of his conciliation efforts shows that he relied to a considerable extent on establishing a common ground of principles to which both sides could adhere. An essential element in this process was to

21. *Ibid.*
22. Hammarskjöld, "Do We Need the United Nations?" Address to Students Association of Copenhagen, May 2, 1959, in Foote, *Hammarskjöld*, p. 200.
23. Hammarskjöld, *Introduction* to the Fourteenth Annual Report of the Secretary General on the Work of the Organization, 1958-1959 UN Doc. A/4132/ Add 1, p. 3.

suggest general standards which had a legal quality, whether as an accepted norm of international law or as a rule which was implied by or closely related to a principle of law. The legal aspect was important in achieving acceptance because it endowed the proposed standards with the authority of pre-existing obligations and the character of a universal rule that would be applied equally in other cases. It thus implied that the solution to be reached would not diverge too sharply from the probable expectations of the states concerned, and for that reason was less likely to involve political difficulties. It also offered an assurance that the conciliation effort was carried out with objectivity and impartiality and therefore without discrimination against either side. Hammarskjöld's awareness of these factors is demonstrated by his frequent recourse to legal rules and precedents which, directly or by analogy, could be applied to the particular situation and accepted as guiding principles by the parties concerned. By a discriminating and skillful use of legal principles, he was thus able to further his diplomacy of conciliation and by its success to reinforce the effectiveness of law.

Although Hammarskjöld often stressed the imperative quality of legal norms, this did not mean that he regarded law as an autonomous force which develops and is applied indendently of political and social factors. He preferred to view law not as a "construction of ideal patterns," but in an "organic sense," as an institution which grows in response to felt necessities and within the limits set by historical conditions and human attitudes.[24] Placed as he was in the center of the political maelstrom, Hammarskjöld could not but be keenly aware of the impact of power relations on the normative structure of international society. He was especially mindful of the fact that the constitutional pattern of the United Nations had been molded largely by the concentration of power in the two major blocs and by the deep conflict between them. He was equally aware of the extent to which internal instability and the demands for radical changes affected the application of existing rules of public order. But it was characteristic that he regarded these factors not merely as imposing limits on the use of law, but in a more positive sense as a challenge which called for creative attempts to find new norms and procedures. In making these attempts in new directions, Hammarskjöld never lost sight of the limiting conditions; he always was conscious that he was nurturing an organic growth, not designing an ideal pattern.

He did not, therefore, attempt to set law against power. He sought rather to find within the limits of power the elements of common interest on the basis of which joint action and agreed standards could be established. In the area of advancing technologies, such as atomic energy and

24. Hammarskjöld in Foote, *Hammarskjöld*, p. 316.

outer space, he pursued efforts to develop new normative arrangements based on the acknowledged factors of interdependence. In the economic and social field, he stressed the mutual interest of the advanced states in combatting the debasement of living standards and human dignity in the impoverished countries of the world. In the most critical arena, the relation between the major power blocs, he devoted himself to seeking balanced arrangements based on the mutual interest of both blocs to survive in a world in which each possessed the power to destroy the other. He did not endeavor to enter directly into big-Power relations, nor in any way to mediate directly between them. But he found opportunities in the peripheral areas, especially in the "power vacuums" that arose in underdeveloped areas and which provoked external intervention and the inevitable counteraction by the other side.[25] In these matters he sought to stave off the dangerous spiral of action and reaction by measures to fill the vacuums and create a viable economy and government by means of economic and financial aid, the building of governmental and administrative machinery, the provision of educational and technical training, and, even as in the Congo, by using armed force to maintain internal order. These measures, commonly described as "executive action," signified for Hammarskjöld a fundamental and decisive advance toward a more effective system of international cooperation, and they have been widely regarded as constituting a major feature of his political legacy.

Although these "operational" measures do not at first seem to be related to international law, it will be evident on reflection that they have an impact on the evolution of standards of international behavior, and the effective implementation of such standards. For it must be borne in mind that collective intervention of the kind described, based on United Nations principles, involves more than "action." It necessarily includes new conceptions of permissible and impermissible interference by individual states, and of the Charter obligations for mutual assistance and co-operation. Moreover, such measures constitute, as Mr. Hammarskjöld observed, practical means and techniques for bringing about compliance with international decisions and principles. They can, therefore, be regarded in a broader and more subtle sense, as a part of the enforcement or sanctioning machinery which is available to the international community to assure observance of its decisions. Viewed in these terms, such practical action will be seen as imparting a new dimension to the efforts to give vigor and efficacy to a normative structure based on the common interests of all peoples.

25. Hammarskjöld, *Introduction* to the Fifteenth Annual Report of the Secretary General 1959-1960, UN Doc. A/4390/Add. 1, p. 4.

Responsibility, Restraint and Ideology in International Secretariats.[26]

Hammarskjöld, as we mentioned earlier, considered the Secretary-General the only "political" officer in the UN Secretariat; all others were non-political civil servants in the classic British sense. It was important in his view that the Secretary-General should be responsible to member governments for the actions of the international staff under his authority. It was equally important that the staff be seen by governments as a truly non-political and impartial body. There was nothing novel in this conception. From the time of the League of Nations, it had become common to describe the Secretariat's role in exceedingly modest terms. An early League report contained a formula that was often repeated: the primary duty of the Secretariat was "to collate the relevant documents and to prepare the ground for decisions without suggesting what those decisions should be." How far the League Secretariat officials departed from this limited conception of their duty is a subject for conjecture, but there is little doubt that many of them enjoyed an influence far beyond that foreseen in the formula. However, the manner in which they exerted that influence reflected the formula: they tried not to appear to be suggesting or making policy decisions. To a large degree, that remained a cardinal principle in the United Nations Secretariat. Yet the requirements of the United Nations for "executive action" and the emergency character of peacekeeping and mediation activities, as well as the demands of economic development and technical assistance, introduced a new dimension to the secretariat. The League formulation no longer fitted, yet the tradition of secretariat restraint and circumspection retained its influence.

Because it is relevant to Hammarskjöld's role, it seems appropriate in this context to reflect on the implications of such restraint and its relation to action by the secretariat. Hammarskjöld had to face these implications in his effort to build an effective international administrative mechanism capable of dealing with political as well as technical matters while maintaining the political neutrality expected of it. (The reflections that follow are more personal than scientific. They are largely impressions based on my experience in the UN secretariat fortified here and there with ideas of more profound thinkers.)

International officials, conscious, as they must be, of their place as civil servants, not political masters, tend to adopt a "low profile" in governmental organs. Only exceptionally do they take issue with a statement of a

---

26. This section and the following section draw upon Oscar Schachter, "Some Reflections on International Officialdom," in Fawcett and Higgins (eds.), *International Organization: Law in Movement, Essays in Honour of John McMahon* (London: Oxford University Press 1974), pp. 53-63.

delegate. Such suggestions as they may make, even on procedural matters, are, more often than not, accompanied by expressions of deference to delegates. Papers or oral statements which indicate solutions or decisions tend to indirection or circumlocution.

A direct and positive style might after all be considered as too assertive. Perhaps that is one reason, though not the only one, why United Nations documents exhibit that "pompous, polysyllabic and relentlessly abstract style" (to quote Edmund Wilson) which characterizes written "bureaucratese."

It is also one of the reasons, possibly the main one, why oral statements by officials sometimes seem so full of inflated compliments to government representatives and self-deprecatory observations about their own role or their suggestions. This public display of deference towards delegates is not infrequently accompanied by private expression of condescension. The transparent manoeuvres, vanities, and ambitions of delegates, the not uncommon gaps in their knowledge, are unfailing sources of secretariat shop-talk. Experienced officials will, by and large, take all this in their stride, as part of the system. However, newer and younger secretariat members tend to be more restive. Many of them will be inclined to contrast the inhibitions placed on their initiative with the opportunity for participation given to equally young and sometimes less qualified delegation members. A recent unofficial survey of a sample of secretariat members reports that most of those interviewed "are frustrated by the vow of silence under which they are obliged to remain mute in conferences while former fellow students and friends who are part of the diplomatic community dominate the spotlight in the verbal area."

The inhibitions placed on international officials are also felt outside the "verbal areas" of conference and committee work. There is certainly some feeling—one cannot say how widespread or intense it is—that the organization prizes the negative virtues—prudence, conformity, restraint—more highly than the positive qualities—initiative, creativity, vigour. It can be said this merely exemplifies the classic model of bureaucracy as first described by Max Weber in which the most valued traits of officials are strict subordination, precision, regularity, skill in technical or administrative routine, and the like. By the same standards, the bureaucracy shows uneasiness, if not outright hostility, when new ideas are advanced or independence and non-conformity manifested. No doubt these are characteristics of most large administrations and we have no hard evidence to enable us to rank international organizations as better or worse. But, putting comparisons aside, there are fairly obvious reasons to support the impression that international organizations tend to favour the more passive and more bureaucratic qualities. What we have already said about circumspection and restraint tells us in part why this is so. Underlying this is the political fact that the international civil service, by and large, operates under a far more limited conception of delegated authority than do national civil services.

It would be surprising if the restraints and inhibitions described above did not have substantial effects on the behavior and attitudes of the individuals. One hesitates to generalize, since conditions, motivations, and personalities vary so widely. We do not have systematically organized data on this and indeed little in the way of scientific research has been attempted in this area. Still, some impressions may be of interest with the caveat that they should not be over-generalized.

I would suppose that the adjustment of individuals to the system is accomplished in large part through the "natural selection" of recruitment and duration of service. Those who find the conditions unpalatable do not enter or soon leave. Once in, many find it easier to resign themselves to, than from, their relatively well-paid positions. Some treat their jobs as secondary and look to other sources of personal satisfaction. They perform their tasks with limited interest and little enthusiasm. It is not unusual for older secretariat members to comment on how they, or others, have lost their drive or have been reduced to apathy. This does not necessarily mean that they express active dissatisfaction. Many will find support for a self-image of dedication by identifying with the goals of the organization, even if in an abstract way, rather than through their direct personal role. On that basis they may adjust to sitting through long and tedious committee meetings in which their role is marginal and barely requires attention. Others will adjust to preparing reports and studies which are no more than compilations or summaries of other published material, sometimes relevant to preparing the way for decisions, more often honoured by ritualistic praise and little more than that.

Those who have joined the international organization with a strong professional motivation may have more difficulty in adjusting to the inhibition and frustration of their jobs. They will have come in to further their careers as experts, challenged by the apparent opportunities in fields like economic development work, international law, social research, political analysis, or the variety of other disciplines represented in the organization. Mere bureaucratic approval is much less important for them than the approbation of experts in their field and acceptance of their ideas. They do not take so easily to the prevailing rule of anonymity under which their papers are presented by, or in the name of, a senior official who has made little if any personal contribution without any attribution to the actual writer. In addition the restrictions placed on scholarly contributions by staff members and an impression that such individual effort is deplored by higher officials are further reasons for dissatisfaction and reluctance to enter the international service. Such "role oriented" professionals are not likely to regard dedication to the aims of international organization as an adequate substitute for a satisfactory professional experience, nor do they tend to think of themselves as civil servants in the usual sense of a career in administration without regard to their particular expertise.

The inhibitions which affect the more scholarly sections of the secretariats probably do not have the same impact on those engaged more directly in operations. These include the thousands engaged in the execution of economic development projects around the world, in the regulatory activities of the specialized agencies, or in the relief activities for refugees or children. I would suppose that the restraints most keenly felt by operational personnel are those imposed by the complicated tangle of authority governing their activity. In an official study, Sir Robert Jackson described the development activities of the United Nations system as "probably the most complex organization in the world."[27] This may be an overstatement but the existence of formidable jurisdictional complexities cannot be doubted. What is distinctive, in comparison to national bureaucratic overlap and conflict, is that the international system lacks the ultimate centralized authority of the national state. There is no single overall parliament, no chief executive, no supreme court to lay down final rules or decisions. The various international organizations involved in the development programmes have their own constitutions and are answerable to no other international authority. "Co-ordination" and consultative procedures permeate the international development process. International development officials feel at times that they are in a morass of inter-agency meetings, endless clearances, and continuous uncertainty as to who decides what.

Contributing to the complexity and pervasive ambiguity is the always uncertain line between the responsibility and authority of the international agency and that of the national government receiving development aid. That the national government is the final authority on what it needs and how to administer it is axiomatic in these programmes, but the injunctions and restraints imposed on the international agencies by their collective bodies cannot be automatically subordinated to individual national decisions. It is apparent that under this complicated system, individual officials must carry out their tasks with circumspect regard for the procedures laid down, and, even more important, with regard for the sensibilities of those in other international bodies and in national governments. One can easily see that the price for this system of fragmented authority may be high in individual frustration—to say nothing of time and energy expended. But while the reasons for this are not difficult to ascertain, it is not enough to convince the officials that the division of authority is inevitable. They must also be persuaded that it is possible for them to carry out the job for which they were hired. At least those with a conscience will need that conviction. There will always be others who can remain satisfied with meeting on

27. R. Jackson, *A Study of the Capacity of the UN Development System* (UN:1969), p. iii.

co-ordination and with the endless movement of papers from office to office. The house-broken official will rarely question the need for restraint. He may, however, share the sentiment expressed in verse by Roy Campbell:

> You praise the firm restraint with which they write,
> I'm with you there, of course.
> They use the snaffle and the curb all right
> But where's the bloody horse?

Even a government strongly in favour of the snaffle and curb for international officials will complain of lack of action on matters which it wishes to have pursued. Numerous resolutions are adopted which entrust the international staff with tasks that demand initiative, judgement, and vigour. There are "bloody horses" to be ridden, even if they have to be kept under tight rein. International organizations have long since shown that they cannot be confined to conference diplomacy and that, gradually or precipitately, they are required to take on tasks that go beyond the traditional functions of conference secretariats.

Certain of these tasks, described as operational or as executive action (a phrase favored by Mr. Hammarskjöld), have acquired a lustre of their own. The international official appears as a man of action, directly engaged in moving men, materials, and funds to places where they are needed: the use of troops for policing, the transport of food for refugees, the sending of technical experts to discover natural resources, the transfer of capital to finance construction. In these cases, he has moved from words to deeds or at least the appearance of deeds. The official can feel that his work is closer to results—the relief of hunger, the suppression of violence, the establishment of a new school, a new road. As a consequence his own role—whatever his echelon—will seem concrete, less concerned with verbal resolutions, more with events. It is not surprising that many of the international officials should find their true vocation in the operational areas and that executive action should be seen by them as the highwater mark of a dynamic international organization.

But there are many mansions in the house of world organization and not all are dedicated to executive action. Nor do all international officials see their role as carrying out operations. If someone drew their attention to the classic fable of Menenius Agrippa about the body politic and its parts, many would regard themselves not as the hands or feet doing what is bidden but as the brain or at least the central nervous system. This would not mean that they question the competence of the intergovernmental organs to determine policy; only that they appreciate the extent to which secretariat studies and reports can mould that policy when issues are complex and difficult.

It is usually good tactics for the staff to present its reports as purely factual, served up to a policy-making body for decision. But it must be

Dag Hammarskjöld in front of United Nations Headquarters in New York, June 1953.

borne in mind that policy-makers are rarely interested in the facts as such. The knowledge they need for policy decisions is knowledge geared to specific goals, institutions, and acceptable solutions. The typical study produced in academic institutions would not, as a rule, meet these conditions. Indeed, studies based on rigorous scientific methodology and precise in their conclusions are generally not suited to the requirements of the policy-maker. An international secretariat cannot afford that kind of intellectual rigour; its sights have to be kept on the ends it serves and on practical necessities. It has a built-in bias because the knowledge which it obtains and conveys must be linked to policy and action. Officials are not paid to waste their efforts or to purvey knowledge for its own sake. They must concern themselves with felt needs and articulated demands. Their product has to meet the tests of feasibility and acceptability. That is a far cry from the kind of independence and flexibility enjoyed by universities and research institutions.

Studies and "background papers" have been used by the international secretariats to initiate or stimulate far-reaching programmes of action. In these endeavours style, strategy, and "organizational ideology" have played important parts. An interesting example can be found in the history of the United Nations Economic Commission for Latin America (ECLA) under the leadership of Raoul Prebisch. In a ten-year period Prebisch and his colleagues presented to the Commission a steady stream of explanations, predictions, objectives, and measures designed to bring about reform in economic policy on both the international and national levels. A principal element was a conception of international stratification, exemplified by a "centre" of industrialized countries and a "periphery" of agricultural raw material producers, the latter suffering from long-term decline in the terms of trade and from short-term fluctuations in the export price for raw materials. Also put forward was a set of functional goals, principally industrialization, the "technicalization" of agriculture, and central planning and programming for the national economy. A third component was a series of specific means to achieve these goals of industrialization: for example, import substitution, protectionism, agrarian reform, and income redistribution.

Whatever the economic merits of the ECLA theory and programme of action (and many economists have been critical of both) Prebisch did win considerable support among the member governments of the region and among their national elites concerned with economic policy. The criticism (which was probably greater outside than in the region) did not greatly weaken the image of rationality and planning projected by the secretariat. Their ideas seemed a welcome contrast to the usual policies of stop-gap measures forced by political pressures. What is interesting for our present purpose is that the secretariat proclaimed its innovative and heterodox approach. Prebisch declared "ECLA is heretical by nature" and that its thinking had to depart from accepted canons. He called for boldness and originality, often in dramatic and emotional language. Over the years a sizeable and diversified corps of supporters appeared throughout the Latin-American region. A recent study sums up the key elements of that support:

In these circumstances, Prebisch appealed to the Latin American nationalists by emphasizing inward-oriented growth. He attracted the modern liberals by emphasizing the state's responsibilities in the guidance of the economy. The intellectuals appreciated his theoretical skill and his appeals for bold, new ideas. Impotent governments supported his putting on the center countries the responsibility for international commodity agreements, extended financial and technical assistance; and other concessions. As for his advocacy of industrialization, it was appealing to all these groups, and also perhaps to the reactionary forces, because it could be construed, presumably, as a way to avoid difficult political and social reforms, particularly agrarian reform. Finally, both to Latin American and to the ECLA Secretariat's staff, Prebisch offered a coherent explanation of the reality to be transformed, a clear delineation of the means to be used to transform it, and the identity of the opposition to be tackled. Finally, in addition to personal charisma, Prebisch projected the image and the reality of professional competence as an economist. This was crucial in strengthening his authority and organizational loyalty.[28]

Few international officials have been as successful as Prebisch in achieving an impact on national attitudes. Several have similarly made efforts to give direction to, and win support for, their activities by basing them on broad unifying concepts or doctrine. John Boyd Orr, for example, while head of the FAO, sought for a doctrine of agricultural welfare based on the use and disposal of surpluses. In the WHO, Brock Chisholm attempted to use an extended concept of good mental health (a concept in the WHO constitution) as a basis for a programme to combat aggressiveness and violence. Gunnar Myrdal made a valiant effort in 1948-49 to bridge the East-West division in Europe through ideas of planning the use of common resources and trade on a continental basis. At one time in UNESCO Julian Huxley sought to formulate a philosophy of scientific humanism as a foundation for global programmes.[29] In the ILO David Morse built wide support for an expanded programme on the basis of a doctrine of economic development and social progress, and Wilfred Jenks formulated a conception of a common law of mankind, based on perceived mutual interests, as a foundation for economic and social rights.[30]

Professor Ernst Haas of Berkeley has characterized these ideas as examples of "organizational" ideologies which "make possible the articulation of shared objectives" and can "bind and fire the organization's staff."[31] Lacking such ideologies, the organizations (in Haas' view) tend to "opportunistic decision-making" and "subgoal-dominated programming" that "degenerate into survival policies." They then do not undertake the

28. Pierre-Michel Fontaine, *Regionalism and Functionalism in International Organization* (unpub. Ph.D. dissertation, University of Denver 1968), pp. 352-3.
29. W. Laves and C. Thomson, *UNESCO* (Bloomington, Ind.: Indiana University Press 1957) p. 49.
30. W. Jenks, *The Common Law of Mankind* (New York: Praeger 1958).
31. E. Haas, *Beyond the Nation-State* (Stanford, Cal.: Stanford University Press 1964), p. 445.

programmatic innovation required to maintain sufficient support by the members (that is, by the various "interest coalitions" of the members). With such ideologies they are better able to persuade clients and supporters that "constantly revalued objectives linked to new demands and new expectations in the environment can be met only by strengthening the organization."[32]

Whether or not one accepts the thesis that organizational ideologies are necessary, it is evident that just as facts become meaningful when they move into ideas, so ideas gather strength as they are linked together in a coherent interrelated pattern. In an international organization a coherent doctrine that combines various goals can attract diverse supporters, each group finding its own benefit in the totality. Under skilful leadership it can impact a sense of mission to staff and members alike. To be sure, this will not work unless the doctrine reflects or expresses the goals shared by members. Huxley's doctrine of "scientific humanism" was rejected by the members who did not accept it as expressing their goals.[33] Moreover, a viable doctrine must have a cutting-edge: that is, it requires sufficient specific content to influence decisions; a vague abstraction is no more than rhetoric. (Perhaps that vagueness was the weakness of Chisholm's doctrine of good mental health.) A third requirement is that the ideas should be validated in practical implementation. Mere slogans or catch-phrases may appeal to some and win applause, but their value is likely to be short-lived. In sum, it is not enough to describe the Promised Land. A way must be shown and it must be demonstrated in actuality, to be the right way.

While no one can be especially optimistic that intellectual initiatives by international officials will meet these exacting requirements, there are indications that opportunities for such initiatives may well increase in the next few years. A factor of some significance, in my view, is the growing recognition of the need for more comprehensive and better integrated approaches to problems previously dealt with in separated discrete segments. This has been evidenced particularly in two broad areas of current concern to the international organizations: one, development and modernization of the less developed countries; and the other, environmental deterioration. I might also add to this the question of the sea-bed and the regime of the oceans. In these fields, the emphasis has moved dramatically from specialized professional techniques to interrelationships and comprehensive planning. It has become more apparent than ever before that developmental and environmental goals must be sought on a global basis, global in the sense of both geography and intellectual discipline.[34] A

32. *Ibid.*, p. 127.
33. Laves and Thomson, *UNESCO*, p. 50.
34. The problems and dilemmas presented by a global perspective in regard to resource management and international institutions are examined in Oscar Schachter, *Sharing the World's Resources* (New York: Columbia University Press 1977).

natural consequence is that the responsibility for preparing adequate strategies will fall increasingly on the staffs of the global institutions. National governments, of course, will share the responsibility, especially as they command the greater part of the resources required, but the global character of the problems and their interdependencies are strong reasons for turning to an international mechanism. That is not to say that the present international staffing is sufficient, only that there is a need and consequently an opportunity for the international secretariats to play a central role in the formulation of the required strategies. This has already been recognized in the extensive endeavour of the major organizations to appraise the lessons of the first development decade and to formulate a new world-wide strategy of development for the next decade. We have seen also the beginnings of a similar effort in response to the growing and widespread demands to stem the world-wide deterioration of the natural environment.

From a broad intellectual perspective these developments may be seen as having a greater significance than opening up opportunities for international officials or even advancing the solution of the problems to which they are directed. They can be seen as revealing indicators of the penetration into the international consciousness of the importance of scientific inquiry and approach. (I do not, of course, mean here the natural sciences or engineering techologies, but rather the outlook and methods that characterize the scientific approach in whatever area it may be applied.) When international groups of experts or for that matter of non-expert officials enter into a common effort to solve the problems of, say, underdevelopment or of environmental damage they tend, more and more, to discuss their approach on the basis of a common set of concepts and methodologies of inquiry. There will of course still be statements of preference for particular political ideologies or social systems but these are subordinated, as a rule, to analysis that relies on a frame of reference accepted by diverse political and ideological groupings. It may be said that this phenomenon is a natural consequence of a multi-partisan, "multi-ideological" group trying to deal with a common problem. They have to be ecumenical if they are to proceed with the business in hand. That is probably true and not unimportant. It is also evidence that there has been a world-wide diffusion of the scientific approach and a realization that its rationality and objectivity are needed to produce reliable knowledge, the kind of knowledge that has predictive power and enables men to exert control over their environment. I cannot emphasize this point too heavily for it seems to me to be the solid rock on which the intellectual contribution of the international secretariat must rest.[35]

35. Hammarskjöld's views on the importance of science and scientfic method are well expressed in his address "Science and Human Relations," given at the Atoms for Peace Award Ceremony at the Rockefeller Institute, Jan. 29, 1959. See Foote, *Hammarskjöld*, pp. 194-199.

That rock, though necessary, will not however be sufficient. An international administration cannot be effective in promulgating ideas or in carrying out operations without imaginative vision and a wise and courageous leadership. "Imponderabilia" though these may be, without them the international staffs will consist largely of busy bureaucrats, intent on means rather than ends, and of ill-co-ordinated experts, each of whom (as Sir Isaiah Berlin once observed) "sooner or later becomes oppressed and irritated by being unable to step out of his box and survey the relationship of his particular activity to the whole."[36] To be sure, leadership cannot be simply placed on order. We have no ready formulas to produce officials with vision, directive wisdom, and courage; yet on occasion they have appeared (some will say almost by accident) at the head or in the higher echelons of the international civil service. There is no sure ground for believing that they will continue to appear, only a hope that the inadequacies of purely national efforts will drive home to governments the need for a vigorous and creative international public service.

36. Isaiah Berlin, as quoted in Henry Brandon, *Conversations with Henry Brandon* (London: Deutsch 1966), p. 25.

Peter Steiner

Dag Hammarskjöld, Secretary-General of the United Nations, was born on 29 July 1905, in Jsnkoping, Sweden. In 1933, he was Assistant Professor in Political Economy at the University of Stockholm. He had a notable career in the field of finance. From 1936 to 1945, he was Secretary-General of the Swedish Government's Department of Finance. In 1946, he held the position of Specialist in Finance in the Swedish Foreign Ministry. He also served as Chairman of the Executive Committee of the Organization for European Economic Cooperation. He became his country's Minister of State in 1950. Mr. Hammarskjöld served as Vice-Chairman of the delegation of Sweden to the 6th Session of the United Nations General Assembly, and as Chairman to the 7th Session. He assumed his duties as Secretary-General of the United Nations in April 1953, and served until his death on 17 September 1961.

4
An Informal Retrospection on Dag Hammarskjöld's Commitment to Economic and Social Development

Philippe de Seynes

Philippe de Seynes started his career in the Ministry of Finance of France. In 1949, he joined the French Mission to the United Nations as Economic Counsellor. In 1954, he became adviser to Prime Minister Pierre Mendès-France. In 1955, he was appointed Under-Secretary-General of the United Nations in charge of Economic and Social Affairs, where he remained until 1975. He now heads the "Project on the Future" in the United Nations Institute for Training and Research (UNITAR).

My relationship with Dag Hammarskjöld came to be quite close and this, rather rapidly, after I had assumed my position in the Secretariat. When we first discussed the future of the economic role of the United Nations, we discovered that we were very much on the same wave length. This was probably due in part to the fact that the pattern of the higher education systems which we had both followed had been permeated by similar traditions. It was very largely what was called in Europe "political economy," which now seems split into different sub-disciplines. Also, he became involved in international economics mostly within the Organization for Economic Cooperation and Development (OECD), or rather its predecessor—the Organization for European Economic Cooperation (OEEC)—at the time when I was myself involved in multilateral economic diplomacy as a member of the French Delegation to the United Nations.

At the personal level, there had already been a number of contacts between the two institutions, although I had not met Hammarskjöld before November 1954, when he first interviewed me. At that time, I could feel that he had a great inclination to plunge into economic problems, as he saw quite clearly that there would be a rapid and vast expansion in that field, linked to the emergence of the Third World. It was, at the same time, quite clear that his mind was also attracted elsewhere, to the political arena, not just by the necessity of his functions but also because these were new problems for him, and his mind was always alert to and even in quest of new problems. On the occasion of this interview, he ventured this remark, that still startles me, given the time at which it was made: "From now on, the two main problems occupying the United Nations will be Africa and the atom." He had not yet suspected how quickly and deeply he would become absorbed in the intricate politics of the Middle East and other areas of conflict.

As to the private character of his existence, not one of his close colleagues was able to penetrate his private life, nor did any of us really seek to do so. Working with him was in itself sufficiently enriching, and it was a constantly renewed source of enrichment. Outside the work, there was also a small amount of free time that could occasionally be spent with him at lunch or dinner, or during travel periods. But there was no temptation to use these opportunities to try to pierce the mystery of his private life, as his conversation covered such a wide range of interests: political, social and cultural. I for one never had enough of it. The few who thought they may have had a claim on his privacy soon burned their fingers. Occasionally, it dawned upon us in one or another fleeting remark, that he had his own "secret garden" that he was preserving jealously. This became clear only with the publication, after his death, of *Markings*. His public life and his private life however were in my view quite separate. I have always been impatient with authors who, writing on him, were trying to discover links between one or the other entry in his private diary and what had happened on the same day in the Security Council or the General Assembly. And I was also very irritated with those of my countrymen who came to dislike him intensely and propagated the notion that he was "listening to voices," or having visions, when he was taking political initiatives. In my view, nothing could be further from the truth. I have never met any person striving with so much insistence to develop a juridical construction as the basis for even the most minute decisions. In this sense, he was a true positivist. There is nothing strange or unique in such a dichotomy between public and private life. It probably is reconciled at a certain level of philosophical reflection, which he did not have the time to fully develop and communicate.

But as to the work relationship, as I have already hinted, it was enriching but also exacting, mainly because he was so allergic to platitudes. This feature also influenced his personal relations, (although these could be quite relaxed) and this forced one to be always on the alert. But it was highly stimulating to try to adjust to that frame of mind . . . a real learning process. He was also very demanding in respect of papers submitted to him, either memoranda for action, or draft speeches which he was to deliver. He had a rigorous discipline in respect of internal staff meetings. They took place every Friday at 9:30 a.m., and I cannot recall his ever being late. His briefings were often quite illuminating, and they always reflected the power of analysis that he was able to apply to current matters.

Hammarskjöld's conception of the office of Under-Secretary-General for Economic and Social Affairs was quite explicit. He thought it should be occupied by someone well-versed in political economy, neither a pure diplomat nor a narrow specialist, but someone able to deal with general problems, as he felt that so many would be rushing in rapidly. He had a somewhat exaggerated opinion of the high level of the French Civil Service, particularly the Corps of "Inspecteurs des Finances" and in 1954, as he was searching for a candidate to fill the job, he was definitely trying to enlist a member of that Corps. That is how I came in the picture. But there was something else, perhaps more important, which an anecdote can illustrate. He was discussing this matter with Prime Minister Pierre Mendes-France with whom I was working at the time, during the negotiations in Geneva on Indochina. He was inquiring about people whom he had met in OECD, and who were far better known than I was. At some point in the conversation, however, Georges Boris, who was the closest confidant of Pierre Mendes-France and who was attending the meeting, told him: "If I were you, I would forget about the people you have mentioned. I think you should consider Philippe de Seynes because he believes in it." This, Hammarskjöld told me much later, had been quite decisive for him. I think it also illustrates an aspect of his scale of values and his attitude toward the United Nations.

In the second half of the 1950's it had become clear that the role of the United Nations in economic and social affairs was bound to evolve rapidly. The shape and nature of the problems were changing. At the beginning, the minds were obsessed by the memories of the 1930's, and it was natural to look for policies of international cooperation which would, through anticyclical measures on a worldwide basis, avoid the "beggar-thy-neighbor" syndrome of the pre-war period. Some outstanding reports emanated from the Department of Economic and Social Affairs, produced by experts of the highest rank. Looking back on these early approaches, it is interesting to see that some of their parts are still relevant to the problems of today as far as the industrial economies are concerned. What, however, was much more novel, and was perceived only gradually, was the specificity of the predicament of the developing countries. It was difficult to resist the temptation to apply to new problems a type of recipe that had already found so much support in the current literature, both theoretical and empirical. In fact, this reflected an almost inevitable lag in the development of economic concepts. For instance it is only recently that the excessive emphasis on trade and capital transfers as remedies to underdevelopment has been seriously questioned within official circles, and it still at times comes as a surprise, breeding disbelief, when it is suggested that the flows of goods and money from North to South may not in all circumstances have benign effects.

This may say something about a certain intellectual inertia in the life of institutions, because some of the forerunners of the now fashionable notion of self-reliance—Kaleczki, Myrdal, Raoul Prebish, Arthur Lewis and Hans Singer—had served for varying periods in one part or the other of the United Nations. Yet the thoughts which they had expressed in their academic work did not fully permeate the thinking of the United Nations. Rather, the institution settled for a set of assumptions relating to the identification of foreign exchange and saving *gaps,* known as the *"two gaps theory."* Although this approach represented real progress over previous analyses, inasmuch as it recognized a structural asymmetry between the economies of the developing world and the industrial countries, it did not do full justice to the complexity of the interractions between national and international factors. These early positions have had a determining effect on the history of the last twenty-five years both in the United Nations and in national governments. The somewhat indiscriminate emphasis on the role of international trade and capital transfers as the engine of national development, has encouraged, in the countries of the South, outward-looking development policies which now are often seen as a serious impediment to their further progress.

There were another aspect important for the early orientation of the United Nations. That was the institutional set-up. The Founding Fathers were highly aware that the Organization should have an economic and social component on the same level of constitutional prestige as peace and security, and decolonization. They however were not as successful in devising the instrument. This was partly due to the fact that the Specialized Agencies which had already been created or were being created around that period, were virtually independent of the U.N. Organization or only loosely related to it through the concept of "coordination."

Some of these bodies were endowed with a power of decision far greater than had been given to the Economic and Social Council (ECOSOC), supposedly the linchpin of the whole system. As ECOSOC became a preserve of the diplomats, the decision-makers of the national economic systems ceased to personally participate in its deliberations and as it was slow in expanding its membership, it lost the confidence of the Third World. The alternative to make it a true "chamber of reflection" would have required a far greater apparatus of research and analysis, together with the practice of hearings on an international basis. This would have entailed financial resources of a different magnitude than the international community was prepared to provide, and perhaps also political risks which it was not ready to confront.

Yet, in spite of its original weakness, when Hammarskjöld took over,

Hammarskjöld's Commitment to Economic and Social Development

Dag Hammarskjöld resting in New Zealand, after an official tour, February 1956.

the United Nations had already carved out for itself a place in the economic field, still embryonic but indicative of the direction which future expansion would take. There was in the Secretariat a strong corps of outstanding professionals, producing important reports and it was gradually realized that the United Nations, through its various forums which became every year more numerous, and its ubiquitous presence in all parts of the world, could exercise a considerable power of influence. The volume of reports, already oriented in a different direction from the classical theory of international relations, could not fail to impress upon the industrial countries the importance and very specific "problematique" of the Third World.

I expressed these thoughts in a lecture dedicated to the memory of Dag Hammarskjöld and delivered at Strasbourg University in 1964 in the following manner.

> A new channel—or circuit—is being established through which gradually all problems are being routed, even those whose considerations was previously reserved for more antiseptic and reassuring forums; a channel characterized by a different combination of forces and a special ideology, one in which new criteria are applied to national policies and through which the world community is constantly confronted with proposals which the major centers of decision making cannot indefinitely overlook.[1]

In fact, the development of the institutional framework itself considerably exercised the mind of Hammarskjöld. For example, he became aware very early of the great value of the regional economic commissions and made it a point to attend most of their sessions, which in that period took place annually. He took advantage of this to visit a number of the governments of each region.

One of the important, and to him intriguing, aspects of these institutional developments was the functioning of the arrangements set up for their coordination. This was the prestigious Administrative Committee on Coordination (ACC) that twice a year brought together with the Secretary-General the Heads of the Specialized Agencies. These gatherings at times brought up problems of protocol which in turn irritated or amused Hammarskjöld. It threw some useful light on the "sovereignty" of international institutions, a matter which has been somewhat neglected in political science and international law. Hammarskjöld, however, felt very accutely the importance of these discussions even if they did not induce any move toward a systemwide integration, and he always enjoyed great respect and esteem from his colleagues on the Committee. Gradually he, like some of us, came to feel the advantages of pluralism, particularly if, as happened toward the end of the 1950's, more intellectual exchanges at various levels took place under ACC auspices. The Agencies themselves also gradually came to understand better the importance of touching base with the Secretary-General on matters of their competence with a political content, such as programs in the Middle East or Africa.

In the Department of Economic and Social Affairs, Hammarskjöld paid great attention to the annual *World Economic Survey,* which was an

---

1. Reproduced in A. Cordier and W. Foote, eds., *The Quest for Peace* (New York: Columbia University Press, 1965), p. 189.

ongoing project when he arrived in 1953. He thought there was a possibility of influence there which was not fully exploited. He had known of the equivalent document in the League of Nations and found its successor too mechanical and perhaps "neutral." When I arrived, he decided to convene a blue-ribbon group of economists to get their views on the matter. The meeting was not altogether illuminating and I suggested to him that we could improve the *Survey* on the strength of our own resources and judgement. There was a remarkable group of professionals in the Department, as the early recruitment, in the first flush of enthusiasm for the United Nations, had been outstanding. Yet there also were political constraints which we were better placed to judge than were outsiders. These pertained to the heterogeneous membership, which made it difficult even in the mid-1950's, to use the League of Nations as a model in such matters. We had to rely even more on the "objectivity" of statistics, and the art of manipulating data to squeeze every bit of useful information from them. Jack Mosak, who was given the responsibility of the *Survey,* was a master in that art, with also great pedagogical gifts which enabled him to recruit and train new staff. The *Survey* was improved, and it carried, for years, in addition to the report on "Current Trends," a special feature on one of the important sectors of international economics. It remained austere but, on its own terms which were valid, it became authoritative. As the membership of the United Nations rapidly changed, and as the majority tilted overwhelmingly on the side of the developing countries, something more openly policy-oriented became not only necessary, but also politically possible. But this change also entailed the demise of ECOSOC in favor of UNCTAD and the General Assembly, as the primary advocacy organs for the Third World. New institutions were also created under the General Assembly. In retrospect, one has to conclude that ECOSOC was somewhat of an abstract concept of the Founding Fathers, and was not so constituted that it could take in its stride the momentous changes which were taking place in the international community. This, however, was not fully realized during Hammarskjöld's time. It is interesting that in one of our last conversations, shortly before he departed for the fateful trip, he said to me in a half-serious, half-jocular mood: "Before you and I depart from the scene we must do something with *that* ECOSOC."

In contrast to ECOSOC the United Nations' program of technical cooperation rapidly became a force in international relations. A small program had been started as early as 1948 almost as a matter of "giving something to do to the UN." Hammarskjöld, however, was convinced of its value and was ambitious for its development. He sensed the special advantage of a multilateral approach, through which, for instance, countries that had reached independence early in the postwar period could bring their experience to bear on more recently-independent ones. He even at times talked about a United Nations *"economic trusteeship,"* a concept publicly denounced by Nkrumah from the podium of the General Assembly. He encouraged a scheme which would have provided new governments at their request, with experts exercising executive responsibilities for a period of time. This, however, became controversial. There were few applications and the scheme fizzled out. But other forms of technical cooperation expanded rapidly and new institutional instruments were created. For instance, Hammarskjöld was very active in the establishment of the "Special Fund," (later to become the UNDP) which was in fact a substitute for the "capital development fund" which the rich countries, in spite of lengthy studies, obstinately refused to sponsor. Hammarskjöld brought Paul Hoffman to lead the Special Fund—one of the foremost personalities of the Marshall Plan—and this insured the successful launching and rapid ascent of one of the most interesting ventures of the post-war period.

The relationship with the Colonial Powers was, of course, a very thorny area since Hammarskjöld's tenure of office coincided with the very intense period of decolonization that started in 1955, more particularly the process of African emancipation. Very early in this period he saw the potentialities of a "mediating" role through the technical and economic cooperation programs of the United Nations. The Department of Economic and Social Affairs started, I believe in 1955, a very modest training course for those who were to fill the higher echelons of African administration. This concentrated mostly on the subject of negotiations for financial and technical cooperation with international institutions as well as private banks. This intergovernmental program benefitted from the assistance of the Specialized Agencies, including the World Bank and the IMF. The courses consisted of twenty officials mostly from Africa but also a few from Asia, and were organized in the form of very intensive sessions at the location of the various international institutions and national donor agencies. It also included visits to the Soviet Union and other Socialist countries. In the case of countries which were still under colonial rule—and this was the case for most French-speaking countries until 1958—the participants were selected in consultation with the metropolitan government.

This program was much appreciated by the participants and in a practical and positive manner it demonstrated Hammarskjöld's interest in mobilizing the forces of the United Nations system to assist Africa in the difficult process of achieving economic independence. Happily, this did not create real frictions with the metropolitan powers. The occasion for friction came, and in a very sharp manner, in the Fall of 1956 with the Suez crisis and the United Nations-induced withdrawal of the invading troops. I well remember a small dinner party at Hammarskjöld's home, in honor of French Premier Guy Mollet and his Minister of Foreign Affairs, when they were taken to task by Ambassador Entezam of Iran, an extremely courteous, subtle and forceful dialectician. After the granting of independence to

African sub-Saharian countries by President De Gaulle in 1958 the skies did not suddenly clear up. For example, on the occasion of De Gaulle's official visit to the United Nations, as was customary, Hammarskjöld invited him to the United Nations for a luncheon which was to include members of the Security Council and some other heads of missions. In his letter of invitation he expressed the desire to have a chance to discuss with De Gaulle the complementarity which he saw between the actions of the United Nations and France in Africa. This irritated De Gaulle, who replied, with his usual "grandeur" and in his aphoristic style, in a hand-written note of three lines indicating that he had no intention to come to the United Nations, adding "Comment les rencontrerais-je puis qu'elles ne seront pas en session." (How could I meet them since they will not be in session?) He, however, invited Hammarskjöld to meet with *him* at the Waldorf-Astoria. Although Hammarskjöld was not amused, he went for what was not much more than an exchange of courtesies.

Then came the Congo (now Zaire) crisis. De Gaulle thought for a moment that the scheme he had nurtured for some time, of a tripartite (American, English, French) directorate would be the ideal instrument to solve what he saw as a difficult situation. Nobody else, however, was of that opinion. There was little doubt at that time that the Colonial Powers preferred Tshombe to Lumumba and did not favor the intervention of the United Nations which Lumumba was requesting. Hammarskjöld foresaw a vast operation of technical and administrative cooperation, and for awhile all the principal officers of the Secretariat were mobilized to that effect. I was sent to Brussels with my colleague Henry Bloch to negotiate the transfer of the funds and responsibilities of the "Banque du Congo" to the central authority of the Congo in what was still at that time Leopoldville. This showed the Belgian side of the problem. It was not an easy undertaking given the mood prevailing in Brussels, but I was greatly helped in it by Raymond Scheyven, the Belgian Minister in charge of Economic Affairs of the Congo and his remarkable entourage who all showed great foresight. A large number of UN experts were sent to the Congo, and even one or two were given direct administrative responsibilities in such technical fields as telecommunications, under the scheme alluded to previously. It seemed particularly relevant in a situation like that of the Congo, with only a handful of university graduates, capable of taking over technical and administrative responsibilities.

Later, there was the crisis arising from the bombing of Bizerte in Tunisia. Hammarskjöld did not hesitate to respond to the appeal of President Bourguiba, and he left for Tunis without delay. He did so as a matter of principle, and also in gratitude for the help he had received from Tunisia in establishing the United Nations force in the Congo. Although upon his return, he asked to be received by the French government, this was refused. On the whole I would say the difficulties he encountered with the Colonial Powers were, objectively, unavoidable. They perhaps were greater than they might have been with another Secretary-General, because Hammarskjöld always was a "maximalist" in his ambitions for the role of the United Nations.

Hammarskjöld's economic philosophy might be called a mixture of Keynesianism and what was to be labeled later "functionalism." He died before the limits of this approach (which really was the Social Democractic approach) in terms of practical policies had been reached or at least perceived. Sweden epitomized the success of this approach and, having been active in labor relations, Hammarskjöld retained an optimistic faith in its continuing validity.

There is really no sign that he was ever touched by the emerging theory of "unequal exchange" or the interpretations of imperialism to be found in the writings of some of the new historians. He worked in a period of soaring material expansion, with in particular, a great development of technical and also financial North-South cooperation, emancipation and regionalism; being "maximalist" for the United Nations, he perceived a vast area ahead to be conquered through new programs, and interventions which would gradually lead to a more structured and efficient international society, constantly widening in the process the role of international institutions. As far as I can see, he did not view as inexorable the resilience of the world capitalist system, to survive and rebound with the help of always-more-subtle means of domination and exploitation.

The most momentous of the changes in the United Nations occurred after his death, and I have often speculated on how he would have reacted to them. In some of us, there was a rapid philosophical evolution. Perhaps it was somewhat slower for him as he was less constantly exposed to the Third World economic and social reality, having to spend so much of his time on diplomatic matters. Yet he responded to every experience, and was alert to every signal. Something has to be said here about our mentality as "enlightened Westerners" devoted to the cause of the Third World. At the beginning, we thought that "Western enlightenment" would bring to the Secretariat adequate credentials. It took us some time to understand that the geographic distribution of posts was a strong requirement of the Third World as well as of the Socialist countries. Perhaps in the Hammarskjöld period we were slow in redressing the initial imbalance, and perhaps also we found an easy excuse in the article of the Charter which gives top priority to "proficiency" among the criteria for recruitment and promotion. All this we recognize with "hindsight" and Hammarskjöld would no doubt also have recognized it.

I have no doubt, either, that he would have been enthralled by the development of the 1970's which brought the role of the United Nations to a very high point of influence and visibility, through the series of conferences on global problems that resulted in international programs in fields such as environment, food, population, and habitat. Such occurrences were certainly part of his vision and ambitions.

And he would also have supported the continuing efforts of the Third World to acquire a voice in international monetary matters. He was the only Secretary-General ever to be invited to speak (and yet only once), at the annual meetings of the IMF and the World Bank. He never quite accepted the idea that the United Nations Organization should be debarred from discussing these matters and from seeking to influence them even if it could not hope to assume operational responsibilities for them.

Dag Hammarskjöld being welcomed upon his arrival at Gaza airfield by (then) Col. I. J. Rikhye, Chief-of-Staff of the United Nations Emergency Force, and Brig. Gen. Amin Hilmy (saluting), Chief-of-Staff of the Egyptian Liaison Staff in Gaza, December 1958.

5
Hammarskjöld and Peacekeeping

Indar Jit Rikhye

Born in Lahore on July 30, 1920, and educated at the Central Model School, Government College Lahore and at the Indian Military Academy, Dehra Dun, Major-General (Ret.) Rikhye saw active service during World War II in the Middle East and Italy. Following India's independence, he participated in the Kashmir operations and later commanded a special force in Ladakh.

In October, 1957, he was appointed Commander of the Indian Contingent with the United Nations Emergency Force in Gaza and subsequently Chief of Staff of the Force. Dag Hammarskjöld first met him in Gaza and selected him for a future U.N. assignment.

An opportunity soon arose with the establishment of U.N. operations in the Congo in July 1960. Hammarskjöld appointed Rikhye as Military Adviser. As a member of the "Congo Club," Rikhye joined the intimate group of Hammarskjöld's advisers.

> Asked if I have courage
> To go on to the end,
> I answer Yes without
> A second thought[1]

The name Hammarskjöld has become synonymous with peacekeeping. The term "peacekeeping" is open to many different definitions. Though it has been applied to the many roles of the United Nations in the maintenance of international peace and security, it undoubtedly applied to U.N. observer groups and U.N. forces established on territories by consent of the governments concerned. Since 1946, the U.N. has established a number of observer groups to monitor ceasefires and armistices; however, it was Dag Hammarskjöld who accepted the challenge of the General Assembly to organize and introduce a U.N. Emergency Force in Egypt to end the

---

1. Dag Hammarskjöld, *Markings,* trans. Leif Sjoberg and W. H. Auden (New York: Alfred A. Knopf, 1964), p. 206.

fighting in the Middle East and to deal with the consequences of the Suez War in 1956. An idea first mooted by Lester Pearson, Minister of External Affairs of Canada, to establish an international force in the Suez Canal area was eventually forged by Hammarskjöld into the use of military contingents for peacekeeping as an innovative and powerful instrument of diplomacy. The first U.N. Emergency Force (UNEF) became an example for the future, and four years later Hammarskjöld was called upon by the Security Council to set up another peacekeeping force to deal with the civil war and subsequent Belgian military intervention which followed the independence of the Congo (now Zaire). *Operations des nations Unie au Congo* (ONUC) turned out to be the most complex and the largest peacekeeping effort by the U.N.

Hammarskjöld nurtured UNEF and ONUC with great personal care. He concerned himself with every detail and supervised every discussion in deciding their organization and operations. He personally negotiated operational arrangements for the peacekeeping forces with the host governments. In fact, there was hardly an aspect of these operations that did not carry a Hammarskjöld mark. Such personal involvement by a Secretary-General in these types of U.N. operations has never been repeated.

Hammarskjöld's commitment to peacekeeping operations stemmed from his early realization that these operations could be developed into an effective tool for furthering the process of peaceful settlement of disputes. Also, having analyzed past U.N. experience in the maintenance of international peace and security, especially as related to the Korean crises, he understood the futility of coercive actions by the U.N. in the face of division between the great powers. Therefore, there had to be another way, and when the opportunity appeared, he succeeded in developing a novel use of military forces not to wage war but to make peace.

In these early days of the evolution of the use of military forces for peacekeeping in a non-force role, there was need for high qualities of leadership, diplomatic skills and a thorough understanding of the military. Hammarskjöld more than matched these qualities. Having spent his early years as Secretary-General in reorganizing the secretariat, improving conditions and morale of the staff, he had won the respect and loyalty of the international staff. Word had reached the U.N. military observers in the Middle East and in Kashmir, and through them their military establishments, that the new Secretary-General was a leader amongst men. His success in obtaining the release on August 1, 1954, of the downed American B-29 crew in China, brought him international acclaim and greatly enhanced his prestige.

Hammarskjöld had many other gifts. His upbringing, his scholarly and artistic interests, his experience with the Swedish government were all assets. Added to these, his smart bearing, his shy smile, his steel-blue penetrating and honest eyes pervaded confidence. His quiet humor, a sympathetic word here and there during his visits and his informal manners delighted the peacekeepers in the field. He took keen interest in the conditions in which peacekeepers had to operate, and by timely visits to the forces, he succeeded in establishing a rapport with the civilians and soldiers, which is an essential quality in great leaders.

He showed immense courage[2] not only in diplomacy but also in taking personal risks. As he wrote in his notebook, "Do not seek death. Death will find you. But seek the road which makes a fulfilment."[3] He was never afraid for his life and chided those who were responsible for his security for trying to prevent personal contact with people. He was amongst the first to fly with UNEF troops from Coppadacino[4] to Abu Suweir,[5] and again he personally led ONUC troops into Elisabethville,[6] in the face of Kantangese[7] threats.

Hammarskjöld was endowed with another rare quality that endeared him to all echelons, from the highest to the lowest. Although an intellect, he could take equally genuine delight in trivial interests. He spent the Christmas of 1958 with UNEF. He heartily laughed with the Indian soldiers at the antics of their officers playing an exhibition field hockey game on mule back and he revelled with the Swedish soldiers in singing their drinking songs, just as he joined with gusto in singing their Christmas carols. Brian Urquhart, in his book *Hammarskjöld*[8] writes that "He was . . . a born bachelor." It equally can be said that he was a soldier's man.

When Hammarskjöld joined the U.N., the General Assembly was preoccupied with the Korean situation. During the difficult climate of the cold war, Trygve Lie, the first Secretary-General, actively supported the Security Council's approval of the United States' decision to use force to resist the North Korean invasion of South Korea. In the face of Soviet censure and refusal to communicate with him for over two years, he had resigned on November 10, 1952. Thus, when Dag Hammarskjöld was appointed to succeed Trygve Lie, the United Nations was still mainly occupied with the Korean situation. However, the armistice was in the air, and Hammarskjöld soon realized that there was little the U.N. or he could do till there was an end to fighting, and even then at best he could only play a peripheral role.

The Security Council's approval of the use of force under Chapter VII of the Charter to deal with North Korea's invasion across the 38th parallel

2. See note 1.
3. *Ibid.*, 159.
4. Near Naples, Italy.
5. Just south of Ismalia, Egypt.
6. Now called Lumumbashi.
7. Now called Shaba.
8. Brian Urquhart, *Hammarskjöld* (New York: Alfred A. Knopf, 1972), p. 26.

caused a serious rift between the United States and the Soviet Union. The Security Council has refrained from taking enforcement action since. Understanding the mood of the U.N. membership, especially of the permanent members of the Council, Hammarskjöld realized from the outset that, "The possibilities of the Organization to use military force are limited to acts of coercion in the name of the world community against a nation which violates the peace. Such an action requires unanimity of the Great Powers."[9]

Brian Urquhart in *Hammarskjöld* sums up Dag Hammarskjöld's philosophy on the role of the U.N. in the settlement of disputes:

> Hammarskjöld saw as the primary function of the U.N. the day-to-day effort to control and moderate conflicts that were a threat to peace, through a system of mediation and conciliation developed on the basis of the sovereign equality of estates. This primary function went hand-in-hand with a long-term effort to attain wider social justice and equality both for individuals and, in the political, economic, and social sense, for nations. He believed that progress in this direction must be based on a growing respect for international law and an emergence of a truly international civil service, free from all national pressure and influences and recognized as such by governments.[10]

Hammarskjöld's understanding of the resolution of conflicts through mediation and conciliation was not only based on his sense of the prevailing mood of the U.N. member states but on a conviction of the uselessness of war, certainly of major war, as a useful tool for diplomacy. In speaking on this question, he said, "To the diplomat of the middle of the twentieth century, war is something that must be averted at almost any cost. . . . Just as the diplomat of today must rule out war as an instrument of policy, so he must recognize that in the new state of interdependence between nations, war anywhere becomes a concern of all."[11]

Besides the futility of war as a diplomatic tool, Hammarskjöld felt that the sacrifice of life demanded by war did not justify the end results. He felt strongly that the U.N., in spite of its past shortcomings, must strive "to save succeeding generations from the scourge of war."[12] In an address he said that [The Organization (U.N.) was born out of cataclysm of the Second World War. It should justify the sacrifices of all fighters for freedom and justice in that war. I remember the bitter lines of a great Anglo-

---

9. Dag Hammarskjöld, "Do We Need the United Nations?", address to Students Association, Copenhagen, May 2, 1959, published in Wilder Foote, ed., *Servant of Peace*, (New York: Harper and Row, 1962).

10. *Ibid.*, 47.

11. "New Diplomatic Techniques in the New World," an address to the Foreign Policy Association, New York, October 21, 1963, published in *Servant of Peace*.

12. United Nations, *Charter*, 1.

American poet (W. H. Auden) who wrote in "Epitaph on an Unknown Solider:"

> To save your world, you asked this man to die,
> Would this man, could he see you now, ask why?

It is our duty to the past and it is our duty to the future, so to serve both our nations of the world as to be able to give a reply to that anguished question.[13]]

In developing principles for the operations of U.N. peacekeeping forces, Hammarskjöld from the start wanted to ensure that the troops would only be used for peaceful settlement and in a non-enforcement role. Since troops were armed, Hammarskjöld provided a "clean delineation" as to when they could use their arms when needed. His interpretation of the relevant General Assembly resolution in respect of UNEF was:

> ... men engaged in the operation may never take the initiative in the use of armed force, but are entitled to respond with force to an attack with arms, including attempts to use force to make them withdraw from positions which they occupy under orders from the Commander, acting under the authority of the Assembly and within the scope of its resolutions.[14]

In setting up the Congo peacekeeping operation, Hammarskjöld followed the UNEF pattern in defining the limits of the use of force by U.N. troops, i.e., military units would be entitled to act only in self-defense. In amplification of this definition, he said that acting under the authority of the Secretary-General and within the scope of its resolution, "the basic element involved is clearly the prohibition against any initiative in the use of the armed force."[15]

However, as the threat of civil war increased, the Security Council on February 21, 1961, "authorized the use of force, if necessary, in the last resort"[16] to prevent the occurrence of civil war. During the discussion preceding this resolution, the members did not have in mind to change the legal basis of the U.N. peacekeeping force or Hammarskjöld's original interpretation that the U.N. troops were "prohibited against any initiative in the use of armed force." Therefore he authorized the troops, for the first time, to take up positions for the purpose of preventing civil war clashes, for example, in support of ceasefire arrangements and neutralized zones. In

---

13. "The World and the Nation," commencement address at Stanford University, Palo Alto, California, June 19, 1955, published in *Servant of Peace*.
14. United Nations General Assembly, A/3943, October 9, 1958, paragraph 179.
15. United Nations Security Council, S/4389 Add 1-6, SCOR, supplement for July, August, September, 1960 (July 18, 1960), pp. 16-24.
16. United Nations Security Council, S/4741.

case the troops were attacked while holding such positions, they could exercise the right of self-defense.

Hammarskjöld realized that for a peacekeeping force to be effective in a consent type of operation, it must enjoy freedom of movement to enable it to carry out its operational responsibilities. This and other matters relating to privileges and immunities for the members of the force were incorporated in a Status of Forces Agreement for UNEF signed with Egypt. A similar agreement was negotiated with the Congolese Government in respect of ONUC and initaled by Justin Bomboko, the Foreign Minister. Soon thereafter, Prime Minister Lumumba was removed from power. However, Hammarskjöld insisted that the agreement stood as initialed by Bomboko and provided the basis for ONUC. It is interesting to note that the U.N. has failed to negoitate Status of Force agreements for subsequent peacekeeeping operations.

Besides UNEF and ONUC, the first and largest of the peacekeeping forces, respectively, Hammarskjöld also was responsible for establishing a U.N. Observer Group in Lebanon—UNOGIL. An analysis of Hammarskjöld's role in these three peacekeeping operations is described below.

United Nations Emergency Force

After the breakout of fighting between Israel and Egypt in the Sinai and the landings by Anglo-French forces in the Suez Canal area on November 2, 1956, the General Assembly, acting under the terms of the "Uniting for Peace" resolution[17] called for a ceasefire; a halt to the movement of military forces and arms into the area; urged all parties to the GAA[18] promptly to withdraw all forces behind the Armistice lines, to desist from raids across the Armistice Lines into neighboring territory, and to observe scrupulously the provisions of the GAA.[19] This resolution formed the basis upon which the functions of UNEF were defined.

In another resolution on November 4, the General Assembly requested the Secretary-General to "submit to it within forty-eight hours a plan for the setting up, with the consent of the nations concerned, of an emergency United Nations Force to secure and supervise the cessation of hostilities in accordance with all the terms of the aforementioned (November 2) resolution."[20]

Beginning with the afternoon of November 3, when the idea of an international force was first put forward by Lester Pearson, Hammarskjöld

---

17. United Nations General Assembly Resolution 377A(v), November 3, 1950, paragraph A.i.
18. General Armistice Agreements 1949.
19. United Nations General Assembly Resolution 997 (ES-1), November 2, 1956.
20. United Nations General Assembly Resolution 998 (E.S.-1)

had been in close consultations with his staff associates, Andrew Cordier, Executive Assistant to the Secretary-General, and Ralph Bunche, Under Secretary for Special Political Affairs. He was also in touch with his friend Hans Engen, Permanent Representative of Norway to the United Nations, and also with India's Permanent Representative, Arthur Lall. After the November 4 Assembly resolution, Hammarskjöld and his associates were able to start more detailed planning for the U.N. Force. In the absence of military expertise within the Secretariat,[21] Hammarskjöld sent an urgent cable to Major-General E. L. M. Burns of Canada, Chief of Staff, UNTSO[22] at Jerusalem seeking his views on the size, type and equipment of troops that would be required. The force, initially at least, would be placed under the command of Burns, and his recommendations were required in time for the Secretary-General to submit his report to the Assembly on the night of November 5.

The choice of Burns turned out to be a good one. As Chief of Staff, UNTSO, he was well acquainted with the situation, but what was even better was that he was a highly experienced World War II veteran field commander. Though first appointed as chief, he was later confirmed as commander and never was a better choice made to give practical shape and provide effective leadership in the field for the first experiment in the use of a military force in a non-enforcement role.

In his communication, Hammarskjöld had told Burns that he understood that the functions of the force would be to insure the safety of the Canal and to police the withdrawal of troops to the demarcation lines. Burns based his suggestions on some assumptions, i.e., that Egypt would agree to a force being stationed in the Canal Zone; the area between the Suez Canal and the International Frontier would be kept as a demilitarized zone with only lightly armed Egyptian police until the conclusion of peace; the Israelis would be made to withdraw to their side of the International Frontier, and that it would be politically possible to leave the Gaza Strip under Israeli occupation. As it turned out, only the first assumption proved entirely correct.

According to Burns,

> Based on these assumptions, I stated that I thought the force should be so strong that it would be in no danger of being thrust aside, pushed out, or ignored, as the U.N. military observers had been in Palestine — mainly by the Israelis, but on occasion by other parties. I thought such a

---

21. A Military Staff Committee (MSC), consisting of military experts of the five permanent members of the Security Council established under Article 47 of the Charter, had proved ineffective since the beginning of the cold war. Regardless of this fact, the use of MSC for UNEF was ruled out because France and the U.K. had landed troops in Egypt.

22. United Nations Truce Supervision Organization.

force, in view of the strength of the armed forces of Israel and Egypt, would have to be about the size of a division, with a brigade of tanks, and attached reconnaissance and fighter aircraft units—the whole organized as an operational force capable of fighting.[23]

Hammarskjöld had a different composition in mind. Of course, Burns was not fully aware of the evolution of ideas on the thirty-eighth floor of the U.N. Secretariat. The establishment of UNEF was the condition upon which the ceasefire would be brought about; the Anglo-French and Israeli forces could only be persuaded to withdraw after effective deployment of the U.N. troops. Therefore, the speed with which the force could be organized and moved into Egyptian territory was of vital importance.

The composition of the force was primarily based on the fact that it was not intended to fight or to enforce peace. The members of the force only needed light weapons for personal, camp, installations and Headquarters' protection. The troops belonging to the parties to the conflict were also excluded. Having devoted his early years to the reorganization of the Secretariat, the principle of wider geographical representation had brought fruitful results in improving the effectiveness of the organization. Now Hammarskjöld advocated the same principle for the composition of the force. The force required consent of the country before it would be deployed on its territory. Lastly, nations contributed troops and equipment on a voluntary basis. These guidelines, developed by Hammarskjöld for UNEF, were adopted for ONUC and for future peacekeeping forces.

Most of the nations that could have contributed logistic and technical troops were politically excluded. Because of this, it was not possible to obtain composite units for UNEF, a problem that has beset all peacekeeping forces so far. Eventually, Canada provided signal communications, logistic units and transport aircraft. Only India contributed a composite unit, and its communications and logistic elements were combined with similar Canadian units for operations.

The Secretary-General made his report on the formation of UNEF to the General Assembly on November 5. He recommended that a U.N. Command be set up, with Burns as Chief of Command, on an emergency basis and that officers from UNTSO be made available to assist while the Commander recruit his staff. On receiving Assembly approval, Hammarskjöld instructed Burns to visit Cairo to discuss plans for the deployment of the force.

A number of troop-contributing countries dispatched military representatives to Headquarters in New York. Hammarskjöld organized them in a working group. General John B. Cutler, U.S. Army, then the Agent

---

23. Lt. Gen. E. L. M. Burns, *Between Arab and Israeli* (New York: Ivan Oblensky, Inc., 1963), p. 188.

General of the U.N. Korean Agency, was temporarily assigned as Military Adviser until the arrival of General I. A. E. Martola of Finland.

The Assembly, having set up the force and a command, had left to Hammarskjöld the responsibility of negotiating its entry, the composition, the nature of the force and the condition under which it would operate in Egyptian territory. These negotiations proved to be the most difficult aspects of establishing UNEF. Hammarskjöld had hoped to have advance parties arrive in Egypt within thirty-six to forty-eight hours, but Egypt raised a number of questions that had to be dealt with first. The Egyptian Government, while agreeing to accept the force on its territory, attempted to more clearly define the functions of the force by asking the following questions: Would the force move up to the Armistice Lines and would the governments concerned agree to occupation of areas astride these lines? Would the force be deployed in the Canal and how long would the force stay? Once again, the arrangements made by Hammarskjöld for UNEF became guidelines for the future, i.e., the force would be temporarily stationed in Egypt with the consent of the Egyptian Government; the U.N. troops would not be used to force a solution of the Canal. In other words, it was not intended to use UNEF to force a political solution, and while the views of the host country in regard to selection of national contingents would be carefully considered, the Secretary-General would make the final choice, insuring that the force would be international in character (this dealt with Egypt's objection to Canadian troops since they owed allegiance to the British Queen).

After receiving assurances on Egypt's sovereign right of consent to the introduction of UNEF and with outstanding differences on the question of UNEF's stay, the Egyptians agreed to receive UNEF on November 14. Hammarskjöld, having agreed to visit Cairo to discuss outstanding questions, flew to Abu Suweir on November 15.

The major issue to be resolved during Hammarskjöld's visit to Cairo was an Egyptian request for clarification of the question how long it was contemplated that the Force would stay in the Armistice Demarcation Lines area. As the decision to establish UNEF was taken under Chapter VI of the Charter, it was obvious to Hammarskjöld that the resolution to establish UNEF did not in any way limit the sovereignty of the host country. Therefore, the problem was how to limit this right of Egypt to withdraw the Force before its task was completed.

Hammarskjöld recognized that the emergency character of the Force linked it to the crisis envisaged in the General Assembly Resolution 997 (ES-1) of November 2, 1956. Therefore, when the crisis did not warrant continued UNEF presence, it would require negotiations between the parties. However, UNEF could only operate and stay with the consent of Egypt.

The ideal arrangement would have been to tie Egypt by an agreement in which they declared that withdrawal should take place only if so decided by the General Assembly. Another possible solution could be that the U.N. and the Egyptian Government should agree on withdrawal. Since Nasser proved most reluctant to surrender any part of Egyptian sovereignty, Hammarskjöld finally succeeded in reaching a "good faith" agreement, and its key paragraph as follows:

> The Government of Egypt declares that when exercising its sovereign right on any matter concerning the presence and functioning of UNEF, it will be guided in good faith by its acceptance of the General Assembly Resolutions 997 (ES-1) and 1000 (ES-1), in particular the U.N. understanding, this to correspond to the wishes of the Government of Egypt reaffirms its willingness to maintain UNEF till its task was completed.

The object of this formula was to recognize Egypt's undisputed right to request the withdrawal of UNEF, but to get from Egypt an agreement by which the government would limit its freedom of action by making any request for withdrawal of the Force dependent upon the completion of the Force's task, a question that obviously would have to be submitted for interpretation to the General Assembly.[24]

Hammarskjöld's agreement on the question of withdrawal of UNEF proved fragile, when in May 1967 Egypt decided to call for the withdrawal of UNEF. Neither the Security Counil nor the General Assembly, which had established the Force, chose to discuss Egypt's request to the Secretary-General for its withdrawal. In the absence of any action by the U.N. organs, U Thant felt obliged to withdraw the Force, leading to the June 1967 Arab-Israeli war and much controversy over his action.[25]

Hammarskjöld returned from Egypt with heightened prestige. He raised the authority and the influence of the office of the Secretary-General to a level never enjoyed before. The British and the French, having failed in their political and military venture to impose a solution of the Suez Canal dispute on Egypt, had been soundly rebuffed by the international community. Israel had equally been rebuked for having joined in this venture. Therefore, these three nations looked for ways to belittle the U.N. and Hammarskjöld in particular. On the other hand, Egypt wished to take advantage of the international political support that it had received and viewed every move with suspicion to insure that their antagonists did not gain an advantage. All this slowed the pace of negotiations to find a solution to the Suez Canal crisis.

The Anglo-French forces withdrew from Egypt on December 22. By this date the Israelis had pulled back fifty kilometers in the Sinai. Burns had by now deployed U.N. troops in the Canal Zone and interposed his men

---

24. Urquhart, *op. cit.*, pp. 193-194.
25. For details, see Indar Jit Rikhye, *The Sinai Blunder* (London: Frank Cass, 1980).

between the Israelis and Egyptians in the Sinai. As the U.N. had no mandate to prevent Egyptian movement of troops across the Canal, all that Hammarskjöld could do was to ask Egypt not to cross the Canal and to instruct UNEF to insure a separation of Egyptian and Israeli forces. The latter, taking no chances, tore up the roads as they withdrew, even slowing down the advance of the U.N. troops.

While the Suez Canal clearance operations were first under negotiation and subsequently started, Hammarskjöld had to maintain the momentum of negotiations to deal with a number of critical issues. Israeli forces had to be persuaded to withdraw from the Sinai and somehow Egypt had to be persuaded preferably not to send its forces back into the Sinai; and if they must, to limit their numbers and weaponry. Israel had gone to war because of Egyptian-supported fedayeen raids from the Gaza Strip and the blockade of the Straits of Tiran. The Israelis had declared that they were prepared to hand over Sharm el Sheikh and Ras Nasrani, where the Egyptians had placed guns for the blockade of the narrow straits at the entrance to the Gulf of Aqaba, to UNEF if they stayed till a peace treaty was signed. As for Gaza, they were willing to withdraw their troops, but insisted on maintaining administrative and police responsibilities.

Hammarskjöld understood the Israeli need of security against a threat from Gaza and of freedom of navigation through the straits of Tiran to open up the new port being built at Eilat. The Egyptians, on their part, were adamant on matters relating to their sovereignty, and as to Gaza, the GAA of 1949 clearly had placed the responsibility for the administration of this territory on Egypt. Pressures on Hammarskjöld increased with a General Assembly resolution of January 19,[26] to pursue his efforts to secure Israel's withdrawal.

After a series of negotiations, Hammarskjöld, in a report to the General Assembly on January 24,[27] set out guidelines for future negotiations: 1) The U.N. could not force a settlement; 2) The GAA remained the basis for all future arrangements and, accordingly, Egypt had been given responsibility for Gaza; 3) Broader functions of UNEF in Gaza would require Egyptian consent; 4) The stationing of UNEF troops at Sharm el Sheikh and Ras Nasrani should be part of their deployment in the Sinai, following the withdrawal of IDF;[28] 5) UNEF operations, by preventing raids and consequent reprisals, should create conditions that would preclude the need to deploy sizeable forces on either side of the armistice lines.

As the pace of negotiations slowed down, Hammarskjöld chose to make the effectiveness of UNEF his major card for furthering the objectives

26. General Assembly Resolution 1123 (XI).
27. General Assembly Resolution 3512.
28. Israeli Defense Forces.

of the General Assembly. Suspicious of a new kind of legal arrangement being suggested for UNEF, the Egyptians had prolonged the negotiations. At one time Hammarskjöld even sent a cable to President Nasser to impress upon him the novelties of the agreement. The U.N. had to maintain a balance between national sovereignty (of Egypt) and the authority of the U.N. over the U.N. force. What was even more important was that the force must have no semblance to an occupation force nor should it look like NATO or Warsaw Pact troops stationed on foreign soil. The U.N. force must retain freedom of movement to perform its functions within the mandate given to it and must remain under the authority of the U.N. Furthermore, the maintenance and support of the force must be without interference, and its personnel should enjoy certain privileges and immunities to enable them to perform their responsibilities effectively. Ably assisted by Constantin Stavropoulos, the U.N. legal counsel, Hammarskjöld finally succeeded in obtaining Egyptian approval by February 8. The final draft included the unprecedented clause, which was Hammarskjöld's own idea, that unlike other multinational forces, UNEF personnel would remain under the criminal jurisdiction of their own countries. This new formula was reaffirmation of national sovereignty. In practice, if a conflict arose between Egyptian criminal procedures and privileges of the national contingent, UNEF personnel, whenever held by Egyptian authorities, would be handed over to UNEF for custody by its own contingent and produced before Egyptian authorities for evidence and to complete their procedures. Thereafter, national criminal laws applied in dealing with the case. Although some contingents smarted over their personnel being initially held by Egyptian authorities for misdemeanors, in the end it saved Egyptian pride and sovereignty and permitted the national contingent to deal with the case in accordance with its own laws. Each troop-contributing nation had to deal with such cases, bearing in mind its own relations with Egypt.

Because of Israel's firm stand on guarantees regarding Gaza and the Gulf of Aqaba, as well as the future administrative control of Gaza, the negotiations shifted to Washington. The United States firmly suported the Armistice Agreement on the question of Gaza and equally supported the international status of the Gulf of Aqaba in respect to the necessity for freedom of movement. After receiving United States assurances of the support for the exercise of the right of free and *innocent* passage through the Straits of Tiran, an arrangement was finally reached that more or less conformed to the guidelines recommended by the Secretary-General to the General Assembly on January 24, 1957. By early March, UNEF troops had replaced the Israelis at Sharm el Sheikh and were deployed along the Armistice Demarcation Line in the Gaza Strip, while the Egyptians assumed administrative responsibilities of Gaza in accordance with the GAA. Within a short time, UNEF was able to create conditions that brought peace and tranquillity to this area for the first time since the creation of the state of Israel.

The effectiveness of the UNEF operation and the confidence that it created in the usefulness of this diplomatic tool led some member states, particularly the United States, to advocate the establishing of a standing U.N. force. However, Hammarskjöld was not convinced that the international organization had developed sufficiently to assume such a responsibility. As stated earlier, a study he ordered of UNEF experience only recommended that nations wishing to contribute troops for future U.N. operations should prepare their personnel and have them available on a standby basis.

In establishing UNEF, Hammarskjöld clearly emerged as the outstanding personality on the international stage. His great intellect, his enormous capacity for work, his negotiating skills and his great courage, led member states and important leaders of the world community increasingly to rely on him and ask him to assume greater and greater responsibilities. In the U.N. corridors, the word was "Let Dag do it."

United Nations Observer Group in Lebanon

The Suez debacle increased the popularity of President Nasser. The fluid and often unpredictable relations among Arabs and the revolutionary change generally believed to be sponsored by Nasser and the Soviets had led the Western powers to support conservative regimes in the region. Nasser had not only rejected the offer by John Foster Dulles, the United States Secretary of State, to join CENTO to safeguard the Arab nations against Communist expansion, but had actively worked against this military alliance and prevented many Arab states from participating in it.

Early in 1958, Egypt and Syria formed a new nation, the United Arab Republic. Anxious to prevent a Soviet-supported take-over of the Middle East by Nasserites, Iraq and Jordan, the two Kingdoms already connected by *Heshemite* blood, formed an Arab Union. However, further developments heightened western concern and added fuel to the smoldering fires in Lebanon. The pro-western King Saud of Saudi Arabia turned over power to his brother, Prince Faisal, known to be a Nasser sympathizer, and a coup in July in Iraq placed in power a pro-Nasserite, Brigadier Abdul Kassem.

The Palestine refugees had upset the balance between Christians and Moslems in favor of the latter, and President Chamoun's lean towards the West had increased opposition within Lebanon. But when he tried to amend the Constitution to stay on in office for another term, civil war broke out.

The West viewed Nasser and his supporters, as they did the Soviet Union, with grave suspicion and believed that Communists were behind all the trouble. Chamoun appeared to them to be a patriot. By mid-May, the

Lebanese Army had established a semblance of order in the main towns. Chamoun's inquiry about the possibility of United States assistance was met with caution. However, the American sixth fleet was moved closer to Lebanon. On May 22, Chamoun called for a Security Council meeting to consider a Lebanese complaint of massive, illegal and unprovoked intervention[29] and accused the UAR of acts of terrorism, arming of rebels and infiltration of armed bands from Syria.[30]

The first draft resolution that emerged in the Council, suggested by the United Kingdom and the United States, included the establishment of an observer group to insure that there was no illegal infiltration of arms and personnel. When Hammarskjöld objected on the grounds that he had no authority to provide the necessary observers and administrative support, a revised version was approved by the Council.[31]

Hammarskjöld viewed the U.N. Lebanese operation as "a classical case of preventative diplomacy,"[32] and indeed it proved to be so. Hammarskjöld had advised against establishing a peacekeeping force like UNEF because he wished to avoid a U.N. involvement in the civil war and because the Lebanese complaint of outside interference required observers along the border and all points of entry into Lebanon. Furthermore, Hammarskjöld's brilliant and innovative mind realized that a great deal of political sophistication was required in analyzing and dealing with complaints. He therefore suggested a high-level team, consisting of three distinguished men representing different regions, to head the observer group. This team would analyze the reports of the military observers and would be responsible for diplomatic contacts with leaders and their parties who were involved in the region. General Odd Bull, Chief of Staff, the Royal Norwegian Air Force; former President Galo Plaza of Ecuador; and Rajeshwar Dayal, former Permanent Representative of India to the United Nations, were selected to head UNOGIL with some six hundred military observers and support personnel.

Shortly after setting up the operation, Hammarskjöld visited the Middle East. The Lebanese Moslem Prime Minister, Samy es-Sol agreed that fighting between the two communities must be stopped. Hammarskjöld assured the Jordanians that he was determined to implement the Council's resolution. In Jerusalem Ben-Gurion was unconcerned and strangely suggested that a U.N. force be placed in Lebanon, an idea that Hammarskjöld had found impractical from the start.

It was in Cairo that Hammarskjöld had to convince Nasser to cease support of the Lebanese opposition. His two main arguments were that any evidence of Egyptian support for the opposition would prejudice the future

29. Official Records Security Council's 823rd meeting, June 6, 1958.
30. United Nations Security Council S/4007, May 22, 1958.
31. United Nations Security Council S/4022, June 10, 1958.
32. Urquhart, *op. cit.*, p. 265.

of UNEF, and that an intervention by the Americans and the British could have an adverse effect on the relations between Egypt and the West. Hammarskjöld left Cairo with Nasser's assurances that military assistance to the opposition would cease and propaganda against Chamoun's regime would stop. Now he could turn his attention to isolate the Lebanese internal situation from outside influences.

The first UNOGIL report showed little evidence of infiltration across from Syria. The Western nations, however, refused to accept this report and showed a long list of violations to the Secretary-General. A comprehensive analysis of day and night reconnaissance by U.N. aircraft failed to provide any clear evidence. This provided added fuel to the Western media and to their political leaders to question the integrity of UNOGIL.

On July 14, Brigadier Kassem overthrew the Hashemite monarchy of Iraq, killing King Faisal, the Crown Prince and Prime Minister Nuri es-Said. A Lebanese request for American military assistance was inevitable. The United States landed troops in Lebanon on July 15, acting under Article 51 of the Charter.[33] In the meanwhile, King Hussein had requested British assistance, which also had been accepted.

Henry Cabot Lodge, representing the United States, informed the Security Council that the U.S. forces in Lebanon had been instructed to cooperate with UNOGIL, but Hammarskjöld already had instructed the Observer Group that there was no basis of cooperation other than matters relating to the access to Beirut airport.

On July 16, 1958, the United States put forward a resolution to the Council requesting the Secretary-General to start consultations on what amounted to the setting up of a peacekeeping force to be deployed along the Lebanese borders. In the view of the United States, such a step would make it possible for them to withdraw their forces. Hammarskjöld, on the other hand, was admanant that UNOGIL had already proved effective and must remain the basis of the U.N. operations in Lebanon. Therefore, in spite of opposition, including at one time from the Swedish Government, he pressed for the expansion of UNOGIL. After a Japanese initiative in the Council to enlarge UNOGIL failed to materialize, and finding Soviet support for the enlargment of the Observer operation, Hammarskjöld, boldly acting on his own, put forward a plan to enhance the capability of UNOGIL that would enable the U.N. to find a way out of the dangerous situation. In the absence of any dissent, and assuming that he had the tacit approval of the Council members, he set out to enlarge the group to over six hundred personnel and added to the number of aircraft and helicopters.

Hammarskjöld's courageous initiative in dealing with the consequences on Lebanon of the coup in Iraq had left his flanks wide open. He required more active support of member states. He found the answer to this question

33. See United Nations *Charter*, Article 51, pp. 18-19.

by setting up a consultative group along the lines of the UNEF Advisory Committee.[34] He invited the same countries in their exclusive personal capacity. By the end of July, in spite of American and British efforts to undermine the credibility of UNOGIL, the findings of the U.N. did little to help President Chamoun. The United States started the search for a compromise candidate, and General Chehab, the Lebanese Chief of Staff, appeared a likely candidate. On July 31, Chehab was elected President.

Hammarskjöld now turned his attention to help create conditions for the withdrawal of American troops from Lebanon and British troops from Jordan. In deciding his next steps, he had to take the whole Middle East

34. United Nations General Assembly Resolution 1001 (ES-1) of November 7, 1956, paragraphs 6 and 9.

environment under consideration. UNEF was keeping quiet along the Armistice Lines between Egypt and Israel. He therefore concentrated on seeking ways to reduce the vulnerability of Jordan and especially the threats to the King. He chose to increase the observation capability on the West Bank and establish a larger UNTSO office in Lebanon. With the election of Chehab as President, he hoped the situation in Lebanon would soon stabilize so he could replace UNOGIL with some form of U.N. presence in Beirut. He felt that with UNEF in Gaza and the Sinai, UNTSO astride the Armistice Lines, a larger U.N. presence in Amman and a presence in Beirut, the U.N. might well be able to establish a "Cordon Sanitaire," which would break the trend toward a military encirclement of Israel.[35]

On August 8, Hammarskjöld addressed the Third Special Session of the General Assembly and set out his ideas for accommodations in the Middle East. After some debate, the Arab States submitted a resolution on August 21[36] that was unanimously adopted. The resolution took note of the American and British governments' declaration of withdrawal, reaffirmed that all member states should stop interference in other states in this region, and requested the Secretary-General to make practical arrangements in connection with governments to uphold the Charter in relation to Jordan and Lebanon. The Arab resolution added a reference to the Arab League's Charter, requiring strengthening of relations within the Arab States.

Hammarskjöld had triumphed again.

United Nations Operation in the Congo

The U.N. operations in the Congo were the last major occupation of Dag Hammarskjöld before his death. On gaining its independence, the Congo plunged into civil war. The Belgians and the new Congolese leaders had expected tribal clashes following independence, but the mutiny of the Armée Nationale Conglais—ANC (formerly Force Publique) came as a surprise. The Belgians had been permitted to retain three military bases in the Congo after independence. When the clashes led to beating and killing of blacks and whites, looting, burning and destruction of property, the Belgians first intervened with troops from the military bases to protect the white population and their property and later brought metropolitan troops from Belgium as anarchy increased with the spread of mutiny amongst the ANC.

On July 11, 1960, Prime Minister Patrice Lumumba appealed to the U.N. for military assistance to help reorganize the Congolese Army and to restore law and order. At about the same time, the President of Katanga (Shaba) Province, Moise Tshombe, declared the independence of Katanga and seceded from the Congo.

35. Urquhart, *op. cit.*, p. 288.
36. General Assembly Resolution A/3893, Rev. 1.

Hammarskjöld had foreseen difficulties in the Congo following its independence. During a tour of Africa early in 1960, he had witnessed the lack of preparation. The country was large and had enormous natural wealth. It was a difficult country to govern, and the powerful vested interests were going to be a major factor after independence. Anticipating problems, Hammarskjöld had sent Ralph Bunche, his Under-Secretary for Special Political Affairs, to Leopoldville before independence was declared so he would be available to advise the new government.

There was heavy fighting between the Belgian troops and the Congolese in Port Matadi, and at Tshombe's request, Belgian troops had intervened in Elisabethville (Lumumbashi). On July 13, the Belgians had also occupied the Leopoldville (Kinshasa) airport and the white part of the town, which included the Government offices and Parliament. These actions heightened tensions across the Congo and raised doubts as to the intentions of the Belgians. Anxious to stem the tide of Belgian military takeover and to restore some order, Lumumba appealed to President Kwame Nkrumah of Ghana for military assistance.

Hammarskjöld realized that any U.N. operation in the Congo was going to be most difficult and extremely complex. The role of the U.N. troops in the restoration of law and order under the prevailing conditions of anarchy was going to be dangerous and delicate. After the complete breakdown of the colonial regime, large-scale civilian assistance would be required. There were foreign vested interests, and the crisis had a potential to become a cold-war issue besides the inevitable clash between anti-colonial forces and Belgium supported by its allies. The politics of a U.N. role was going to be complicated, and in the light of great-power interests, it would have to be under the authority of the Security Council.

After hearing reports on developments in the Congo on July 13, Hammarskjöld was convinced that only the U.N. could get the Belgian troops out and help prevent a complete breakdown of law and order. Invoking Article 99[37] of the Charter for the first time in the history of the U.N., Hammarskjöld requested a meeting of the Security Council.

On July 14, the Security Council called[38] on the Belgians to withdraw from the Congo and requested the Secretary-General to report back. The substance of the resolution was: "Decides to authorize the Secretary-General to take necessary steps in consultation with the Government of the Republic of the Congo, to provide the Government with such military assistance as may be necessary until, through the efforts of the Congolese

---

37. Article 99—The Secretary may bring to the attention of the Security Council any matter which in his opinion may threaten the maintenance of international peace and security.

38. United Nations Security Council Resolution S/4387.

Government with the technical assistance of the United Nations, the national security forces may be able, in the opinion of the Government, to meet fully their tasks. . . ."

The final Council resolution had followed Hammarskjöld's recommendations in the formulation of U.N.'s role. Although the mandate approved was somewhat vague, as is often the case, it provided an adequate basis for the Secretary-General to plan the operation and report back to the Council on July 18.[39] Unquestionably, Hammarskjöld dominated the decision-making process, and it was to him that the Council turned to provide the leadership.

Hammarskjöld gave his immediate attention to organizing ONUC, i.e., arranging contribution of troops, setting up ONUC Headquarters, obtaining the civilian experts through agencies and above all selecting the higher leaders in the field. He appointed Ralph Bunche as his Special Representative in the Congo. Hammarskjöld could not have been better served. Bunche knew Africa, had won a Nobel Peace Prize for negotiating the GAA between Israel and the neighboring Arab states, had assisted the Secretary-General in the establishment and later in the operation of UNEF, and above all he was a kindly man who was greatly regarded by his associates and subordinates. At the head of the military and civilian operations, he appointed two Swedes. Selection of these two top-level officials from the same nationality was somewhat unusual for Hammarskjöld, who was committed to geographical distribution. The choice of Sture Linner, even though he was new to the U.N., was understandable, because he had already been appointed the Resident Representative in the Congo for U.N. Technical Assistance. However, the choice of Carl von Horn, Chief of Staff, UNTSO, to serve as Force Commander proved to be ill-conceived. An affable man who had served the Secretary-General satisfactorily in UNTSO, but by disposition, experience and training, he was unsuited for command of a large force operating virtually in combat and under difficult conditions. Instead of being replaced when his inadequacies became know, he had to be short-shrifted frequently, which neither did his humor any good nor made for smooth relations between the Secretary-General's aides and the Commander and his staff. Somehow the U.N. staff muddled through, and in spite of frictions, were able to make the operations effective.

The U.N. military operations in the Congo turned out to be a major undertaking. With the Congolese security forces in mutiny and taking sides in political and tribal conflicts and with the breakdown in all local services and the enormous distances involved (1600 kilometers between Leopoldville and Elisabethville), the conduct of military operations required

39. United Nations Security Council Resolution S/4389.

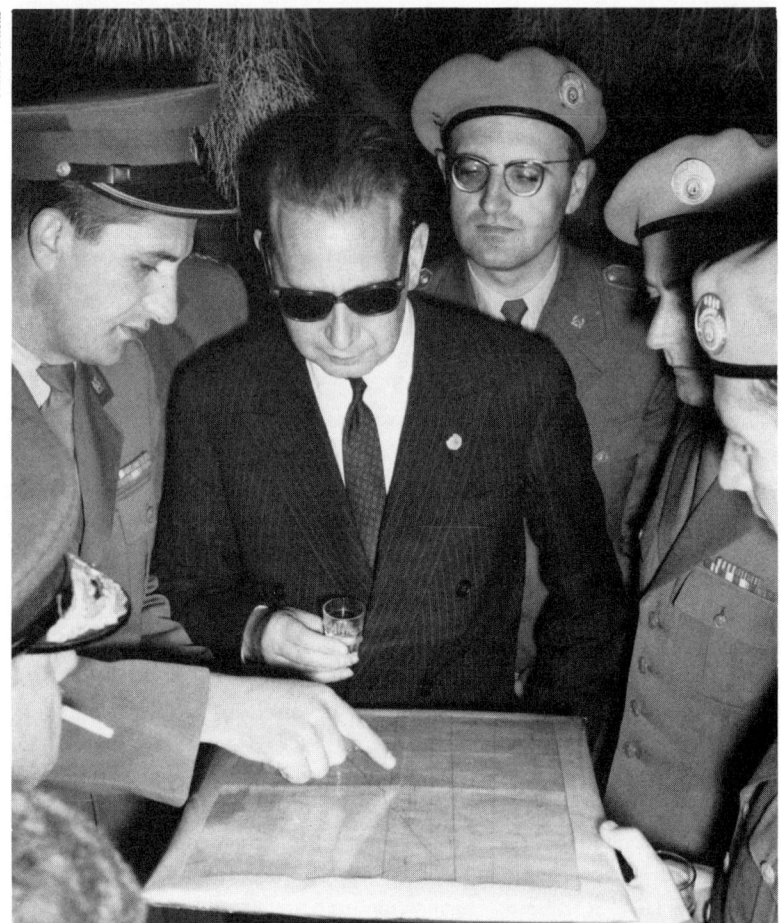

Dag Hammarskjöld visiting a Yugoslav Battalion of the United Nations Emergency Force, at El Arish (Sinai), December 1958.

ingenuity and huge human and material resources. With the exception of the poor choice of the Force Commander, Hammarskjöld's wise leadership pervaded every aspect of the Congo operation. Although he did not live to see the end of the operation, it was his conception, planning, organization, and his vigorous pursuit of his objectives selected by him with the approval of the U.N. organs that led to ONUC's success.

To assist him at Headquarters, Hammarskjöld appointed an experienced civil and technical assistance administrator, Sir Alexander MacFarquhar (U.K.), Special Adviser on civilian operation, Heinz Wieschoff (U.S.), an experienced U.N. hand, as the Political Adviser, and the author as the Military Adviser. Other aides who assisted the Secretary-General were Andrew Cordier, Ralph Bunche, after his return from Leopoldville, and C. V. Narasimhan in what came to be known as the "Congo Club." At various times, Francis Nwokedi (Nigeria), Godfrey Amachree (Nigeria), Robert W. Gardiner (Ghana), and Tareh Sahbani (Tunisia) were also included.

Hammarskjöld was praised, criticized and attacked for his conduct of the Congo operations. Since these operations include political aspects, civilian assistance and military aspects, only the military role in peacekeeping is considered in this chapter.

The mandate provided by the Security Council was vague, but clearly placed the responsibility on the Secretary-General for the conduct of the operation. An Advisory Committee, along UNEF lines, was set up. It provided Hammarskjöld with an opportunity to listen to views, draw a consensus, and present his ideas. Realizing that he needed strong political support, he often referred to the Security Council for endorsement or an additional authorization.

The main tasks of ONUC were: 1) to arrange the withdrawal of Belgian forces and consequently remove the threat to international peace and security; 2) to assist the Congolese government in restoring law and order, including the training and reorganization of the Congolese Army (ANC); and 3) to assist in the restoration of essential services and to help organize and train the Congolese to run these services. In carrying out these functions, the U.N. had to fill the vacuum created by the removal of Belgian colonial administration and to keep the cold war out of the Congo.

Hammarskjöld first set out to obtain troops, establish a force command and logistics support. The ad hoc nature of peacekeeping operations creates many inherent problems, and the Congo operation was no exception to this. Hammarskjöld decided to build the force largely from African troops. In order to give it an international character, he obtained Scandinavian, Irish, Indonesian and Malayan troops. Canadians, Indians and Pakistanis provided signal communications and logistics, and Latin Americans the air crew. Hammarskjöld tried to involve the Eastern Europeans, but only succeeded in obtaining Yugoslav air crew for transport aircraft. The Force Headquarters represented national contingents and some others to give it a wide geographical representation.

As the troops were being flown in, they were speedily deployed to assist in restoring law and order. The withdrawal of Belgians depended on ONUC's capability to protect life and property and to facilitate normal life.

Von Horn did not reach Leopoldville until July 17. In the meanwhile, Major General H. T. Alexander (U.K.), Chief of Staff of Ghana, had arrived with his troops and felt obliged to assume command without the authority of the U.N. In order to fill the gap of higher command, Hammarskjöld appointed Bunche as acting Commander. This bit of "ad hocry" created as many problems as when, in November, he appointed his Military Adviser as Acting Officer-in-Charge, ONUC. Such unusual appointments create friction and cause resentment, sometimes permanently damaging personal relations.

Von Horn was allowed to bring some observers from UNTSO to serve on his staff. Burns had resorted to the same practice in establishing UNEF. The difference between the two, however, was that Burns, of his own choice, reorganized his staff to be more representative of the troops in his Command and sensitive to the politics of peacekeeping, whereas Von Horn resented the changes made later by U.N. Headquarters. The UNTSO observers were on temporary loan. Besides, the criteria for selecting a good observer are not always the same as those for a good staff officer.

As more troops were inducted, the entire Command was reorganized. Under force headquarters a number of area headquarters were established; each of these generally conformed to Congolese provinces and, as far as possible, became the responsibility of one of the national contingents. The logistics, signal communications and air transport were unified for smoother operations. Some conditions were established to persuade the Belgians to withdraw.

In addressing the Katanga problem, Hammarskjöld insisted on peaceful entry of U.N. troops. The earlier efforts of Bunche had been aborted by the Katangese. This had made Lumumba seek U.N. military action in support of an ANC enforcement action. However, Hammarskjöld was determined to resort to negotiations to persuade the Belgians to implement the decisions of the Security Council in all aspects, especially in regard to Katanga.

The gap between the Congolese leaders and Hammarskjöld was gradually widening. Lumumba's first meeting with Hammarskjöld had turned sour, but now the Congolese leaders were openly critical of the Secretary-General and accused him of being one-sided in favor of Belgians and Europeans. Realizing that Lumumba might turn to the Soviets, who might well decide to bypass the U.N., Hammarskjöld returned to the Security Council for a new mandate in respect to Katanga. When the Council met on August 8, he urged the Council to state explicitly that the previous resolutions on the Congo applied specifically to Katanga and pressed for speedy action to avoid a possible danger of war in the Congo. The Council resolved[40] to call on the Belgians to withdraw immediately from Katanga under modalities to be determined by the Secretary-General, authorized ONUC to enter Katanga and reaffirmed that force would not be used to influence the final outcome of any internal conflict.

Hammarskjöld now took one of the boldest steps in his U.N. career. After informing Leopoldville, Elisabethville and the Belgians of his plans, he flew into Elisabethville with the advance troops of ONUC's Swedish contingent. A journey which could have proved disastrous was turned into a success by his daring. During the following weeks, more troops were flown in to secure civil services and the industrial installations and to protect the opposition, which Tshombe was ruthlessly eliminating with the

---

40. United Nations Security Council Resolution S/4426, of August 9, 1960.

Dag Hammarskjöld in Katanga, the Congo (now Zaire), at Elisabeth Airport, August 1960.

help of his Belgian-led Katanga gendarmerie. As Hammarskjöld pressed the Katangese, the Belgians and other western powers with interests in the mineral-rich province to further implement the Council resolutions, ONUC ran into increasing opposition and conflict. The subsequent developments in Elisabethville led to open fighting between ONUC and the Katangese. It was on a journey to end the fighting that Hammarskjöld died in an air crash.

On his return from his first visit to Katanga, Hammarskjöld stopped at Leopoldville to meet Lumumba and Bomboko. Instead of being warmly received, he was attacked for his actions. Lumumba declared that the U.N. was required to provide military assistance in consultation with the Congolese government. Therefore, the U.N. resources should have been placed at the disposal of the Congolese. Lumumba charged that the Secretary-General had connived with Tshombe and called for the replacement of Irish and Swedish troops by African troops and ANC. The chasm between Hammarskjöld and Lumumba had widened. Hammarskjöld, of course, could not accede to any of these requests without violating the basic principle of peacekeeping and the Council's mandate.

Just as differences were growing between the U.N. and the Congolese leaders, the Congolese government was coming apart. The Belgian compromise solution of having the three most prominent leaders in key positions, i.e., Joseph Kasavubu as President, Patrice Lumumba as Prime Minister, and Moise Tshombe as head of Katanga, did not resolve their basic rivalries, which had tribal overtones. Tshombe had already chosen his own way. After Lumumba launched an ANC attack on Katanga, with support of Soviet aircraft on loan to Ghana and vehicles provided by the Soviet Union for civilian assistance, his differences with Kasavubu and the Army Chief of Staff Colonel Joseph Mobutu increased enormously. The Congolese invasion forces, unable to land in Katanga, were being airlifted and moved by road to Kasai. Lacking supplies, they looted the local population and became involved in tribal fighting, causing a mass exodus of people living in the bush and a large-scale refugee problem. The Western nations, opposed to Lumumba's attempts to resolve the Katanga crisis by force, had made them openly hostile to Lumumba. With the support of the Western nations and mining interests, Kasavubu removed Lumumba as Prime Minister. After a few days of mutual recrimination, Col. Mobutu— with the encouragement of the Western group of nations and conservative countries like Morocco, which had a large contingent in ONUC—" neutralized" the President and the Prime Minister, thereby assuming power over the State.

The *coup d'etat* by Mobutu only added further confusion to the situation. Mobutu had little control over the Congolese Army, and his command over troops in the capital was also doubtful. The Congolese troops spread terror throughout the city of Leopoldville, some taking sides with Lumumba, others with Kasavubu.

The removal of Lumumba from the government created a serious political crisis in the U.N. Because of the current importance of the Congo in world affairs and the key role of the United Nations, many world leaders had gathered in New York. The Secretary-General's Special Representative, Ralph Bunche, had been under attack in Leopoldville, just as his chief was under attack in New York. On Bunche's suggestion that he would be more useful in New York, Hammarskjöld recalled him and sent Andrew Cordier to assume acting charge in the Congo.

On arrival, Cordier encountered the complex situation between the Congolese leaders after the military take-over by Mobutu. The Congolese Army was on the rampage and endangered U.N. life and property, killing and wounding the civilian population and destroying their property. In the meanwhile, the Congolese army in Kasai had created anarchy and large-scale destruction of life and property. Cordier's efforts were directed towards controlling these events and bringing some order out of this chaos. The Congolese leaders were freely using the national radio for mutual attacks and for rabble-rousing. Congolese and Soviet aircraft continued to airlift troops and supplies into Kasai for Katanga. In order to put an end to all this, Cordier closed the airports and the Congolese radio to political leaders. These measures, though considered important to control violence at that time, added to the political problems facing the Secretary-General. While Lumumba was cut off from access to the radio and travel, Kasavubu, Mobutu, and their friendly politicians were being provided facilities across the Congo river by the authorities in Brazzaville. Thus, the U.N. action in closing the radio and the airports was taken to be against Lumumba.

As stated earlier, it is not the intention to discuss in any detail the political aspects of the Congo operations. However, a reference has to be made to political developments that had a direct bearing on the military operations. The U.N. force had no recognized Congolese authority with which to deal. This made liason and negotiations with the Congolese Army factions difficult, and in some cases almost impossible. The removal of Lumumba from the government led to his Deputy Prime Minister, Gizenga, establishing what he declared to the Central Government at Stanleyville. Later, Albert Kalonji, at one time a member of Tshombe's cabinet, encouraged by mining interests, also declared the cessation of Bakwanga. Now the Congolese Army was clearly divided in four factions, i.e., Tshombe's forces in Katanga, Kalonji's troops in Bakwanga, pro-Lumumba forces in the Oriental and partly in Kasai provinces, and elements of troops in Leopoldville province partly with Mobutu, while the others shifted their loyalty from day to day. The U.N. had to stretch its resources to cope with the new violence—almost two hundred thousand refugees in Kasai and factionalized Congo. It was with this background that Hammarskjöld faced his worst political crises, when Soviet Premier Kruschev called for his resignation in his address to the General Assembly.

After the tumultuous General Assembly Session came to an end and once the Kings, Presidents, Prime Ministers and Foreign Ministers had departed, Hammarskjöld turned his full attention to resolving the Congolese political dilemma. President Kennedy, after his inauguration, had appointed Adlai Stevenson—a liberal Democrat and at one time a political rival—as the American Permanent Representative to the U.N. Hammarskjöld expected the new American administration to improve its relations with the Soviet Union and to take a more sympathetic view of African nationalism, which would facilitate political reconciliation in the Congo. In an address to the 1961 General Assembly Session, Kennedy later confirmed these hopes when he said, "We prefer world law, in the age of self-determination, to world war in the age of extermination."

Anxious of the charismatic influence of Lumumba on the Congolese soldiers in the Thysville military camp where he was being held, Kasavubu and Mobutu had transferred him to Katanga. African and many other world leaders feared for his life. On February 13, 1961, Hammarskjöld informed the Council of Lumumba's death while in the custody of Katangese authorities.

The killing of Lumumba once again exposed Hammarskjöld to severe criticism of his role in the conduct of the U.N. operations in the Congo, and for the first time to the personal rancour of many African and Third World leaders. Lumumba's death was followed by violence and revenge. In his address to the Security Council, which met to consider Lumumba's death and consequent developments in the Congo, Hammarskjöld again emphasized that local armed conflict was likely to lead to a widening of the conflict into the international arena.

Hammarskjöld urged the Council to take strong measures to deal with the situation in the Congo. He suggested that besides ordering an investigation in Lumumba's death, the Council should: a) authorize ONUC to protect civilians against attacks by ANC; b) authorize ONUC to forestall clashes between ANC units; c) reactivate efforts to reorganize ANC and remove it from political conflict; and d) eliminate foreign, especially Belgian, political and military personnel. On February 21,[41] the Council adopted Hammarskjöld's recommendations. The Council recognized that the Congo situation was a threat to international peace and security. In an expanded mandate, recognizing that there was a widespread threat of civil war, it authorized the U.N. to act to prevent this and included the use of force, if necessary, in the last resort. The Council realized that immediate withdrawal was required of Belgian and other military personnel, advisers, and specifically mercenaries.

In May, Paul-Henri Spaak formed a government in Belgium, and the EEC concerned itself to resolve the Congo problem. In the meanwhile, Hammarskjöld pushed ahead with the implementation of the new U.N. mandate. In spite of the opposition of the Leopoldville-Bakwanga-Elisabethville axis, he persuaded the Congolese to reconcile their differences. A reconvened Parliament on August 2 decided on a government of national unity with Cyril Adoula as the Prime Minister. The new govenment enjoyed universal support in the country, except for Katanga, which continued its secession. His hand strengthened by the new Congolese leadership, Hammarskjöld and his aides in the Congo relentlessly pursued the implementation of the February 21, Security Council resolution.

ONUC re-entered the port of Matadi on June 18 and opened it for operations. On August 28, the U.N. troops launched a limited military operation in Elisabethville to round up mercenaries. After achieving initial success, the operation was halted by mutual consent of the U.N. and Katangese authorities. Tshombe's government, the Belgians, and the consulates of the nations from where the majority of mercenaries had been

---

41. United Nations Security Council Resolution S/4741.

recruited agreed to cooperate in the removal of mercenaries and advisers. The implementation of this arrangement moved slowly, and it soon became evident that many of the removed persons were re-entering Katanga and rejoining Tshombe surreptitiously. Anticipating more difficulties ahead, the U.N. continued further strengthening of its troops in Katanga.

By the first week of September, it became obvious that the western consulates and Tshombe were reneging on an agreement made with Connor Cruise O'Brien, ONUC Representative in Katanga. The Belgian Council had given asylum to a large number of officers, and the Western governments were critical of U.N. action against mercenaries. Sture Linner, now Officer-in-Charge, ONUC, and Mahomoud Khiary (Tunisian), ONUC Chief of Civilian operations, who had since his arrival in the Congo played a key political role, reported to the Secretary-General that some two hundred of the five hundred mercenaries had gone into hiding. O'Brien suspected that the mercenaries might well carry out a *coup de main*.

The senior staff at ONUC urged the Secretary-General to undertake a diplomatic offensive to persuade Tshombe to accede to the Security Council resolution and become reconciled with the Central Government. In case Tshombe failed to comply within a given time limit, ONUC troops should seize the Elisabethville radio station, as they had done on August 28, apprehend Tshombe's secret police and round up mercenaries. Hammarskjöld advised caution and decided to consult a number of governments who were concerned with the problem of Katanga. He also talked with the main western powers concerned, i.e., the United States, Britain, Canada and Belgium. Hammarskjöld found support for more pressure on Tshombe. However, Tshombe still expected to maintain his independence.

In an exchange of communications, Hammarskjöld summarized his views to Linner and redefined the role of ONUC in implementing the U.N. resolution. The basic point was that the U.N. mandate only permitted the use of force in self-defense. Acts of violence, incitement of population or troop movements would incur U.N. protective measures, but the U.N. could use force only in the last resort. In other words, the Security Council had not fully authorized any enforcement action. He therefore did not wish ONUC to undertake any action without his authorization.

Now started a chain of events which led to a renewal of fighting in Katanga. On September 10, Tombelaine, an assistant of O'Brien's, was arrested in Elisabethville. After obtaining his release, O'Brien demanded the expulsion of Belgians in the Katanga Secret Police. About the same time, Hammarskjöld decided to travel to Leopoldville on an invitation from Adoula, with the hope that he might be able to provide some face-saving device to Tshombe to come to Leopoldville. While he had permitted Linner to implement their plan, he had cautioned him that no action would be taken before consulting him in Leopoldville.

While Hammarskjöld was en route by air to Leopoldville on September 13, fighting started in Elisabethville. There are many causes attributed to the renewal of fighting. Khiary and O'Brien advocated strong action. O'Brien, living through the nightmare existence in Elisabethville of animosity, hatred and rumor, was ready for strong action. Khiary, who had played a major role in Congolese reconciliation, seemed to have chosen to end the secession, if not by negotiations, then by force. Linner's position had been weakened by the ability of Khiary and O'Brien dealing separately and together directly with Hammarskjöld. Having been obliged to let Rajeshwar Dayal return to his national diplomatic post, Hammarskjöld dealt with Linner, Khiary and O'Brien himself. On top of it, the military leadership in the Congo, bereft of higher politico-military advisers, lacked political comprehension to cope with the ever-changing Congo scenario.

Although the U.N. military action achieved a measure of success, it was greatly hampered by the use of armed aircraft by Katanga against ONUC troops and transport aircraft. The U.N. troops, through inept planning, repeated their previous plan of action, thereby losing the element of surprise.

On reaching Leopoldville on September 14, Hammarskjöld realized that what was supposed to be a non-violent action to gain control of the radio in Elisabethville and round up mercenaries, had developed into a sort of battle. While the Africans and Asians lauded the strong U.N. action, Belgium, Britain and Northern Rhodesia reacted strongly. Hammarskjöld's major concern was to end the fighting.

On September 16, O'Brien offered to meet Tshombe anywhere in Katanga without U.N. escort. Hammarskjöld instructed O'Brien to suggest an immediate and unconditional ceasefire and resumption of negotiations to bring Tshombe and Adoula together. He also proposed a meeting between Tshombe and himself. On September 17, Tshombe agreed to an immediate ceasefire, but demanded that the U.N. troops be confined to their camps and all U.N. troop movements be halted. He agreed to meet Hammarskjöld at Ndola, Northern Rhodesia.

Hammarskjöld took off in the ONUC Command aircraft DC-6B Albertina at 4:50 p.m. The plane had previously flown General Sean McKeon, the U.N. Force Commander, to Elisabethville and had been shot at while at the airport. The damage had been repaired, and the aircraft declared fit for flying. Because of the Katanga air activity, the flight plan was not revealed. The flight ended in a disaster some six hours later near Ndola airport, killing all aboard except Sgt. Harry Julien of the U.N. Security Force, who remained in a coma for a week prior to his death. Hammarskjöld's brilliant career and his life came to a sudden and tragic end.

Hammarskjöld's Contribution to U.N. Peacekeeping

In assessing Hammarskjöld's contribution to United Nations peacekeeping, few will question his enormous contribution. In fact, he most likely is to be remembered for using the Secretary-General's office to weld peacekeeping into an important diplomatic tool to resolve armed conflicts, thereby enlarging the scope of his office and the role of the world organization itself. His two great achievements were the evolution, establishment, and conduct of the first UNEF—to keep the peace between Egypt and Israel after the Suez war in 1956—and the peacekeeping operations in the Congo.

His handling of the Sinai and Gaza peacekeeping operation was carried out with such great skill that it became a model for the future. Although peacekeeping operations are not similar in political contexts and in format, it is generally agreed that guidelines did emerge from the experience of UNEF that became the basis for such future operations.

The conduct of UNEF was greatly facilitated due to a most effective commander in the field, General E. L. M. Burns. The Canadian general's expertise combined his World War II experience as an armored corps commander during the campaign in Italy with his years as chief of staff of UNTSO. Thus, Burns was able to provide the diplomatic and military leadership that has become an essential requisite for the command of peacekeeping operations. Unfortunately, in the Congo operation the choice of Carl von Horn as commander of ONUC by Hammarskjöld proved faulty. This complex and difficult operation required highly skilled and experienced leadership. Both qualities were lacking in von Horn. This Swedish officer had satisfactorily performed his duties as chief of staff of UNTSO and was keen and readily available for the command of a peacekeeping force. In addition, the appointment of Burns already had established a precedent. Thus, having placed von Horn in command, Hammarskjöld found it difficult to remove him without jeopardizing his relations with his countrymen, on whose support he relied. By the time von Horn was transferred back to his previous assignment, as chief of staff of UNTSO, great damage had been done in organizing ONUC into a cohesive operational force, and, worst of all, the vital ingredient of creating an *esprit de corps* in the U.N. command remained elusive thereafter.

The Congo operation created a most grave threat to the future of the United Nations. Hammarskjöld's conduct of the operation so annoyed the Soviet Union that during the General Assembly's Session in 1960, Chairman Krushchev called for Hammarskjöld's resignation and demanded that he be replaced by a troika. By the end of ONUC's mandate, the United Nations faced its most serious financial crisis, causing a dangerous diplomatic confrontation between the United States and the Soviet Union because of the latter's refusal to contribute towards the cost of peacekeeping operations. Many member states believe that had the nature of the operations and the financial costs been foreseen, the Congo peacekeeping operation may not have taken place.

In drawing a balance sheet of ONUC, there is little doubt that the

Congo operation prevented a major civil war, with dangerous and perhaps even direct superpower involvement. The United Nations was able to achieve reunification of the Congo and assisted in restoring law and order to a level where it became possible for a government to be approved by parliamentary process. Furthermore, the U.N. provided massive assistance in order to restore normal life in the Congo and became a conduit for much of the bilateral aid to the young country, which lacked trained manpower, and enabled it to deal with the total breakdown of the civil administration at a critical time in its history. The concept and the implementation of most of these ideas can be attributed to Hammarskjöld, and subsequent achievements of the United Nations can be attributed to the sound plans that he laid out.

On the debit side of the Congo operations, there are three main criticisms voiced to Hammarskjöld's conduct of the operations. Firstly, that Hammarskjöld failed to prevent what many believe was the unconstitutional removal of Prime Minister Lumumba and the subsequent coup d'etat by Mobutu, and consequently most of the Third World nations, particularly the Africans, became skeptical of the usefulness of the U.N. peacekeeping operations as a result of the Congolese experience. It was Lumumba who invited the United Nations to the Congo, yet the United Nations failed to keep him from becoming the first political casualty, even though at the time it had almost twenty thousand troops in the Congo. Hammarskjöld was also blamed for not having prevented the murder of Lumumba. Related to the role of Lumumba, Hammarskjöld also was held responsible for the action taken by Andrew Cordier, temporarily in charge of the Congo operations, when he ordered the airports to be closed and denied the use of the radio station in Leopoldville to political leaders. This action prevented Lumumba from communicating with the Congolese while, imperceived by ONUC, Brazzaville was providing broadcast facilities to his enemies. ONUC also prevented Lumumba's attempts to invade Katanga to end secession.

In deciding policy in regard to the internal power struggle amongst the Congolese leaders, Hammarskjöld wisely chose not to intervene. Hammarskjöld's difficulties in providing security to Lumumba stemmed from a number of developments. These included (1) the inability of the U.N. to counter activities of some foreign embassies in the Congo, which were actively opposed to Lumumba, (2) ONUC efforts to avoid a major military confrontation between its troops and the Congolese army, which would have been necessary to bring Lumumba out of Congolese custody, and (3) the possibility of Lumumba being killed during a rescue operation. As to Cordier's action to close the airports and the radio station in Leopoldville, at that time it was perceived as a necessary action to control and limit the civil war and the consequent blood bath of innocent civilians. As stated earlier, this action did prove to limit Lumumba's political activities.

While the Third World and the Socialist countries have been critical of Hammarskjöld's leadership of the Congo operation as it related to Lumumba, it was the West that was critical of Hammarskjöld's conduct of operations in Katanga. Operation RUM PUNCH by ONUC on August 28, 1961, to round up white mercenaries serving with the Katangese forces, was an implementation of the provisions of the Security Council Resolution of February 21, 1961,[42] and as a result, Tshombe agreed to the expulsion of mercenaries as also to cooperate with the United Nations. The Belgian and other western consulates in Elisabethville, representing the countries of origin of the mercenaries, had undertaken to expel these men arrested by ONUC. The consulates failed to do so, as most of these men were able to return to Katanga while the U.N. was engaged in negotiating with their home governments to prevent further travel of mercenaries to Katanga.

Two weeks later, ONUC launched operation MORTHOR. This operation did not have the approval of the Secretary-General, nor had the Military Adviser been consulted. It was carried out on the initiative of Mahmoud Khiary of Tunisia, the head of the U.N. civilian operation, and Conor Cruise O'Brien, the U.N. Representative in Katagana. Hammarskjöld only realized the full implication of this operation when he arrived in the Congo on September 13, by which time the operation had run into serious difficulties. This operation has already been mentioned, including the comment that the higher command structure, after the departure of the Secretary-General's Special Representative, Rajeshwar Dayal, lacked cohesiveness in the field. Hammarskjöld dealt with Sture Linner, the Swedish officer in charge in the Congo and also with Mahmoud Khiary, based in Leopoldville, who played an extremely active role in the political negotiations, and O'Brien in Katanga. General Sean McKeon, the Irish ONUC commander, dealt with Linner; whereas Brigadier Raja, the Indian commander of the U.N. troops in Katanga, was dealing with O'Brien. Thus, the military political leadership was confusing in the Congo, because each of the senior actors was dealing directly with Hammarskjöld, sometimes not fully knowing what the other was doing. There were reasons why Hammarskjöld lived with the situation, but it was one which led to grief.

Hammarskjöld was unable to find a suitable replacement for Dayal, an able administrator and an experienced diplomat. Therefore, he chose to exercise greater personal control by appointing Linner, then the officer in charge of civilian operations. Both Khiary and O'Brien were brilliant and proved skillful, the former dealing with the Congolese on important political matters beyond his appointed responsibilities, and the latter dealing with the Katangese. Thus, communications between Hammarskjöld in New York and Linner, Khiary and O'Brien in the Congo were sent to the individual concerned. Of course, Hammarskjöld dealt with

42. United Nations Security Council Resolution S/4741.

McKeon on military matters, but Raja in Katanga, aware of O'Brien's direct link with the Secretary-General, accepted instructions from the latter.

Hammarskjöld's direct personal control of ONUC may be likened to the historic instances of the removal of an army commander in the field and the assumption of direct command by a theater military commander. In this case, Linner's role as officer-in-charge of ONUC in the chain of responsibility became confused, while the able and forceful Khiary held the political strings in Leopoldville, and O'Brien, because of his somewhat independent position as ONUC representative in Katanga, was required to deal with the Secretary-General anyway (while keeping Linner informed). However, as far as the chain of command of ONUC troops was concerned, this arrangement of political control proved detrimental. Raja's superior was McKeon and not O'Brien, and only the commander of ONUC could have authorized operations like the second round.

In regard to UNEF, with the able direction of Hammarskjöld, and later Ralph Bunche during the period of U Thant's Secretary-Generalship, the peacekeeping operation in the Sinai and Gaza Strip was managed in exemplary manner. It was the withdrawal of UNEF on May 16, 1967, that raised considerable controversy. U Thant and Ralph Bunche were certain that they complied with all relevant resolutions of the General Assembly, including the arrangements negotiated by Hammarskjöld with Egypt on the question of withdrawal of the force, i.e., the Good Faith Agreement.[43]

According to this agreement, Hammarskjöld was only able to persuade the Government of Egypt to declare "that when exercising its sovereign rights in any matter concerning the presence and functioning of UNEF, it will be guided in good faith by its acceptance of the General Assembly Resolution 1000 (ES-1) and 997 (ES-1) in particular the U.N. understanding, this to correspond to the wishes of the Government of Egypt reaffirming its willingness to maintain UNEF until its task is completed."

Hammarskjöld sought to develop from a basis of cooperation, an arrangement that would also have the approval of the General Assembly. However, he was unable to obtain an Egyptian commitment that only the Assembly should decide when to withdraw UNEF after it had determined that its task was completed. He knew that it was a peacekeeping operation by consent and therefore there could be not hint of it being an enforcement action. Hammarskjöld was negotiating with Egypt from a relatively weak position, since Israel had refused to accept any part of UNEF to be deployed on its territory. Therefore the consent of Egypt to accept UNEF on its territory became cardinal, and when this consent was withdrawn, there was no way for UNEF to remain in Egypt.

The central basis of the UNEF operation, i.e., Egypt's consent, was lost

---

43. United Nations General Assembly 3375 (Annex) of November 20, 1956.

on critics of U Thant when he conceded to the Egyptian request to withdraw UNEF, fully realizing the consequences. These critics attributed this decision to U Thant's sympathy and admiration for President Nasser. They felt U Thant was anti-Western in his attitude because he had failed to keep UNEF in Egypt, contrary to the wishes of the western powers. On comparing U Thant with Hammarskjöld, his critics said that Hammarskjöld would not have given in to Nasser. Indeed, the personal style of diplomacy of both men was different, but once Egypt had decided to withdraw its consent, UNEF could no longer stay on Egyptian soil. Besides, U Thant fully complied with the arrangements agreed to by Hammarskjöld in this respect.

In conclusion, Hammarskjöld's role in peacekeeping remains an example that has yet to be surpassed. His enormous personal energy, personal courage, sagaciousness, political, diplomatic and administrative skills place him among the great. He enhanced the office of the Secretary-General and the ability of the United Nations to do what it must do first: strengthen its capability for maintenance of international peace and security. In spite of the many difficulties, i.e., the ad hoc nature of peacekeeping operations, the conflicting interests of member states, the complexity of the political issues, the enormous distances between New York and the area of U.N. peacekeeping operations, reliance on the telex as the only means for speedy communications, as well as the problems encountered from within the areas of conflict, Hammarskjöld's conduct of peacekeeping operations have become classic studies in this type of diplomacy to resolve conflicts through peaceful means.

Hammarskjöld was a great Secretary-General and a superb chief.

6
Hammarskjöld's Conception of the United Nations' Role in World Politics

Mark W. Zacher

Mark W. Zacher is Professor of Political Science and Director of the Institute of International Relations at the University of British Columbia. His major field of research is the politics of international organizations and law-making. He has written one book on Hammarskjöld's views on the United Nations' roles in international politics, *Dag Hammarskjöld's United Nations* (Columbia University Press, 1970), and another on the roles of global and regional organizations in conflict management, *International Conflicts and Collective Security, 1946-1977: The United Nations, Organization of American States, Organization of African Unity, and Arab League* (Praeger, 1979). He is the co-editor of *Conflict and Stability in Southeast Asia* (Doubleday, 1974) and *Canadian Foreign Policy and the Law of the Sea* (University of British Columbia Press, 1977), and the co-author of *Pollution, Politics, and Internatioanl Law: Tankers at Sea* (University of California Press, 1979).

Few would question that Dag Hammarskjöld was a resourceful and articulate diplomat and Secretary-General. As Secretary-General he probably gave more time than his predecessor and successors to reflecting about the role of the Organization in world politics, and he certainly left a more extensive record of his thoughts than any other occupant of the office. He was a man who regarded himself as having a mission ("Your prayer has been answered, as you know, God has a use for you. . ."),[1] and he wanted the imprint of his mission to be recorded not just in his actions but in his own words as well.

His conception of the United Nations' role in global politics can be conceived as falling under two general headings: the kinds of actions which the Organization could and should undertake to affect particular types of

---

1. This appeared in *Markings* and was written in 1953. Dag Hammarskjöld, *Markings* (New York: Alfred A. Knopf, 1964), p. 89.

international problems and the institutional developments which could and should be realized in our historical era. His views on these two interdependent issues, which developed gradually over the years 1953-61, were and are still controversial, and it is therefore valuable two decades after his death to reflect on them. They should, in fact, be a central ingredient in any diplomat's, scholar's or citizen's analysis of the past and future evolution of the United Nations' role in international politics.

The United Nations' Role in Conflict Management

The overriding concern of Dag Hammarskjöld as Secretary-General was international security relations. His tenure in office predated the emergence of the Group of 77, the formation of UNCTAD and the explosion of meetings and bodies within the UN system dealing with North-South economic issues. The issues which most concerned him and most governments—including those of the developing countries—during the years 1953-61 were the possibility of an East-West military conflict and the promotion and protection of the political independence of Third World nations. These were interrelated issues as crises such as those in the Middle East in 1956 and the Congo in 1960 showed only too well. The above comments do not indicate that Hammarskjöld and national statesmen were not concerned with the promotion of economic equality between the developed and developing countries. They certainly were, as is indicated by the growth of UN technical assistance programs and the debate over the creation of the Special United Nations Fund for Economic Development (SUNFED). However, the overriding issues on the UN agenda and in the minds of statesmen at the time were the prospect of the Cold War's becoming "hot" and the attempts by the Third World nations to achieve and protect their political independence. It was hence logical that Hammarskjöld would turn his considerable intellectual capabilities and diplomatic talents to these matters. In the early 1980s they may not have the priority which they had in the 1950s and early 1960s, and they may have assumed quite different dimensions as a result of changes in international political relationships. However, their salience is still very high, and Hammarskjöld's strategies concerning the Organization's activities in them deserve examination.

The central distinction that Hammarskjöld made in international conflicts was between those "clearly and definitely within the orbit of present day conflicts between the power blocs" and those outside.[2] (This particular terminology did not emerge until 1960, but his perception of these two different sets of conflicts can be seen in previous statements.)[3]

---

2. Wilder Foote, ed., *Servant of Peace: A Selection of the Speeches and Statements of Dag Hammarskjöld* (New York: Harper and Row, 1962), p. 302.

3. See his introductions to his 1954-55 and 1955-56 annual reports. Ibid., pp. 120-24, and UN Doc. A/2911, July 8, 1955.

What precisely distinguished conflicts that were inside or outside the orbit of the blocs he never made clear. However, his analysis leads one to think that it was the locus of the interests in dispute. Those within the orbit of the blocs referred to struggles over the control of governments or territory within the geographical spheres of the two rival alliance sytems. Those outside were logically conflicts in which the integrity of the central alliances was not at stake. This bifurcation, in fact, masks a number of different types of conflicts in each group, although Hammarskjöld's failure to refine his distinctions was probably more a product of the political constraints on someone in his office rather than a lack of understanding of the differences.

When Hammarskjöld first become Secretary-General, it was actually to the central Cold War conflicts that he turned his own and the Organization's attention. In his first report to the members in 1953 he wrote: "The efforts of governments to control and moderate those conflicts that constitute an immediate danger to world peace—and above all the 'East-West' conflict—must command first attention in day-to-day decisions."[4] Despite his successful mediation of the U.S.-China conflict over Chinese imprisonment of American fliers in 1954-55, his views began to change decidedly by 1955,[5] and his diplomatic energies became focused on conflicts in Africa and Asia. His most systematic statement concerning the difficulties which the UN faces in dealing with crises in the central Cold War arena were set forth in his 1960 report to the Members. There, he noted that not only is the Security Council likely to be stymied from acting because of interbloc differences and the Great Power veto, but "the General Assembly would follow lines strongly influenced by considerations only indirectly related to the concrete difficulty under consideration."[6] That is to say, resolutions would merely reflect one bloc's condemnation of another— something which was quite feasible given the numerical predominance of states in the Western system of alliances at that time.[7] He went on to comment that it was also very unwise for the Secretary-General to step in as a mediator in such conflicts since it would "seriously . . . impair the usefulness of his office for the Organization in all other cases for which the services of the United Nations are needed."[8] This would be likely to occur if he alienated one side by putting forth or backing a proposal to which it strongly objected.

4. UN Doc. A/2404, July 21, 1953, p. xi.
5. See his introduction to the 1954-55 annual report, UN Doc. A/2911, July 8, 1955.
6. Foote, ed., op. cit., p. 302.
7. A discussion of the nature and strength of the Cold War coalitions from 1946 to 1977 can be found in: Mark W. Zacher, *International Conflicts and Collective Security, 1946-1977: The United Nations, Organization of American States, Organization of African Unity, and Arab League* (New York: Praeger, 1979), pp. 38-54.
8. Foote, ed., op. cit., p. 302.

These general judgements did not mean that he completely abjured roles for the Organization in such conflicts. However, its activities were not conceived to be central to their management, and he had few illusions as to their impact. In the case of the Soviet Union's invasion of Hungary to prevent it from slipping out of the Warsaw Pact, he did make an oblique judgement of its action, and he privately urged that a committee be established to study and report on the Soviet action. He wanted the Great Powers to realize that they could not commit aggression without suffering an international rebuke, but he had few illusions about the impact of a UN resolution in such a conflict.[9] Hammarskjöld also eschewed any administrative/peacekeeping role in areas controlled or coveted by the major protagonists because it could invoke very hostile stands toward the Organization when consensuses broke down. To suggestions in 1958 that the UN be given control over Berlin, he commented that a UN administration and force

> requires obviously, back of it, somebody who can give the proper kind of directives and instructions, and those directives and instructions, in a case like the present one—the Berlin one—would have to be of a very serious political nature. I would like you to tell me whether you believe that the United Nations at present is so organized, constitutionally, that there is any organ which would be entrusted with that kind of policy decision back of a potential fighting force.[10]

He obviously feared that crucial decisions concerning the operation of a force would have to be made by the Secretary-General and that any action he took would invite the hostility of one side or the other—thus precluding cooperation with his office on other matters.

Hammarskjöld did not completely preclude a role for the Organization in Great Power negotiations concerning their military relationship and confrontation in Europe, but it was to be a minor one during his tenure and was to be concerned primarily with gradually integrating the settlement of their conflicts into the UN framework. He sought to have them hold their negotiations in UN facilities where the norms of the Organization and the mediation of other states and perhaps the Secretary-General might play a role. In 1959 he persuaded the Big Four foreign ministers to meet at the UN in Geneva, and in 1960 he almost succeeded in having a conference of the heads of state held in New York in the wake of the U-2 incident.[11] Regarding the 1959 Geneva meeting he commented: "This is more than a purely formal relationship. It reflects the fact that, should the parties find themselves in need of the kind of assistance the Organization can render in

---

9. Mark W. Zacher, *Dag Hammarskjöld's United Nations* (New York: Columbia University Press, 1970), pp. 136-38.

10. United Nations: Office of Public Information, Press Services, Note No. 1995, May 1, 1959. See also Foote, *Servant of Peace*, p. 206.

11. Zacher, *Dag Hammarskjöld's United Nations*, pp. 64-65.

any other respects, they can ask for such assistance and will get it."[12] The gradual integration of such negotiations into the UN diplomatic system never did evolve as the Secretary-General hoped, but there were few indications that he expected great progress during his years at the UN. He sought solely to lay a foundation on which others might build. The fact that the Great Powers were reluctant to become building blocks for a more encompassing and effective UN diplomatic system certainly did not surprise him.

After several years as Secretary-General, Hammarskjöld began to realize that the utility of the UN during his time in office, and probably long afterwards, would be measured by its contribution to the relationship between the Northern industrialized world and the Southern developing nations. In 1955 he wrote:

> The peoples of Asia today, of Africa tomorrow, are moving towards a new relationship with what history calls the West. The world organization is the place where this emerging relationship in world affairs can most creatively be forged.[13]

Starting with his attempt to resolve problems concerning the armistice agreements between Israel and its Arab neighbors in the spring of 1956, his energies became focused on Third World problems—although they usually elicited the interest and involvement of the Cold War powers and sometimes posed the possibility of a military confrontation between them.

He commented frequently on the UN's role in conflicts outside the area of direct East-West confrontation, but his best reflections came out in the wake of the Congo crisis. He termed the strategy which he had been pursuing "preventive diplomacy" since it was meant to prevent the military intrusion of the power blocs into conflicts—and hence both armed conflicts between them and infringements on the independence of the local Third World countries. He remarked that "[p]reventive action . . . must in the first place aim at filling the vacuum so that it will not provoke actions from any of the major parties, the initiative for which might be taken for preventive purposes but might in truth lead to counteraction from the other side."[14] His judgement was that in case of conflicts in areas of less than crucial concern to them the rival coalitions would allow and perhaps even welcome the introduction of UN peacekeeping operations and mediatory missions "to avoid having a regional or local conflict drawn into the sphere of bloc politics."[15] The developing countries—especially the involved parties—were perceived as backing UN operations in order to protect their own or their compatriots' nonalignment and independence.[16]

12. Foote, ed., op. cit., p. 202.
13. UN Doc. A/2911, July 8, 1955, p. xi.
14. Foote, ed., op. cit., p. 303.
15. Ibid., p. 302.
16. Ibid.

Hammarskjöld did not generally rely on an automatic welling up of Great Power and developing country perceptions that these above interests were and should be paramount and that they dictated a reliance on the UN. On occasions he sought very assiduously to persuade the Great Powers to set aside their rivalries and to agree on common stands. As early as the spring of 1956, he tried to get the major three Western powers to forego ganging up against the Soviet Union and trying to exclude it from the region by introducing a "tripartite" resolution. He succeeded solely on the latter issue but not in getting them to promote a unified stance which would have meant foregoing a competition for allies.[17] Again, he tried to get them to sit down during the Middle East crisis of 1958 and come to an agreement which would have meant some kind of recognition of the neutrality of Lebanon and perhaps other states as well, but it came to naught.[18] In the case of some of his more minor diplomatic forays he was more successful in securing approval from the Great Powers for attempts to promote stabilization. For example, his dispatch of mediators in 1959 and 1960 to settle the disputes between Cambodia and Thailand was cleared with them.[19] In this case the Soviets backed his initiative since for the time being they decided to put a damper on their competition with the West. Such attitudes from both sides, however, were not always forthcoming. In the case of the mediatory mission to Laos in 1960 he did not receive Soviet approval. But he went ahead in any case in trying to promote a return to a neutral foreign policy since he thought the Soviet position arose out of their deference to the Chinese.[20]

A key strategy of Hammarskjöld's in seeking a stabilization of such conflicts was an attempt to secure the backing of the African and Asian countries for the UN's efforts to promote the independence and nonalignment of the directly involved states. This often succeeded as was the case in the Suez crisis of 1956 and the Middle East crisis of 1958. In the latter conflict he urged domestic Lebanese parties to follow their traditional nonaligned stance and the Arab states to reaffirm the Arab League's doctrine on nonintervention, and his approach had some influence on the policies of the regional parties and the Great Powers and hence the outcome of the crisis.[21] In the early days of the Congo crisis this tack also yielded favorable results in that his fostering of unity among the African states was instrumental in bringing the Soviet Union and some of the interested European powers around to an acceptance—albeit a grudging one—of the UN operation. Once the domestic situation in the Congo began to disintegrate, this strategy did not work as well since some of the radical

17. Zacher, *Dag Hammarskjöld's United Nations,* pp. 70-74.
18. Ibid., pp. 63-65, 76-79, 90-93 and 99-103.
19. Ibid., pp. 94-97.
20. Ibid., pp. 102-106.
21. See note 18.

Afro-Asian states and the Soviet Union broke from their previous backing of the operation.[22] Following the Soviets' attack on Hammarskjöld and their proposal for a "troika" in the office of the Secretary-General, Hammarskjöld continued to rest the viability of UN operation in the Congo on the backing of countries from the area. In his now famous speech, and rebuttal to Premier Khruschchev, on October 3, 1960, he stated:

> It is not the Soviet Union or, indeed, any other Great Power who needs the United Nations for their protection; it is all the others. In this sense the Organization is first of all *their* Organization, and I deeply believe in the wisdom with which they will be able to use it and guide it. I shall remain in my post during the term of my office as a servant of the Organization in the interests of all those other nations, as long as *they* wish me to do so.[23]

His efforts to rebuild an Afro-Asian consensus behind the UN operation through informal negotiations and the meetings of the states contributing forces in the Congo Advisory Committee met with considerable success. However, the fact that the consensus had broken down and failed to reemerge in its old form meant that the Great Powers—and more particularly, the Soviet Union—felt free to attack ONUC and his direction of it. This weakened the efficacy of the UN operation and the office of the Secretary-General as well.

This discussion leads logically to another facet of Hammarskjöld's approach to some of the key conflicts in which the UN became involved—namely, his principles for the conduct of UN peacekeeping forces. Most of these were broadly supported and are still followed.[24] However, two of them, non-interference in the domestic politics of the country in which the force is operating and the termination of a force by a UN decision, became quite controversial.[25] In the case of the United Nations Emergency Force (UNEF) in Egypt, the doctrine of nonintervention did not become a major issue (after some initial British, French and Israeli challenges to it) because the primary functions of the force were to supervise the withdrawal of foreign troops and to prevent incursions across an international boundary. In the case of the UN operation in the Congo (ONUC), it became a major issue of contention since the force was operating in a situation of civil disorder—in fact, civil war. Hammarskjöld's policy of having ONUC prevent and terminate acts of violence, of course, had the effect of preventing any group—including the central government—from establishing national control, and it led to vehement calls by some nations for ONUC to defend the central government of the country. In the months

---

22. Ibid., pp. 150-64.
23. Foote, *Servant of Peace,* p. 319.
24. Zacher, *Dag Hammarskjöld's United Nations,* pp. 174-97.
25. Ibid., pp. 177-81 and 189-92.

prior to Hammarskjöld's death and then even more so afterwards, it was realized that a termination of the crisis depended on assuring the Leopoldville government's control of the country. ONUC was able to do this by defeating the Katangese regime under the justification of removing foreign mercenaries and acting in self-defence, but *de facto* it was acting as an agent of the central government.[26]

The principle concerning the force's termination originated with the Suez crisis and the birth of UNEF. Hammarskjöld was very concerned that Egypt might suddenly want to expel the force in favor of troops from a foreign country or in order to initiate military action, and he wanted to create an impediment to this. He thus secured an accord, which was not made public at the time, whereby both the UN and Egypt agreed that withdrawal was dependent on the force's completion of its task.[27] Hammarskjöld and many others interpreted this as requiring approval by the appropriate UN body before withdrawal could occur. This made it impossible for a Great Power or a third of the UN's membership as well as the host state to terminate the force. In the case of serious differences among UN members, especially the Great Powers, as to the direction of the force, it put executive control of the operation in the hands of the Secretary-General. His direction of it was almost certain to engender hostility of the Great Power(s) who opposed its existing policies and wanted it removed. The principle potentially turned approval of the force almost into the signing of a blank cheque for the Secretary-General.

In looking back over Hammarskjöld's central ideas concerning the UN's role in international conflict management, one can judge that some of his ideas were not as refined as they could have been and that others were not appropriate to the existing nature of international relations. With respect to his views on conflicts which were and were not amenable to constructive UN involvement (and the reasons why different groups of UN members would or would not back UN actions), it is quite possible that he did not judge it wise to spell out his thoughts further than he did. He did subsume both interbloc conflicts (between members of the opposing alliances) and intrabloc conflicts in Europe (between members of a single

26. Two studies of ONUC are: Ernest W. Lefever, *Crisis in the Congo: A UN Force in Action* (Washington, D.C.: Brookings, 1964) and *Uncertain Mandate: Politics of the U.N. Congo Operation* (Baltimore: Johns Hopkins Press, 1967).

27. The status and meaning of this accord were subject to a great deal of controversy at the time of Secretary-General U Thant's decision to terminate UNEF in May 1967 following Egypt's request that it withdraw from certain areas. It is our view that irrespective of the merits of the legal arguments on these issues, the principle backed by Hammarskjöld was not a wise one. For analyses of the original accord and the 1967 controversy, see Rosalyn Higgins, *United Nations Peacekeeping, 1946-67: Volume I, The Middle East* (London: Oxford University Press, 1969), pp. 335-67; and Yashpal Tandon, "UNEF, the Secretary-General, and International Diplomacy in the Third Arab-Israeli War," *International Organization* 22 (Spring 1968), pp. 529-56.

alliance) under disputes within the orbit of the East-West rivalry. However, while the politics surrounding these two types of conflicts were quite distinct, Hammarskjöld was certainly correct that in neither one was constructive and successful UN action likely (for example, the Berlin and Hungarian crises).[28]

With respect to conflicts outside the geographic sphere of the two blocs, Hammarskjöld did not distinguish between those in which the Organization could play a major and active role and those in which it could not. In fact, there was a considerable number where the UN was not involved or was only peripherally involved. Those where the Organization could play an active role were largely confined to situations where members of one coalition intervened in a nonaligned state. In such a case the allies of the state using force as well as the nonaligned states and the members of the

28. For a discussion of the UN's involvement in interbloc and intrabloc conflicts and the policies of different groups of states in these confrontations, see Zacher, *International Conflicts and Collective Security*, chapters 1 and 2, especially pp. 54-60, 63-64, and 71-73.

rival bloc opposed the military action. The reasons why the allies of the aggressing state opposed the military action were that they feared that military aid by the rival bloc to the nonaligned state could spark an interbloc conflagration—and perhaps more importantly that the use of force could drive the victim state and its nonaligned compatriots into collaboration with the rival bloc. This was fundamentally the situation in the Suez (1956), Congo (1960) and French-Tunisian (1961) conflicts where the U.S. and many other Western states opposed the actions of the Israelis, British, French and Belgians.[29] Apart from the Soviet invasion of Hungary these were the only three conflicts during the years 1953-61 where a UN deliberative organ came out against the threat or use of force.

If the threat or initiation of armed violence was directed by a non-aligned state against an ally of a major bloc [for example, the Afghanistan-Pakistan (1955 and 1961), UAR-Lebanon and Jordan (1958), and Iraq-Kuwait (1961) conflicts], the ability of the UN to act was constrained by one superpower's backing for the threatening or aggressing nonaligned state.[30] In the Middle East crisis of 1958 Hammarskjöld was able to use very creatively a UN fact-finding group and his own mediatory abilities to promote domestic Lebanese and regional Arab rapprochements, but the UN involvement was constrained by Great Power backing for the involved parties. The only military incursion involving two nonaligned states between 1953 and 1961 (the Egyptian occupation of small areas of the Sudan in 1958) saw the adoption of very impartial stances by the Great Powers and Egypt's withdrawal after about a week.[31] In the case of conflicts between the allies of one military bloc in the Third World, the conflicting parties and more importantly the bloc leaders sought to keep the disputes out of the UN where members of the rival coalition could affect the conflicts' management. There were many confrontations of this type in Latin America and Africa during the years 1953-61, and they were generally resolved in regional bodies such as Organization of American States.[32] What the above observations indicate is that even in most conflicts outside the blocs there are not consensuses for strong UN action to prevent or terminate armed violence.

It is true that with respect to conflicts where there were marked divisions between the major coalitions, Hammarskjöld was sometimes able to exert some influence as a mediator in his independent capacity as

29. Threats and acts of aggression by aligned against nonaligned states are discussed in: Ibid., pp. 54-59 and 73-78; and Zacher, *Dag Hammarskjöld's United Nations*, chapter 4.

30. For a discussion of the UN's involvement in conflicts where there is a threat or act of aggression by a nonaligned state against a member of a major security coalition, see Zacher, *International Conflicts and Collective Security*, pp. 54-62.

31. Ibid., pp. 68-71.

32. Conflicts between Third World members of a single major coalition are analyzed in: Ibid., pp. 54-59 and 64-68.

Secretary-General. His diplomatic interventions were relatively infrequent and often did not bear fruit; but they did indicate how it was sometimes possible for the Organization's executive officer to overcome the axes of conflict which inhibited the deliberative organs. The best known examples were his mediatory activities in the U.S.-China dispute in 1954-55[33] and the Middle East crisis of 1958,[34] but there were others. His dispatch of Swedish and Norwegian diplomats in 1959 and 1960 to assist Thailand and Cambodia[35] in resolving their differences was quite successful, and the same can be said about the activities of a Colombian diplomat and two UN Secretariat officials in settling an Israeli-Jordan dispute concerning the armistice agreement in 1957.[36] On the other hand, the attempts by himself and several personal representatives to affect different facets of the Arab-Israeli conflict in 1956 and 1958-60,[37] the Laotian imbroglio in 1959 and 1960[38] and the Saudi Arabia-U.K. conflict over the Buraimi Oasis in 1959 and 1960[39] were not so successful.

Despite the above cited failures, Hammarskjöld has to be given accolades for his diplomatic ingenuity and skill in initiating and carrying out diplomatic missions and in garnering political backing for his own activities and those launched by the Security Council and General Assembly. He sought the backing or at least the acquiescence of the Great Powers—especially the U.S. and USSR, and was often instrumental in securing approval of the Afro-Asian countries since it was crucial both in-and-of-itself and as a means of obtaining Great Power backing. He was an inventive Secretary-General, but he was not reckless. He sought to buttress himself always by law and the political support of the membership.[40]

Where he can probably be faulted in his approach to conflict management is with respect to his backing of certain principles for UN peacekeeping forces. The principle that the termination of a force requires an affirmative decision of a UN body poses significant impediments to approval by the host states and the Great Powers, and it creates the very real possibility (or probability) that the Secretary-General will have to make decisions to which certain powers and groups of states are vehemently opposed. As occurred in the Congo crisis, this risks the political life of the incumbent

---

33. Zacher, *Dag Hammarskjöld's United Nations*, pp. 112-13 and 128-31.
34. See footnote 18.
35. Ibid., pp. 94-97.
36. Ibid., pp. 83-85.
37. Ibid., pp. 70-74 and 85-88.
38. Ibid., pp. 102-06 and 167-68.
39. Ibid., pp. 97-98 and 118.
40. On his concern for having legal bases for his positions, see ibid., pp. 125-27 and Oscar Schachter, "Dag Hammarskjöld and the Relation of Law to Politics," *American Journal of International Law* 56 (January 1962), pp. 1-8.

Secretary-General—and the office itself. Insistence on the principle for future forces would inhibit their acceptance by host states and the Organization's membership, and actual adoption of it would potentially subject the Secretary-General to political suicide. It is one thing to obtain backing for six-month mandates in order to secure some short-run predictability and stability (as is now general practice), and quite another thing to create a force which can only be terminated by a two-thirds majority or Great Power unanimity. Hammarskjöld's political realism and insight failed him on this issue.

As was noted previously, Hammarskjöld's formulation of the doctrine of nonintervention for peacekeeping forces poses few problems for forces which operate along an international frontier, but in situations of domestic strife it can have serious weaknesses. If the domestic situation is one where there are clearly defined domestic factions living in separate geographical zones and the force is asked to discourage an outbreak of fighting between them (as was the case in Cyprus between 1964 and 1974 and has, to a certain extent, been the case in Lebanon since 1979), Hammarskjöld's formulation can probably work. However, when the international problem is the inability of the central government to assert its control throughout the country, a UN policy of preventing outbreaks of fighting does not fill the bill. In the Congo the UN from 1961 to 1963 was able to mask its acting on behalf of the central government under several legal justifications, but acting on its behalf it was! If in the future UN bodies want to remove the threats to international peace which are posed by certain situations of civil disorder and they want to secure the support of the host as well as some external parties, they are going to have to be willing to uphold the legal government. This may be possible by a reinterpretation of "nonintervention," but it could be done by the formulation of a new principle.

Hammarskjöld was an immensely creative and skillful UN executive officer and diplomat in relating the UN to contemporary international security relations. It is important that we remember and reflect on his contributions, but as with any statesman, we should learn from his errors as well.

Institutional Development

Hammarskjöld was very concerned with the UN's contribution to the settlement or amelioration of conflicts during his years as Secretary-General, but he was also very preoccupied with the long-term significance of the activities of the Organization. He was quite convinced that the Organization was the center and the crucible for the molding of global systems of collaboration, and he wanted to be a force in building cooperative practices and in strengthening the authority of international political institutions.

While he undoubtedly had a strong sense of mission about making the

United Nations a more central force in global politics, it would be quite inaccurate to portray him as a radical visionary who expected world political structures to be transformed overnight. In 1958 he remarked:

> It is difficult to see how a leap from today's chaotic and disjointed world to something approaching a world federation is to come about. To attain such a goal, elements of organic growth are required. We must serve our apprenticeship and at every stage try to develop forms of international coexistence as far as is possible at the moment, if we are to be justified in hoping someday to realise the more radical solutions which the situation may see fit to call for.[41]

Two years later he commented along a similar vein:

> The dynamic forces at work in this stage of human history have made world organization necessary. The balance of these forces has also set the limits within which the power of world organization can develop at each stop and beyond which progress, when the balance of forces so permits, will be possible only by processes of organic growth in the system of custom and law prevailing in the society of nations.[42]

At different times he described the evolution which was taking place as being from "institutional systems of international coexistence" to "constitutional systems of international cooperation" and from "a static conference machinery" to "a dynamic instrument of governments."[43] However, as this terminology and the above quotes indicate, he regarded the evolution as incremental and organic and based on positive experiences with different forms of collaboration within the Organization's structure.

In the institutional evolution of the Organization, Hammarskjöld viewed the growth of the permanent missions at the UN and constant interactions among the diplomats as central to the evolutionary process. He noted that these consultations "often in close contact with the Secretariat—may well come to be regarded as the most important 'common law' development which has taken place so far within the constitutional framework of the Charter."[44] This multilateral process, in his estimation, enabled officials to gain a much better understanding of each other's positions, encouraged the initiation and acceptance of mediatory missions, and tended to produce consensuses on issues which inevitably influenced the policies of the disputing parties. He remarked that on many problems there emerged

> an opinion independent of partisan interests and dominated by the objectives indicated in the United Nations Charter. This opinion may be more or less articulated and more or less clear-cut, but the fact that it

41. Dag Hammarskjöld, "Why the United Nations?", *United Nations Review* 5 (July 1958), p. 16.
42. United Nations: Office of Public Information, Press Services, Note No. 818, March 24, 1954, p. 18.
43. Foote, *Servant of Peace*, pp. 251 and 354.
44. Ibid., p. 224.

exists forms the basis for the evolution of a stand by the Organization itself, which is relatively independent of that of the parties.[45]

He also felt that the informal diplomatic network gave the formal organs of the UN "greater weight in present day diplomacy. The public debate, and the decisions reached, gain added significance when the attitudes presented in public result from practically uninterrupted informal contacts and negotiations."[46] To put his thoughts in other terms, he recognized that a public accord was the tip of a diplomatic iceberg—and that that tip required a much greater mass of diplomatic interactions which supported it—yet was invisible to the outside observer. Hammarskjöld sometimes urged national statesmen to send their best diplomats to UN missions, and he obviously saw them as crucial elements in the strengthening and improvement of the diplomatic system on which pubic accomplishments were based. It is also of interest, as was noted previously, that he tried to persuade the Great Powers to bring at least some of their top-level negotiations into the UN diplomatic framework so that gradually the broader system of interests and facilities at the UN could influence their interactions. He had rather limited success in this area, but his attempts do indicate how he thought the diplomatic framework should and could evolve.

Hammarskjöld's views on the formal legal authority of the UN's deliberative organs, in particular, the Security Council and General Assembly, mirrored conventional interpretations of the Charter. The Security Council's decisions were regarded as binding (although he recognized that states' practices fell short of the prescription), and those of the Assembly as only recommendatory.[47] However, he detected and supported a trend whereby states felt an increasing sense of obligation to comply with them. He noted that the existing legal formula

> leaves scope for a gradual development in practice of the weight of the decisions. To the extent that more respect, in fact, is shown to General Assembly recommendations by Member States, they may come more and more close to being recognized as decisions having a binding effect on those concerned, particularly when they involve the application of the binding principles of the Charter and of international law.[48]

Being a student of history and the law, he did not generally support attempts at this early stage in the Organization's evolution to declare its decisions as legally binding. He remarked once:

> We need to think of the institutions of the United Nations not as parliamentary in character but as a framework within which the govern-

45. Ibid., p. 209.
46. Ibid., p. 224.
47. Ibid., pp. 361-64.
48. Ibid., p. 361.

ments can, by trial and error, build up traditions of world community and mutual responsibility that will over a period of years gradually acquire the force of world law built upon the only sure foundation for any law—well established customs and traditions.[49]

Insofar as he made the Organization a more active and effective framework for collaboration, he contributed to the building of this foundation.

One issue concerning the legal weight of decisions became quite controversial during his tenure as Secretary-General, and it was the obligation of UN members to pay for UN peacekeeping operations. It was Hammarskjöld's contention that these were "expenses of the Organization" under Article 17, paragraph 2 of the Charter, and as such could be assessed on all members. The Soviets and French countered that only the Security Council had the power to levy mandatory expenses for UN forces. Against this point of view Hammarskjöld argued:

> If this provision of the Charter were to be disregarded and the apportionment of the expenses left to the Security Council, this would obviously involve an extension of the unanimity rule in that the approval of all the Permanent Members would be required for the continued financing of peace and security operations. In short, each Permanent Member would then have a continuing veto over the implementation decided on by the Council.[50]

As is now well known, the supporters of this position "backed off" when the crisis came to a head in 1964 and 1965. And in retrospect one can judge that it was probably a desirable outcome—at least as long as there were no accepted procedures whereby a Great Power or a large group of Members could secure the termination of the force in the short run. It is just not within the realm of the politically possible in our age that a Great Power or a major coalition of countries is going to be tied for indefinite periods of time to financing a force whose activities it opposes. Now that the practice of creating forces for a short period (usually six months) has become the norm, a system of obligatory assessments is possibly feasible. However, it is probably not desirable to make it the rule in all cases. Some countries may be rather indifferent—or possibly even slightly opposed—to an operation backed by a large number of states, but would be willing to approve it (or at least abstain) if they would not have to bear the costs. To require their financial backing might lead to their vigorous opposition. Such a flexible stance toward financing certainly has real pitfalls in that it encourages states to be "free riders." However, it is a situation we will probably have to accept in our present system of international relations.

Of central importance to Hammarskjöld's conception of the evolving

49. United Nations: Office of Public Information, Press Services, Press Release SG/373, March 18, 1954, p. 4.

50. General Assembly, *Official Records*, 15th Session, Plenary meeting 977 (April 5, 1961), para. 34.

role of the UN in world politics was the ability of UN organs to launch "executive actions" such as peacekeeping forces, aid programs, etc. In fact, the recognition and exercise of this right was central to the Organization's evolution from "a static conference machinery" to "a dynamic instrument of governments." On this issue he wrote:

> The first one is firmly anchored in the time-honored philosophy of sovereign national States in competition of which the most that may be expected in the international field is that they achieve a peaceful coexistence. The second one envisages possibilities of inter-governmental action overriding such a philosophy, and opens the road towards more developed and increasingly effective forms of constructive international cooperation.[51]

It was certainly in this area of "executive actions" that the Organization broke new ground during his tenure. It is possible to deprecate the significance of peacekeeping forces and to question some of the operational guidelines which Hammarskjöld prescribed, but they were significant departures in international security collaboration within the UN framework. And without his imagination, energy and skill they might never have emerged. It is also noteworthy that even after the tortured history of the Congo operation peacekeeping forces have continued to be utilized by the Organization. They have, in Hammarskjöld's words, "press[ed] against the wall that hides the future."[52]

As has been evident throughout this essay, Hammarskjöld regarded the office of the Secretary-General and the Secretariat as a whole as key elements in the Organization's ability to affect international politics. He once noted that "the main significance of the evolution of the office of the Secretary-General . . . lies in the fact that it has provided means for smooth and fast action, which might otherwise not have been possibly open to the Organization."[53] Concerning the significance of independent diplomatic initiatives he remarked at another time: "Step by step, he . . . builds up a practice which may open the door to a more generally recognized independent influence for the Organization as such in the political evolution."[54] Adlai Stevenson commented on the above points in comparable terms when he remarked that "Dag Hammarskjöld—himself a key part of the machinery—helped make the machinery more workable, more adaptable, more relevant to the immediate political needs."[55] Hammarskjöld was immensely creative as a mediator and counsellor and increased the accept-

---

51. Foote, *Servant of Peace*, p. 355.
52. Ibid., p. 252.
53. Ibid., p. 227.
54. Ibid., p. 209.
55. Adlai E. Stevenson, "From Containment to Cease-Fire and Peaceful Change," in Andrew W. Cordier and Wilder Foote, eds., *The Quest for Peace* (New York: Columbia University Press, 1965), p. 53.

ability and expectations among governments that the office-holder would and should be active in this field. It was, of course, in his role as the official in charge of peacekeeping forces that he broke new ground for the office. On the Security Council's and General Assembly's delegation of these responsibilities to the Secretary-General he wrote that "the development reflects an incipient growth of possibilities for the Organization to operate in specific cases within a latitude of independence in practice given to it by its Member governments for such cases."[56]

Hammarskjöld's views on the independence of the office have not been without their critics. Professor Jean Siotis delivered a rather stinging criticism:

> In law and practice, the manifestation of the international organization's "own will," which is distinct but not "independent" of the wills of its composing elements, is actually subordinated to the wills of the states which are expressed, tacitly or explicitly in its midst. For not having taken account of this reality, Dag Hammarskjöld met a political death, before dying physically; and perhaps the second death was only the consequence of the first.[57]

Joseph Lash made a comparable point when he said that Hammarskjöld

> came close to enunciating a "vox populorum" concept of the Secretary Generalship. The Secretary General was the spokesman of the Organization "in its capacity as an independent opinion factor." There was such an "independent factor" building up he insisted. It reflected the reaction, judgement and evaluation of that vast majority of member nations not directly involved in a dispute for which the principles of the Charter weighed more heavily than direct or indirect partisan interests.[58]

The former Irish diplomat and UN official during the Congo operation, Dr. Conor Cruise O'Brien, directed his criticism more specifically to the latitude of independence which Hammarskjöld advocated for his office in the direction of peacekeeping ventures.

> [R]oughly speaking the theory was this: the Secretary General represented the general will of the international community as a whole, independent of the will of any individual member or group of members; where the other organs of the Charter, the Security Council and the General Assembly, had failed to reach agreement, the Secretary General, and under him the Secretariat, could be, and ought to be, trusted to act in the general interest of all. In this way, and through such situations, the authority of the Secretary General and the Secretariat were to be gradually built up in the direction, it was hoped, ultimately of a genuinely supranational authority—a world government. . . .
> I do not believe however that we are helping the tendency in that

---

56. Foote, *Servant of Peace*, pp. 227-28.
57. Jean Siotis, *Essai sur le Secrétariat International* (Geneve: Droz, 1963), p. 249.
58. Joseph P. Lash, *Dag Hammarskjöld: Custodian of the Brush-Fire Peace* (New York: Doubleday, 1961), p. 201.

direction by pretending that we have already reached a stage which we have not in fact reached: a stage where the Secretary-General and the Secretariat can be implicitly relied on as an impartial instrument in the service of the international community as a whole, influenced by no national policies.[59]

In evaluating these judgements it is important to differentiate between the roles of the Secretary-General as a diplomatic spokesman and mediator, on the one hand, and as the executive officer of peacekeeping operations, on the other. Siotis' statement was directed at both of them, Lash's basically at the spokesman/mediator one, and O'Brien's at the executive one. Lash's point about Hammarskjöld's having a "vox populorum" conception of his office is just wrong. When he thought that most members felt a certain way about a conflict, he would convey this to the parties. Likewise, if he thought that a particular arrangement might be a basis for a compromise, he often stated his views. However, he almost always confined his judgements to private meetings, and he was regarded almost universally by national officials as a paragon of diplomatic tact. This is precisely why he was a party to so many negotiations and was given so many responsibilities. Andrew Cordier once described him as an advocate of "open covenants quietly arrived at."[60] In commenting about the extent to which the Secretary-General could be an "independent opinion factor," Hammarskjöld stated that he "had to accept the limitation of acting mainly on inner lines without publicity," and that "in nine out of ten cases, the Secretary-General could destroy his chances of exerting an independent influence on developments by publicly appealing to opinion over the heads of governments."[61] On another occasion he remarked that "clearly . . . a relationship of mutual confidence and trust would be impossible in an atmosphere of publicity. . . . He [the Secretary-General] should not permit himself to become a cause of conflict unless the obligations of his office leave him no alternative."[62] His behavior in the office, in fact, conformed very closely to the above philosophy. The only conflicts in which he actually voiced his opposition to national policies were his oblique judgements of the aggressors in the Suez and Hungarian crises in 1956 and his criticism of Egypt's refusal to allow the passage of Israeli ships through the Suez Canal in 1959.[63]

59. Connor Cruise O'Brien, *To Katanga and Back* (New York: Simon and Schuster, 1962), pp. 15-16.
60. Andrew W. Cordier, "Methods and Motivations of Dag Hammarskjöld," in Cordier and Foote, *Quest for Peace*, p. 19.
61. Foote, *Servant of Peace*, p. 209.
62. Ibid., p. 47.
63. The statement on the Suez crisis is in: Security Council, *Official Records*, 751st meeting (October 31, 1954), para. 4; on the Hungarian crisis—Security Council, *Official Records*, 754th meeting (November 4, 1956), para. 76; and on the Egyptian refusal to allow passage of Israeli ships—United Nations: Office of Public Information, Press Services, Note No. 2038, September 10, 1959, p. 21.

It is with respect to Hammarskjöld's views on the role of the Secretary-General in the direction of peacekeeping forces that one can be critical. However, Dr. O'Brien overshoots the mark when he speaks of Hammarskjöld's believing that "the Secretary General represented the general will of the international community" and that "the authority of the Secretary General and the Secretariat were to be gradually built up in the direction, it was hoped, ultimately of a genuinely supranational authority—a world government. . . ." In his speech at Oxford University in May 1961 he remarked that the Secretary-General was not "a kind of Delphic oracle who alone speaks for the international community," and then described the means by which he could maintain international impartiality and remain responsive to the wishes of the Members. These were guiding his actions by the principles of the Charter and United Nations legal precedents and obtaining maximum direction from the Members through formal resolutions and informal consultations with advisory committees and individual delegations. However, he then went on:

> Even if all these steps are taken, it will still remain as has been amply demonstrated in practice, that the reduced area of discretion will be large enough to expose the international Secretariat to heated political controversy and to accusations of lack of neutrality.[64]

It is important to note that Hammarskjöld, in fact, was extremely conscientious in seeking advice from member states and urging them to agree on particular courses of action—especially in formal UN bodies and the advisory committees composed of contributors to the peacekeeping forces.

Having recognized the very real and honest attempts by Hammarskjöld to seek advice and promote consensuses, it can still be questioned whether he adhered to operational principles for the forces which almost inevitably forced the office holder into such a degree of discretionary decision-making that vehement attacks on the office and the operations were almost inevitable. First and foremost, he did not allow for the termination of a force within a reasonably short time after the consensus which led to its creation broke down. This consensus would have to include the host state(s), the Great Powers (or at least the superpowers), and any large and important coalitions within the UN membership. It is a fact of contemporary international life that significant "executive actions" by international organizations require the backing or acquiescence of the major actors (or groups of actors) in an issue-area. When consensuses disappear, the operations, the officials in charge and the organizations themselves will be subject to vigorous—if not vitriolic—attacks unless the operations are soon concluded. Attempts to continue with them may well lead to the political death of the officials in charge and to severe difficulties for the operation. And they could severely inhibit the willingness of states to back

64. Foote, *Servant of Peace,* p. 347.

any collaborative activities within the international body in the future. As mentioned in an earlier part of this article, another operational principle which opened the Secretary-General to attack was that of non-intervention (or at least Hammarskjöld's interpretation of it in a situation of civil disorder). If followed scrupulously in such a situation, attacks by the host government and its external supporters are bound to result. There generally has to be support for some *de jure* or *de facto* legal order—and a recognition of what this is before the force goes in. Otherwise, the Secretary-General as the person in charge will find himself in the middle of a maelstrom, and he and his office are bound to suffer some serious political blows.

Hammarskjöld may not have developed his views concerning the roles of the Organization in as great detail as he might have—probably for very good political reasons. And he may have adopted some unwise strategies in certain situations. However, he left a wealth of insights concerning the possible contributions of the Organization to the creation of a more stable and just world through both his statements and his actions. It is almost inevitable that any statesman who seeks to "press against the wall that hides the future" will at times overstep the bounds of what is politically achievable in a particular historical era. To be, in the words of Lady Barbara Ward Jackson, "a man of the next generation"[65] invites both triumph and tragedy. Hammarskjöld's triumphs will be remembered and valued for generations to come.

65. Barbara Ward, "The United Nations and the Decade of Development," in Cordier and Foote, *Quest for Peace,* p. 201.

7

Dag Hammarskjöld: The Private Person in a Very Public Office

Brian Urquhart

Brian Urquhart, Under-Secretary-General for Special Political Affairs of the United Nations, has been a member of the Secretariat since August 1945. Born in Dorset, England, in 1919, and educated at Westminster School and Christ Church, Oxford, he served in the British Army in North Africa, Sicily and Europe from 1939 to 1945. In July 1945 Mr. Urquhart was appointed Personal Assistant to Gladwyn Jebb, Executive Secretary of the Preparatory Commission of the United Nations, and then served for three years, from March 1946, as Personal Assistant to Trygve Lie, the first Secretary-General of the United Nations. He subsequently joined the office of the late Dr. Ralph Bunche, Under-Secretary-General for Special Political Affairs, where he was active in organizing and directing all of the United Nations peacekeeping operations. During Dag Hammarskjöld's eight years as Secretary-General, Mr. Urquhart worked closely with him on all aspects of peace-keeping, most notably in the Suez crisis of 1956 and in the Congo crisis of 1960. In 1972, Mr. Urquhart's biography of Hammarskjöld was published by Alfred Knopf. In 1974, Mr. Urquhart was appointed as Under-Secretary-General for Special Political Affairs and is responsible, among other things, for the conduct of all peace-keeping operations and many other political activities of the United Nations. He is one of the principal political advisers of the Secretary-General.

Some public figures are completely taken over by their public life. Others fiercely guard the inner fortress of privacy and private activity as the centre and true source of their strength and capacity to bear public responsibility. Hammarskjöld was very definitely of the latter school. "Personally," he said in 1955, "I am very happy if I can escape professional talk after 7 or 8 o'clock."

Hammarskjöld was in many ways a paradoxical man—shy but proud, personally modest but highly ambitious for his office, intellectually brilliant but in some ways naive, given to mysticism but severely pragmatic in political arrangements, aristocratic but informal, highly motivated but deeply sceptical. This vein of paradox emerges in the relationship between his carefully guarded private life and the very high degree of public exposure inherent in his job as Secretary-General. There can be no question that Hammarskjöld loved public life and regarded the Secretary-Generalship as the most important thing that had ever happened to him. On the other hand, he never got over his natural shyness and a certain awkwardness in dealing with people, and he intensely resented well-meaning efforts to take an interest in his own personal life. He even kept his friends in separate compartments, each for a particular sphere of intellectual activity, and he did not encourage them to meet each other.

In Hammarskjöld's public performance one always sensed a great inner strength and conviction. The fact that he could shut off his public life at will and engage in private pursuits of a literary, musical or intellectual nature, gave him a reserve of strength and a capacity for recreation which is denied most people. He was unmarried and could therefore lead an admittedly individualistic existence—a tidy and disciplined life, using every waking hour to the maximum.

The fact that he was known to be intellectual and mystically inclined and that he stubbornly refused to talk about this side of his life, gave his public persona an element of mystery and reserve which certainly did him no harm with the press. There was nothing obvious about Hammarskjöld. He avoided organised social life and the various circles of so-called society. His press conferences were often a masterpiece of elliptical statements, circumlocutions and elegant dodging of questions, although when the occasion required he spoke his mind with the greatest clarity. Being hard to get and even harder to pin down was an important asset in preserving the interest of the media and the public.

Hammarskjöld was shy of human contact. It was extremely important to him to escape from the cares of office and from the attentions of well-meaning colleagues into his private world, from which he returned refreshed and invigorated to the herculean labours of the Secretary-Generalship. His apartment on 73rd Street and Park Avenue or his small country house outside Brewster, New York, were oases where he could think, write, or go for walks and commune with nature. His indefatigability and stamina became legendary. When, after several sleepless nights during a crisis someone said "You must be tired," he replied "That would be frivolous." In later years this process of recreation was increasingly related to religious experience and a growing interest in mysticism.

The Secretary-General of the United Nations, for all the eminence of his position, enjoys few of the normal attributes of power or authority. His strength thus inevitably resides mainly in his own integrity, strength of character, ability and moral courage. Hammarskjöld believed strongly that success in public life and politics was pre-eminently to do with those attributes.

Dag Hammarskjöld at his summer residence in Brewster, New York, in April 1957.

'Politics and diplomacy' [he wrote], 'are no play of will and skill where results are independent of the character of those engaging in the game. Results are determined not by superficial ability, but by the consistency of the actors in their efforts and by the validity of their ideals. Contrary to what seems to be popular belief, there is no intellectual activity which more ruthlessly tests the solidity of a man than politics. Apparently easy successes with the public are possible for a juggler, but lasting results are achieved only by the patient builder.'

This belief was very much a part of the Hammarskjöld family tradition. Of his austere conservative father, Hjalmar, who had been Prime Minister of Sweden during World War I and had suffered an irreversible political defeat, partly due to his unwillingness to bend to contemporary opinion, Hammarskjöld wrote:

> A mature man is his own judge. In the end, his only firm support is being faithful to his own convictions. The advice of others may be welcome and valuable, but it does not free him from responsibility. Therefore, he may

become very lonely. Therefore, too, he must run, with open eyes, the risk of being accused of obdurate self-sufficiency.

This was also an extraordinarily apt description of Hammarskjöld's own character.

Coupled with the family tradition of public service was an exceptional intellect and an amazing facility in a wide range of subjects. Hammarskjöld's academic career, especially in law and economics, was outstanding, and he became Under Secretary of the Ministry of Finance and Chairman of the Governors of the Bank of Sweden at the age of thirty. He went on, at a very early age, to major posts in the Swedish Foreign Office, and developed an intellectual self-discipline which enabled him to master new and vast areas of knowledge and to undertake, without apparent effort, extraordinary burdens of work. But for all his great success and gifts Hammarskjöld's early years appear to have been haunted by a sense of discontent and an unsuccessful quest for the meaning of life. His spiritual notebook *Markings* gives strong indications of a pervasive sense of futility during his early years of public success.

His unexpected accession to the Secretary-Generalship of the United Nations, a great international public office, was also a key turning point in his personal development, for it gave him a vocation which dominated the rest of his life. This vocation became the keystone of the arch formed by his other great qualities—intellect, courage, stamina and integrity. Having been unable to surrender himself emotionally, he gladly surrendered his life to this most demanding of all public posts. In the year of his death he wrote:

> From that moment stems the certainty that existence is meaningful and that therefore my life, in submission, has a goal. From that moment I have known what it means " 'not to look back', to 'take no thought for the morrow.' "

and in 1957:

> For someone whose job so obviously mirrors man's extraordinary possibilities and responsibilities, there is no excuse if he loses his sense of "having been called". So long as he keeps that, everything he can do has a meaning, nothing a price.

This accession to one of the world's most demanding and difficult jobs undoubtedly helped Hammarskjöld to find a more positive relationship to other people as well as the beginning of the inner peace he had sought for so long. His official family in the UN, the small group on which he most relied, provided exactly the degree of working friendship and support he needed without intruding on his privacy. Outside this circle, however, his relationships were not always easy. He expected too much of people and was often disappointed. He had little use for those who did not meet his extremely exacting standards of dedication, intelligence or self-sacrifice, and he could be impatient and curt, often with little justification. His judgements of people, sometimes based on a single misunderstanding or mistake, could be harsh and irreversible. He was anything but tolerant of fools, but easily taken in, for a short time at least, by phonies. All of this indicated a residue of personal immaturity and insecurity. On the other hand he was never more loyal to his colleagues, sometimes to his own cost, than when they were in difficulties, and he never hesitated to take personal responsibility for their actions even when these were not what he had intended.

It would be hard to overestimate the importance of Hammarskjöld's personality and character on the Office of the Secretary-General and indeed on the development of the Organisation itself during his stewardship. He had arrived unexpectedly in 1953 at a time of great disillusionment and disarray in the world organisation. His predecessor, Trygve Lie, having struggled manfully to establish the Organisation and to steer its infant steps through the trials and uncertainties of the post-war world, had been rendered almost totally ineffective mainly by two developments. The UN involvement in the Korean war had destroyed his relationship with the Soviet Union, while the McCarthy witchhunt in the United States, for which the UN was a happy hunting ground, had simultaneously mortgaged his relationship with the United States and eliminated whatever confidence the members of the UN Secretariat had had in him. Hammarskjöld therefore faced a dual challenge—to restore the political position of the Secretary-General and to rally the international secretariat.

He was lucky in some ways. In April 1953 the political climate had suddenly improved in various respects—Stalin had died; with Eisenhower there was a new and optimistic United States Administration; and an Armistice in the Korean war was in sight. Hammarskjöld, although scarcely known in the UN world, had a solid background in administration as well as considerable experience, in the Organisation for European Economic Co-ordination (OEEC), of international and multilateral dealings. His personality and character, however, were still his main assets.

He took up his office with great modesty and tact, concealing his intellect and his cutting edge with great skill. He handled his predecessor—who, while roundly abusing him behind his back, wished to stay on to advise him—with a mixture of forbearance and determination which evoked admiration and some amusement. He was approachable and made great efforts, in spite of his shyness, to get to know his new colleagues. He ate in the staff cafeteria and visited the entire staff in their offices during his first three months in New York. As far as public statements were concerned, he confined himself to trying to define his concept of the Organisation and its place in the world and to dispel the excessive hopes and foolish claims which, even in its early years, had created much disillusionment. The United Nations, he said, was "not created in order to bring us to heaven but in order to save us from hell." The Organisation, he wrote, was:

> the beginning of an organic process through which the diversity of peoples and their governments are struggling to find common ground upon which they can live together in the one world which has been thrust upon us before we were ready.

From the outset those who dealt with him were deeply impressed with Hammarskjöld's quiet self-confidence and by his apparently effortless grasp of whatever subject he was dealing with. He mastered with extraordinary ease the tangled and trodden-down jungle of the UN's various staff and administrative rules and regulations and began to re-order them as a means of re-establishing staff morale and opposing the inroads of McCarthyism. He led an intensive survey of the organisation and budget of the UN and introduced effective reorganisation, streamlining and cuts in expenditure. On the political side, though exceedingly cautious in public statements, he resisted pressures from all quarters to make hasty appointments or decisions.

Hammarskjöld was still generally regarded, in his first years in New York, as a cautious non-political bureaucrat, which was one of the main reasons why his appointment as Secretary-General had been unanimously approved. What his sponsors and supporters had not understood was that beneath the careful, civil servant exterior lay a passionate moral sense, an unshakeable integrity and a desire to confront injustice, violence and prejudice with the weapons of humanity and reason. Above all, Hammarskjöld was a strong-minded individual and felt very deeply the basic imperative of personal responsibility.

> I hate talking in personal terms, [he told an early press conference] but it finally boils down to the man . . . Where there is an uncontested right of the Secretary-General, I find it easier to stand up against whatever pressures there might be from whatever corners they might come, because then I can come down to the personal factor and say frankly this is something I would not do. That is sometimes a stronger line of defense. Where you fight it out like a lawyer is, in my experience, in the political sphere a weaker position.

This central characteristic emerged clearly in Hammarskjöld's approach to the crippling personnel, administrative and morale problems he had inherited. In his first year he devoted most of his energy to this central problem, remarking:

> Sometimes when I look ahead, the problems raised by our need to develop a truly international and independent Secretariat seem to me to be beyond human capacity. But I know that this is not so . . .

But he was no sentimentalist or seeker after popularity. He took an equally tough line with the US Government, McCarthy and the FBI on the one side (terminating the latter's presence in the UN building) and with the Secretariat on the other. If the members of the Secretariat had a right to protection as international civil servants they also had an obligation to deserve that right by their integrity and conduct. Some of Hammarskjöld's decisions reflecting this point of view were far from popular with the UN staff until they realised that only this uncompromising approach would in the end enhance their status.

Hammarskjöld insisted on his exclusive responsibility for appointments to the Secretariat which the spirit of McCarthyism had challenged and he reasserted his rights and authority in such a way as both to defend the Secretariat and to maintain its discipline. His successful battle with Washington on this issue was, characteristically, given no publicity. Paradoxically, eight years later in his last months Hammarskjöld found himself fighting, in a different form, the same battle for Secretariat independence with the other nuclear super-power.

On the political side Hammarskjöld's quiet but determined personal approach was slower to become apparent. His reaction to the United States-sponsored overthrow of the Government of Guatemala gave a foretaste of his strongly moral approach to politics, but he was unsuccessful in doing more than making a protest and infuriating the Government of the United States—then in a belligerent mood of missionary anti-Communism. The United States had, with the British and French abstaining, railroaded the Security Council into rejecting the agenda item on the Guatemalan crisis on the grounds that the question was a matter for the Organisation of American States rather than the UN. Hammarskjöld thereupon circulated a statement on the relative jurisdictions of the UN and regional organisations, indicating that he considered the question a matter of principle with serious moral implications. He gave Henry Cabot Lodge, the UN Representative, a legal study of the position—causing an uproar in a State Department still uncomfortable over the public reaction to the Guatemalan adventure—which elicited a threat from Washington that its publication would gravely affect the impartial standing of the Secretary-General.

This episode, and the complications of dealing with the effects of McCarthyism on the Secretariat, seriously strained Hammarskjöld's initial relationship with the United States. It was therefore a happy coincidence that the first full deployment of his powers of diplomatic activism in the political field should have been for a purpose especially important to the United States—the freeing of the seventeen American airmen in China. This episode, of the highest importance for international peace, brought into the open for the first time Hammarskjöld's personal qualities as a negotiator and the resulting potential of his office for executing exceptionally difficult diplomatic tasks. His capacity for on occasion striking up close relationships with key leaders, in this case Chou En-lai, and for developing a coherent line of action backed by solid intellectual preparation, his sense of timing and his nerve in the face of challenges and unexpected difficulties all contributed to a masterly solution of a problem widely believed to be insoluble. This success also established Hammarskjöld as a political force in his own right and gave him a marked taste for challenging international problems.

From this time (1955), the political functions of the Secretary-General's office increasingly overshadowed its administrative functions. In the political field especially, Hammarskjöld's personality and personal style were dominating factors in his conduct of the office, and his successes owed more to private and personal efforts behind the scenes than to formal public efforts. He soon realised that an international official with no sovereign powers and without even a regular constituency could not usually compete publicly with the leaders of sovereign States. In crisis situations especially, national leaders are intensely sensitive to national as well as to international public opinion, and the key to persuading them into a sensible course very often lies in finding a way of saving their face and preserving their prestige. Hammarskjöld was acutely aware of this requirement, as is clearly shown in the rules of conduct he wrote for himself in *Markings*:

> It is more important to be aware of the grounds for your own behaviour than to understand the motives of another.
> The other's "face" is more important than your own.
> If, while pleading another's cause, you are at the same time seeking something for yourself, you cannot hope to succeed.
> You can only hope to find a lasting solution to a conflict if you have learned to see the other objectively, but, at the same time, to experience his difficulties subjectively.
> The man who "likes people" disposes once and for all of the man who despises them.
> All first-hand experience is valuable, and he who has given up looking for it will one day find that he lacks what he needs: a closed mind is a weakness, and he who approaches persons or painting or poetry without the youthful ambition to learn a new language and so gain access to someome else's perspective on life, let him beware.
> A successful lie is doubly a lie, an error which has to be corrected is a heavier burden than truth: only an uncompromising 'honesty' can reach the bedrock of decency which you should always expect to find, even under deep layers of evil.
> Finesse must not mean fear of going on the offensive.
> The semblance of influence is sought at the cost of its reality.

These rules spell out faithfully Hammarskjöld's personal approach to multilateral diplomacy, and he followed them to a surprising degree during most of his Secretary-Generalship, although in his last hectic year his manner and style became more subjective and his customary caution was sometimes replaced by strong public counter-attacks against his critics.

Integrity was a quality to which Hammarskjöld attached the highest importance, and it was the keynote of his approach to political and diplomatic action. He would not, indeed could not, undertake an action he thought dishonest or unworthy, and he was thus valued as a friend and interlocutor even by those with whom he strongly disagreed. Within this imperative of integrity, Hammarskjöld was extraordinarily sensitive to the difficulties and sensibilities of the people with whom he was dealing. He had an exceptional talent for suggesting effective solutions that could be accepted without offence by the parties to a conflict. One key to his success as a negotiator was his ability to retain his mobility and to avoid either getting himself boxed in or committing others to rigid public positions that they would have difficulty in changing. By preserving his freedom of manoeuvre, he could often make local progress even in situations that appeared hopeless. His keen sense of timing allowed him both to keep alternatives open and, at the right moment, to create new and unexpected options for the parties. In an apparent deadlock he had a talent for spinning a new concept that the conflicting parties might be able to grasp at without losing face. Such creations as the UN "presence" and much of "peace-keeping" were initially symbolic and unsubstantial. Their first objective was to gain time for common sense and conciliation to come in at the back door when the conflicting parties could not afford to let them be seen coming in through the front door, and in this process the ideas themselves gradually gained substance and acceptance.

Hammarskjöld was from the start very clear about the nature and limitations of his role, and it was when, at the end, the necessity to fill political gaps drove him to defend and justify it publicly that he ran into really serious trouble, especially with France and the Soviet Union. He was fully conscious that, in matters affecting their own interests, the sovereign governments with and through which he had to deal were not normally responsive to the aims and ideals represented by the Secretary-General. He realised that his role must for the most part be that of a discreet, objective and indefatigable go-between and face-saver, and that when things went wrong the Secretary-General was a very convenient scapegoat. He therefore relied on a highly personal approach, stressing his own position and responsibility as Secretary-General and building up, by frequent contacts and personal correspondence, an intimate and confidential relationship with key leaders and pesonalities.

It was by stressing the *personal* responsibility of the Secretary-General that Hammarskjöld gained access to Chou En-lai in the affair of the American fliers, in spite of China's strong objection to the General Assembly resolution on the matter which had condemned Peking in its absence. His meetings with Chou En-lai were the meetings of two intellectuals who happened to be in politics, and an extraordinary rapport developed. Like many others, Hammarskjöld found Chou En-lai to be one of the most remarkable people he had ever met, and apparently the feeling

Dag Hammarskjöld meeting with Prime Minister Chou En-Lai in Peking, in January 1955.

was, to some extent at least, reciprocated. At the end of his career he went to South Africa under the same formula he had used to gain access to Peking, to discuss apartheid with Prime Minister Verwoerd, and again a sincere personal dialogue developed, only to be cut short by Hammarskjöld's death. Throughout his career, by stressing the personal responsibility of the Secretary-General in matters of international peace and security, he was able to discuss and even to assist in broad political problems for which he had no specific mandate.

The building up of personal relationships—a thin link of mutual human sympathy as he called it—was fundamental to Hammarskjöld's method of work and also typical of his character. Shy as he was, he attached enormous importance to a few selected friendships, and some of these were closely connected with his work as Secretary-General. From the beginning he had regarded Lester Pearson of Canada, who as President of the General

Assembly administered the oath of office to Hammarskjöld, as a confidant and friend. After a very shaky start he developed a close relationship with Henry Cabot Lodge, the United States Permanent Representative to the United Nations. In spite of the Suez fiasco, he liked and trusted Selwyn Lloyd, the British Foreign Secretary, and kept in touch with him on a variety of subjects.

It is perhaps significant that Hammarskjöld's two closest friendships in public life straddled the Middle East problem. David Ben Gurion and Mahmoud Fawzi were, respectively, the Prime Minister of Israel and the Foreign Minister of Egypt, countries at that time in violent conflict. Hammarskjöld conducted an intensive correspondence with both and greatly looked forward to his meetings with them, even when, as often happened, they had serious disagreements. Both, in their very different ways, were exceptional and highly civilised men, and both had interests outside politics in common with Hammarskjöld. Whatever success Hammarskjöld had in his dealings in the Middle East problem owed much to the fact that he could address himself with with the utmost frankness, as a friend, to both Ben Gurion and Fawzi.

The idea of friendship and personal esteem as a factor in the conduct of multilateral diplomacy did not work so well with more Olympian statesmen. Krushchev and de Gaulle would have none of it, although the former put a better face on it than the latter, even stating after Hammarskjöld's death that he was a great man. Nor did his contacts with the new leaders of Africa for the most part develop into the kind of relationship he enjoyed with Fawzi or Ben Gurion. Perhaps the acquaintance was too brief, but his initially favourable impressions of such young leaders as Sekou Touré of Guinea or Patrice Lumumba of the Congo soon turned to disillusionment and recrimination on both sides.

The fact is that Hammarskjöld expected a great deal of his friends, and many were not in a position to live up to his exacting standards. Thus, their number did not significantly increase, and in the storms and difficulties of his last year, he turned increasingly to the few he felt comfortable with, his old friends in Sweden, Pearson, Fawzi, Ben Gurion and the French poet/diplomat, St. John Perse (Alexis Saint-Léger Léger).

In trying to describe Hammarskjöld's personality it is impossible entirely to avoid the subjects of sex and religion. As regards sex, there is little to be said and even less information. The rumours of homosexuality which spring up like weeds around an unmarried man are cetainly nonsense in Hammarskjöld's case. He dealt with this dreary phenomenon in a haiku: "Because it did not find a mate / they called the Unicorn / perverted." The unicorn image is probably as near as one is likely to get to the truth—a desire to preserve privacy as a base for higher purposes, some element of admitted narcissism, and an "obdurate self-sufficiency."

Hammarskjöld's religious development is documented extensively in

Dag Hammarskjöld, outside the White House, with Douglas Dillon, President Eisenhower, and Henry Cabot Lodge in May 1959.

Markings, and it was unquestionably a central part of his life. Religion was closely linked in Hammarskjöld's mind with the concept of service.

> I inherited a belief, [he said in 1954], that no life was more satisfactory than one of selfless service to your country—or humanity. This service required a sacrifice of all personal interests, but likewise the courage to stand up unflinchingly for your convictions concerning what was right and good for the community, whatever were the views in fashion.

In the same interview he spoke of the medieval mystics—

> the explanation of how man should live a life of active social service in full harmony with himself as a member of the community of the spirit, I found in the writings of those great medieval mystics for whom 'self-surrender' had been the way to self-realisation, and who in 'singleness of mind' and 'inwardness' had found strength to say yes to every demand, which the needs of their neighbours made them face, and to say yes also to every fate life had in store for them when they followed the call of duty, as they understood it. 'Love'—that much misused and misinterpreted word—for them meant simply an overflowing of the strength with which they felt themselves filled when living in true self-oblivion. And this love found natural expressions in an unhesitant fulfilment of duty and in an unreserved acceptance of life, whatever it brought them personally of toil, suffering—or happiness.

Hammarskjöld's fascination with mysticism intensified as his involvement in political conflict deepened, and he began to reach a sense of fulfilment, inner peace and an acceptance of his fate whatever it might be.

> Simplicity, [he had written in 1959], is to experience reality not in relation to ourselves, but in its sacred independence. Simplicity is to see, judge, and act from the point of rest in ourselves. Then, how much disappears! And how everything else falls into place

In the point of rest at the centre of our being, we encounter a world where all things are at rest in the same way. Then a tree becomes a mystery, a cloud a revelation, each man a cosmos of whose riches we can only catch glimpses. For the simple, life is simple, but it opens a book in which we never get beyond the first syllable.

Nevertheless, amid the storms and disappointments of his final years his reactions were sometimes less than idyllic.

Obligation to action, . . . [he wrote just before death], . . . is more of a danger than of a privilege. At the present phase, events on all levels and the basic stone-age of psychology of men make it rather difficult to translate contemplation into action and to make action the source material for contemplation. . . .

The rising pressures accentuated Hammarskjöld's mysticism, his loneliness and his scepticism. His last year was not a happy one. He was deeply disturbed by the conduct of many of the actors in the Congo drama and indignant at the personal enmity of de Gaulle which reached a climax over Hammarskjöld's involvement in the Bizerte crisis. His breach with the Soviet Union was a blow which also seriously limited his effectiveness. He was also frequently infuriated by American and British attitudes to the Congo problem and irritated by the attempts of some African leaders to exploit it. He felt misunderstood and betrayed, and his later letters to Fawzi, Léger and his Swedish friends are often bitter and disillusioned. He turned increasingly to the solace of religion and mysticism. He did not relish the idea of retirement or the prospect of inactivity. However, in the late summer of 1961 the situation in the Congo improved, and Hammarskjöld became more cheerful and had time to resume his literary and other pursuits.

It is useless to speculate on what Hammarskjöld would have done if he had lived. There is some evidence that he intended to resign as soon as the Katanga question was settled, as he hoped it would be during the trip to the Congo on which he was killed.

His resilience and energy were so great and his interests so vital and diverse, that it is impossible to imagine him inactive or disconsolate for long. He probably intended to write on political philosophy, and his views and ideas would certainly have been of interest and value. He would have made a uniquely qualified and talented arbiter in the present economic debate between the developed and developing countries—the so-called North-South dialogue.

As it is, most of us are left with the memory of his eight years as Secretary-General. For many of us, that memory—the manner and attitude, the appearance, the tone of voice, the cast of mind—remains surprisingly vivid. Like the unicorn, Hammarskjöld had something of a mythical quality—a quality of uniqueness, unworldliness, purity and elusiveness—which keeps him very clearly in the minds and memories of his colleagues and friends. We are unlikely to see anyone like him again.

Dag Hammarskjöld in 1909 (almost 4 years), in Uppsala.

Dag Hammarskjöld's parents, Hjalmar and Agnes, circa 1930.   Dag Hammarskjöld in the early 1930's.

Dag Hammarskjöld with his mother (Agnes) and brother (Sten) taken in August 1927 in the village of Åre in Northern Sweden.

Dag Hammarskjöld relaxing in a cafe, circa 1956.

Dag Hammarskjöld as a youth.

Dag Hammarskjöld with Swedish Foreign Minister Osten Undén (l) and Foreign Office Cabinet Secretary Arne Lundberg (r), circa 1949-50.

The Swedish Cabinet, circa 1949-50, with Dag Hammarskjöld in the background.

Dag Hammarskjöld as he looked in the 1930's.

8
A Bibliographic Essay on Dag Hammarskjöld

Larry Trachtenberg

Larry Trachtenberg is a Doctoral Candidate in International Relations at the London School of Economics and Political Science, where he is conducting research on the role of the Secretariat and Secretary-General in United Nations peace-keeping initiatives. This work is based in large part on the Personal Papers of Dag Hammarskjöld, Ralph Bunche and Andrew Cordier. He has studied at California State University (B.A.) and Uppsala University, Sweden, and has received his M.Sc. (International Relations) at the London School of Economics and Political Science, where he is currently teaching.

I have been told by a 'usually reliable source' in the USSR delegation that they feel they have made an 'error' in their attack on you. But K himself feels very strongly on this as well as on some other questions which some in the 'delegation' also regard as 'errors.'
Handwritten note from Heinz Weischoff to
the Secretary-General (undated)

The [USSR is scratched out here] informant repeats today his reference to the 'error' that has been made by them regarding the position of yourself as SG. He again referred to the fact that this was a decision by K who had confronted Gromyko with this decision, about a year ago, when disarmament was discussed. He repeated that they thought that you had been very objective. In regard to the sharp attacks on you personally, he shrugged it off as one of 'those things in politics.' Now it was difficult to reverse their position; they thought that Narasiman [sic] would make a good SG.
Handwritten note from Heinz Weischoff to
the Secretary-General (18 March 1961)

Two short notes, found in a file among Dag Hammarskjöld's papers in the Royal Library, Stockholm. As presented here, they are significant as they have never before been published in their entirety[1] and do shed some

---
1. These notes are referred to by Brian Urquhart in his work, *Hammarskjöld* (London: Bodley Head, 1973), p. 472.

light, in the very least, on the political problems, and realities facing the Secretary-General in his final months in office. But if the reader was also told that these two notes from Hammarskjöld's Personal Assistant (who died with him in Ndola) were found, neatly folded in Hammarskjöld's wallet on the day after he died, their significance at once becomes intensified. Is one to assume that Dag Hammarskjöld carried these two notes around with him for exactly six months, drawing strength from the insights he might have acquired in their message? Or rather, did he view them as something of a cruel jest, something to fight and persevere against?

This will, more than likely, remain one of a number of unanswered questions about Dag Hammarskjöld. The writer and receiver of the notes are long dead and the "source" of the information can only be speculated upon. These two notes also tell a story which tends to run contrary to popular history as related since that period, thus making them, without corroboration, a potential source of controversy. But in finding these two notes, and deducing their contents, the researcher sitting in Stockholm with the Hammarskjöld papers before him has the opportunity to explore some more, dig a bit deeper and perhaps, if lucky, come up with more information on the questions raised by these two notes.

This is one of the essential joys of undertaking primary source research, the sense of discovery, the knowledge that new ideas are in the making or that old ones may have to be re-thought. But such undertakings also have their agony, as it is rare when a researcher discovers material that will fundamentally change our outlook on a particular event or make us re-think an established concept. But one never knows the end result until one tries, and if it is material which has not been widely used (or in some cases, for the extremely fortunate, never used), there will always be new things to discover about one's subject. Even in the case of material which has been used hundreds of times in the past by others, when looked at by an individual asking new questions, and coupled with other data, the "old" material can often yield more than those papers which are only just seeing the light of day.

In the following pages, some of the major collections of papers which deal with Dag Hammarskjöld and his eight years as Secretary-General will be examined. The main purpose of this exercise is not so much to provide the potential user with a running account of the contents of these various collections, but rather, to let the researcher know that they exist, that they have been utilised before and that, for the most part, the collections discussed here all have something of value for the scholar interested in Dag Hammarskjöld and his work in the UN. One of the main advantages to the English speaking researcher who uses any of these collections is that in almost all cases, the papers are in English. Hammarskjöld used English in every form of written communication, with the exception of some hand-written letters to very close Swedish friends or his family (which were almost always in Swedish). A reading knowledge of Swedish would be a necessity for anyone who was interested in exploring the more personal side of Hammarskjöld's life, as well as his relationships with a variety of Swedish colleagues. There is, of course, a variety of correspondence from delegates and friends of different states, but most of these have usually been translated into English by the time they arrived on the thirty-eighth floor (either at the point of origin or by Secretariat staff). The exception here is correspondence in French, which is almost always found in its original form, as this was a language in which Hammarskjöld was fluent.

Lastly, it should be noted that in most cases, limited photocopying can be undertaken in the collections described below, though in all cases where it is permitted, the material in question will be vetted by the individual responsible for the collection. Use of any photocopied material in publications resulting from the research will normally be based on the permission of the individual responsible for the papers. The name and address of the individual responsible for each collection discussed below is provided at the beginning of each section. Questions relating to access and restrictions on the use of material are touched upon at the end of this paper.

Dag Hammarskjöld Papers[2]

The private and personal papers of Dag Hammarskjöld are located in the Manuscript Department (Handskriftsavdelningen) of the Royal Library in Stockholm, Sweden. The papers are stored in various parts of the Library (most of which is underground) and can only be retrieved by the head of the Manuscript Department. The Collection is divided into two parts, both physically and in terms of the original source. One part of the collection originates from the Secretary-General's Office in New York and the other portion from Hammarskjöld's New York apartment and from Sweden prior to his taking up his UN job. Within these two divisions are numerous other physical subdivisions, which come about due to the manner in which the papers are stored; they are housed in filing cabinets and safes similar to those originally used by Hammarskjöld himself in his office and his home. It is safe to say that, while one collection, the two parts are rather distinct, with the former being the political, and the latter being the more personal. Nevertheless, the two parts heavily interlock and a great deal would be lost by not treating the two as holistic.

The first part of the collection comprises those papers issuing from the United Nations. This is the most useful and one of the most interesting of all the known material dealing with Dag Hammarskjöld. These papers are divided into five parts, representing fairly closely the manner in which they were originally kept in the United Nations. Each part is represented by a

---

2. Dr. Harry Järv, Handskriftsavdelningen (Manuscript Department), Kungliga Biblioteket (The Royal Library), Box 5039, S-102 41 Stockholm, Sweden.

double-locked four drawer filing cabinet and these are numbered SD-I through SD-V. All of these papers, with the exception of those which are found in SD-V, were stored in safes and filing cabinets similar to those on the thirty-eighth floor. These were a small safe and cabinet behind the Secretary-General's desk and four filing cabinets and a large safe located in the office of Hammarskjöld's secretary. When the collection was put together, the papers and documents in Hammarskjöld's files were moved sequentially into SD-I, SD-II, and so forth, as they were found and with no known changes made to the files or the order of the papers. None of the files were numbered at this time and all filing, at least in the Secretary-General's office, was done on a subject basis. Numbering as it now exists was created for the purpose of facilitating some sort of indexing of the contents of the collection.[3]

It would be inordinately difficult to surmise accurately the contents of SD-I through SD-V without going into substantial detail. However, certain observations may be made. It will be noted that the organization of these five cabinets is rather aimless which obviously makes the task for the researcher more difficult. It also raises questions about procedures in the Secretariat, though space limitations prevent a discussion of these aspects in this chapter.

> *SD-I*—contains items relating to Secretariat activities (ranging from administrative and personnel matters to the UN Gift Shop to Hammarskjöld's Meditation Room), all outgoing correspondence relating to United Nations business from 1953 to 1961 and all of the Secretary General's personal financial records. It should be noted that correspondence relating to a subject for which there exist separate files, such as the Suez Crisis or the Congo, will be found within these subject files rather than in the correspondence files of SD-I.
>
> *SD-II*—contains the Secretary-General's travel files for 1953 to 1961 and a wide assortment of miscellaneous political items, including, in the whole of the fourth drawer, what is entitled "The Suez Story." These are the details of the Suez Crisis and subsequent UN activities as put together by Hammarskjöld himself. Included are all of the official and unofficial documents, memoranda, correspondence and Hammarskjöld's personal observations on the situation.
>
> *SD-III*—found in this section is a wide assortment of items relating to political matters, including the UNOGIL operation, Laos and the Congo. This cabinet also contains a larger number of documents dealing with the Middle East in a variety of areas, such as the shooting of UNSTO observer Lt. Col. Flint at Mount Scopus in May 1958, the on-going problems of the Suez Canal and the territories occupied by Israel, and the question of the economic development of the region.
>
> *SD-IV*—here one finds the remainder of the files dealing with Secretariat matters from 1959 through 1961, the bulk of the material on the Congo

---

3. See discussion on page 161 regarding duplication of many of these papers in the United Nations archives.

Operation, (both the military and civilian aspects) and additional material on the Middle East, including all the code and clear cables from UNTSO and code cables dealing with UNEF and the Suez Canal Clearance Operation.

SD-V—this final section of the UN side of the collection is devoted mainly to speeches and correspondence relating to speaking engagements, though it also contains some items regarding Hammarskjöld's death at Ndola, (cables, public statements and letters of condolence) as well as all of the Secretary-General's entertainment files.

The second part of the Hammarskjöld Papers is made up of two main components, though these are physically divided into five cabinets in the same manner as the first part of the collection. The first of the two components consists of Hammarskjöld's papers from, 1) his New York apartment at East 73rd Street and 2) those papers from Stockholm which were left behind by Hammarskjöld when he came to New York in 1953, (these latter papers were in storage during Hammarskjöld's stay in New York). These two components of the Secretary-General's life are housed in three cabinets marked SD-VI, DH-1, and DH-3.

Cabinet SD-VI contains all of the papers found in Dag Hammarskjöld's apartment in New York after his death, while DH-1 holds the main bulk of papers from Stockholm, including correspondence with family and friends, and items dating back to his days at Uppsala University. DH-3 holds items of a more collateral nature, such as honorary degrees, citations, photographs and printed matter from both Stockholm and New York.

The second component of this second part of the collection is rather unique, almost a collection within a collection. This is itself physically divided into two cabinets, DH-2 and DH-4. DH-2 contains a miscellanea of items which at one time or another were in Hammarskjöld's possession, as well as that portion of the private papers of Judge Emil Sandstrom dealing with his work as a member of the General Assembly's Investigation Committee on the Ndola crash—after the Judge's death, his will called for the deposit of these papers in the Hammarskjöld Collection. Also included in this cabinet are some assorted personal notes and letters from acquaintances and close friends of Hammarskjöld's, such as St. John Perse, Barbara Hepworth and John Steinbeck. Much of the rest of the cabinet contains items that, in one manner or another, relate to Hammarskjöld's final days; i.e., the contents of his briefcase found at the crash site, his writings from this period (including the beginnings of his translation of Buber's "Ich und Du") and, rather significantly, as has been shown, his wallet.

In DH-4, one encounters numerous items, none of which actually belonged to Hammarskjöld during his life. They are all things that were presented to or sent to Hammarskjöld's brother Bo, after the Secretary-General died. The majority of these items relate to his death and funeral, including press clippings, eulogies, condolence messages, etc.

What has been provided here is essentially the maximum detail one would gain from an examination of the collection's "index," approximately forty pages of typescript which lists subjects on the basis of how they appear in the files themselves. There is no detailed cataloguing system, but simply the typed or hand-written heading on each file itself. In the case of SD-I through SD-IV, the listing is made by cabinet, from the top drawer down and for each drawer from the front to the back. In cabinets SD-V, SD-VI, and DH-1 through DH-4, the listing is made from the top shelf down and for each shelf from left to right.

So, SD-I, Top Drawer, 1st File is the very first item one encounters on the "index" or finders' aid. It is entitled "Background file on UNICEF organization (blackbound), 1952/53," and this is the extent of the information one receives on this file. There is no indication whether there is one piece of paper in it, or papers five inches thick with hundreds of items. And so it goes with the entire collection. This represents one of the miseries (and joys) of doing research on this collection. Searching can thus be extremely time-consuming and ultimately worthless with regard to the original expectations.

To illustrate the contents of this collection and the often arbitrary manner in which items can be uncovered, we can examine the subject of the UNOGIL operation of 1958.

When scanning the "index" the first actual mention of Lebanon, or the UNOGIL operation is in SD-II, Top Drawer, in a travel file for 1958 marked "Trip to Lebanon, 17 to 26 June." This however, turns out to be just what it says—basic details of travel arrangements to the Lebanon where Hammarskjöld held talks with the Observer Group and various Middle East leaders. Included here are itineraries, payment vouchers, hotel reservations and cables relating to various protocols, and additions and changes to the itinerary. It tends to be rather insubstantial material and the temptation is to move on immediately to potentially richer ground.

But if the researcher had glanced in the folder just before that one, headed "Trip to ME/Geneva/ME, 25 August to 13 Sept. 1958," he would have found, along with the types of documents mentioned above, a thought-provoking letter to Egyptian Foreign Minister, Mohammed Fawzi, dated 15 August, 1958, in which the Secretary-General makes an appeal to Fawzi that "some special brakes" be maintained by Egypt during the changeover to the new government in Lebanon. It was typical of the style of preventive diplomacy Hammarskjöld often utilised and telling at this particular moment, when a peaceful outcome to the dispute was far from certain. But one has to ask why it was in this travel folder. There were no other items like it in this particular folder, though they would appear randomly in other areas.

The next file that is explicitly marked Lebanon or UNOGIL is in this same drawer, the second of SD-II, at the very back and is marked "UNEF

A Bibliographic Essay

Dag Hammarskjöld conferring with officials of the United Nations Observation Group in Lebanon (UNOGIL) in Beirut, September 1958.

(GAZA/UNOGIL (Lebanon)/Operational Principles and Experience), 1959." Included here are two confidential documents, one of which examines the functioning of UNOGIL's Military Staff, and the other a more general account of the overall functioning and practices of the UNOGIL operation. Both documents are highly informative and contain a prodigious amount of previously unpublished data as well as self-criticism by the Military Staff themselves with useful recommendations for future operations. One can find in these documents the basis of numerous changes which were instituted in the field operations of the UNEF in 1959.

The next, and most important, part of the UNOGIL documents is to be found in the Top Drawer of SD-III, in a group of 15 files collectively marked "Lebanon Story (UNOGIL)." In these files one finds all of the cables, correspondence, and UN documents relating to the operation which either passed through or emanated from, the office of the Secretary-General. Of particular interest are the documents to be found in file Number 3 marked "Mission: Personal Notes (key documents) records of conversations during SG's trip June 1958." It is here one finds a classic example of Hammarskjöld's very personal form of diplomacy which he used so effectively.

In talks with Egyptian President Nasser on the evening of 22 June, 1958, the Secretary-General notes that he made it clear that he was "personally convinced of [UAR] military cooperation with the rebels which had taken the form of quite an extensive infiltration and delivery of arms." He went on the state that the UAR should have "no illusions that [the western powers] would all go in [to Lebanon] under certain circumstances."

Nasser went on to defend his point of view, but in the end, "he summed it up by saying that he would give [me] his promise that all military infiltration and arms traffic would halt. I replied that that was alright, but I did not want his promise, as I would not promise him anything myself. For me it was much more important that I had had the impression that he had fully grasped what I wanted to convey . . . I added that his statement of intention was appreciated as confirming this view . . . As he must understand, I very often ran into discussions about his person. What was then said to me was anything but flattering to him. I had one stock-reply which I always used: 'However that may be, he has never gone back on anything he has said to me personally.' " Nasser replied to Hammarskjöld at this point that "I do wish to maintain that record, and that is the reason why I have to be very exact."

Hammarskjöld's openness and dependency on personal relationships in his diplomacy was strongest in his dealings with Middle East leaders and his relations with Nasser are a poignant illustration of this. Other examples abound, such as in Hammarskjöld's conversations with David Ben-Gurion, Mohammed Fawzi and Camille Chamoun. The Secretary-General kept meticulous notes of all conversations (or had an aide, such as Bunche, take notes) and these were immediately written up following the meeting in question, in the form of a partial reconstruction of the dialogue and salient points of the conversation, including Hammarskjöld's personal observations. It is as close as one will come in the Secretary-General's papers to finding a "diary" or personal recording of political events.

Continuing through the "index" one encounters no further direct references to Lebanon or UNOGIL, but careful searches through the collection will reveal additional substantive material on UNOGIL in approximately 30 or other files, such as among correspondence or field reports from representatives of the Secretary-General on other official duties. This is a collection which demands of the researcher a great deal of patience and an even greater willingness to devote large amounts of time (months as opposed to weeks) to the task at hand.

The Hammarskjöld Papers are of extremely high value to any researcher interested in Dag Hammarskjöld, the Office of the Secretary-General or the role of the United Nations in all areas of activity during Hammarskjöld's tenure. The United Nations' scholar will wish to make use of the entire collection, examining the political papers in the first part, as well as the more personal papers in the second part, as the two sections do heavily interlock. Those individuals enquiring into the more intellectual and spiritual side of Hammarskjöld's nature will find the second part of the collection most useful and could probably pass over most of part one.

The overall quality of a collection such as this is difficult to judge, as there are so many elements which make up the total of the papers, as there are different elements making up the total of an individual and his life. As the individual in this case was unique, so are his papers. The lack of a comprehensive index means more work for the researcher, though a more detailed itemization would probably steal a great deal from the sense of discovery one so often feels when working one's way through Dag Hammarskjöld's Papers.

Ralph Bunche Papers[4]

Dag Hammarskjöld and Ralph Bunche both worked selflessly in the United Nations for the goal of world peace and justice. They shared many of the same values, goals and hopes which in their lifetimes they were able to see, at least partially, achieved. But Hammarskjöld and Bunche came from totally contrasting social and cultural environments, and entered UN service from entirely different backgrounds. This difference is clearly reflected in the Papers of Ralph Bunche, housed in the Special Collections Department of the University of California at Los Angeles, Bunche's *alma mater* as an undergraduate.

Ralph Bunche's papers are an important part of any research on Dag Hammarskjöld or the United Nations for two reasons: first, as Under-Secretary-General for Special Political Affairs under Hammarskjöld, Bunche was one of the Secretary-General's most trusted political advisors, among the small circle of individuals who were always in Hammarskjöld's close confidence. This position made Bunche privy not only to most of the key political decisions taken by the Secretary-General, but also a preeminent decision-maker in his own right. This leads to the second reason why a close scrutiny of Bunche's Papers is a necessity. During his almost twenty-five years of service to the United Nations, Bunche's involvement in international affairs made him a hard act to follow for any individual. His insight, political acumen, and skills as a negotiator are legend in UN circles, not to mention the fact that he is the oft unmentioned guiding hand behind most of the United Nations peacekeeping activities between 1956 and 1970. He directed UN efforts in the area of trusteeship and non-self governing territories during the organisation's first ten years and was pivotal in laying the groundwork for UN action on the subject of the Peaceful Uses of Atomic Energy. This remarkable career makes it essential that his papers be examined, but all the more so disappointing when one has concluded the research.

The Bunche Papers are housed in 160 large packing boxes and were put together as a collection by Bunche's daughter Joan with the assistance of a foundation grant. The manner of organization is slightly more ordered than that found in Hammarskjöld's Papers, though the fifty-two page 'finders' aid is very similar to that of the Hammarskjöld Papers in its lack of detail

---

4. James V. Mink, Department of Special Collections, University Research Library, University of California, Los Angeles, California 90024 U.S.A.

Dag Hammarskjöld conferring with Under-Secretary-General Ralph Bunche during the 10th Session of the General Assembly.

about the contents of individual folders. It is however a decidedly more wieldy collection in which to conduct research; one will discover from the beginning that if a folder is marked "Palestine Mediation" that is a fairly exact description of the subject of the contents. No odd letter or memorandum concerning the Congo or Laos will appear; Ms. Bunche did an excellent job sorting her father's papers into comprehensive categories and this undoubtedly makes any research easier. Of course, lack of further detail about file contents means that the above-mentioned file on "Palestine Mediation" could contain a single letter or 1500 items describing the entire course of the mediation effort in 1948-49. This lends itself to the same frustrations encountered in the Hammarskjöld collection, without any of the joys of finding the occasional surprise.

What makes this collection unique, is that it represents, with a few important exceptions to be mentioned later, the sum total of one man's life. There is no doubt that Ralph Bunche had a great sense of his growing place in history, as did his redoubtable grandmother, "Nana," who raised him from the time he was twelve years old. In boxes 126 through 131 of the collection, one finds what is referred to as "Biographical Material," over three hundred files relating to Bunche's childhood, early schooling and family history. Included here are essays and exams from high school, information on Bunche's favourite songs, recipes, anecdotes as well as scripts for films and television shows about Bunche (most of which were never made).

Boxes 1 through 33 contain correspondence from 1927 until 1972, in most cases both incoming and outgoing. To give the researcher some idea of the scale of the collection, Box One contains correspondence from 1927 through 1946, the period of Bunche's life prior to his entering United Nations' service. This box contains twenty-five files holding about 3,200 items; multiply this by the approximately 1,000 files of correspondence that exist in boxes 2 through 33 and the researcher is faced with perhaps 130,000 or more letters. But, making the task even more daunting is that this section represents correspondence only with individuals. Boxes 104 to 120 contain the complete collection of correspondence, notes, reports, etc., relating to Bunche's affiliation with the dozens of organisations and schools on whose boards he served, such as the American Political Science Association, the Council on Foreign Relations and the Rockefeller Foundation. It was an impressive and busy life, and equally so prior to the period when Bunche began his UN tenure.

Bunche's academic career is extremely well-documented in twenty-seven boxes, with seventeen of these devoted to his work at UCLA, Howard and Harvard Universities, including the complete lay-out and notes for his Ph.D. dissertation. Also included in this section is an entire ten boxes dealing with Bunche's collaboration with Gunnar Myrdal on Myrdal's classic study of race relations, *An American Dilemma*. There is also a vast collection of Bunche's memorabilia, as he was a great collector of souvenirs. One finds dinner menus, press clippings, match books from places he ate or stayed, and, rather touchingly, in Box 153, Bunche's UCLA basketball uniform, from the days when he was a star athlete in basketball, baseball and football, as well as a superlative academic.

Perhaps the best documented aspect of Bunche's life to be found scattered throughout this collection are his achievements as a black man in an environment (e.g., American Academia and Washington, D.C., in the 1930s, 1940s, and 1950s) that was well known for its racism and discrimination. And there is no doubt that while outwardly humble about his successes as a black man, Bunche was inordinately proud of himself and what he had accomplished. This is most apparent on some of the tape recordings found in the collection of radio interviews Bunche gave during his career. But for the researcher looking to examine Bunche's work in the United Nations, his relationships with Hammarskjöld and other colleagues, and so forth, a void slowly becomes apparent.

While meticulously documenting Bunche's life outside the UN, this collection generally fails when it comes to providing more than a glance at

Bunche, the Under-Secretary-General and Hammarskjöld's trouble-shooter. This vacuum is ultimately even more frustrating in that this absence of substantive material is not really apparent until one has toiled through the entire collection. Only then, can one sit back and reflect *and* presume that the man obviously led two lives; one inside and one outside the United Nations, but the majority of that part of this life spent inside the UN is, simply, missing. Where is it? Obviously, a man who so carefully documented every other aspect of his life would undoubtedly have done so with that part which represented his major private successes. These papers that we seek are, primarily, in the archives of the Office of the Under-Secretary-General of the UN; a set of papers under the ultimate control of the Secretary-General himself.

Given this important absence of material (for reasons discussed below) the Bunche Papers are not highly recommended for scholars seeking research material dealing primarily with Hammarskjöld or the office of Secretary-General. Nor, for that matter, are they recommended for the researcher who is interested in the work of the United Nations in the field of UN peacekeeping, though as a source of secondary and peripheral information, some very interesting items on the Middle East and the Congo can be found. One striking example is a letter from Bunche to his son Ralph Jr., dated "Friday night, 8 July 1960, The Stanley Palace Hotel," the very day Belgian troops re-entered the Congo in an attempt to 'restore order.' Bunche writes to his son that "I cannot be positive at this moment if I will ever be able to mail" this letter as ". . . there are some heavily armed Congolese soldiers down in the lobby right now ordering people around pretty roughly at gun point. It is touch and go when one of them may erupt and start banging away with one of those automatic rifles they carry. This morning at about 11.30, all of our rooms were invaded by gun-toting soldiers who ordered me and all the rest of us down into the lobby, where we were kept standing around looking sheepish for quite awhile . . . We are all rather scared inside, of course, but we keep up good spirits and cheer each other up . . . Well, if things work out all right in the end this predicament we are all in now will later seem quite amusing. Wouldn't it be ironic, though, if I should now get knocked around here in the very heart of Africa because of anti-white feeling—that reason being that I am not dark enough and might be mistaken for a 'blanc'! Well, life is full of ironies." This little burst of personal insight is especially rewarding as Bunche would rarely, if ever, commit himself in writing to anything regarding his personal feelings about his work. It should be stressed that this type of material is the exception rather than the rule in these papers.

The Bunche Papers are a collection which come highly recommended to the researcher interested in the work of the UN Trusteeship Council. Until 1954, Bunche was the Director of the Department of Trusteeship and Non-Self-Governing Territories in the Secretariat. There is extensive documentation regarding the establishment of this component of the organisation in 1945 and its subsequent operations through its sixteenth session. Many US scholars consider Bunche's work in this area to be by far his greatest achievement, yet his work in Trusteeship is totally unrecorded in the secondary source material. Closely related to these papers, and equally valuable, are the numerous boxes of material containing Bunche's notes and records of his field trips to Africa in the 1930s, to Kenya, Togoland, Dahomey, etc. His notes on his travels to South Africa, especially from a racial perspective, are especially fascinating.

Most importantly, however, this is a collection for someone who wishes to look at Bunche himself. At least two works have been written about Bunche since this collection became available and neither author availed themselves of its contents. The need for a comprehensive general biography certainly exists. Almost every speech, article and letter written by Bunche is to be found within this collection; the individual who undertakes such a work will have 90% of the necessary material in one place, a unique opportunity that would make most researchers and biographers thoroughly envious.

For the researcher who remains determined to seek the more substantive of the political documents missing in the Bunche Papers, or perhaps wants to fill the occasional gap in the Hammarskjöld Papers, we turn now to look at the United Nations Archives in New York City, the largest depository of papers on the United Nations in the world.

United Nations Archives[5]

Housed on several floors of an office building on Park Avenue in New York City, the United Nations Archives represent, on both paper and microfilm, the sum total of UN activities from the very inception of the organisation. It is a vast collection of official documents and all of the minutia that went into their creation. To the researcher working on Hammarskjöld or any aspect of the UN, these archives are an essential stop and one which should always prove rewarding. It would be impossible to go into any great detail about these archives due to their sheer volume and scope, but a look at the files of the Office of the Secretary-General will provide some idea of the type of material available.

The Archives of the United Nations are divided into Archive Groups and Sub-Groups, and the Office of the Secretary-General represents a separate Archive Group. Within this group are such Sub-Groups as the Office of Under-Secretary-General for Special Political Affairs and the Office of the Executive Assistant. Each Sub-Group is further divided into subject areas, so that information on the Congo Operation could appear in

---

5. Mr. Alf Erlandsson, Chief, Archives Section, United Nations, New York, New York 10017 U.S.A.

either of the above Sub-Groups, as well as in the separate and quite massive Archive Group headed ONUC (United Nations Operations in the Congo). In the Congo files under the Sub-Group of the Office of Under-Secretary-General for Special Political Affairs (Ralph Bunche during this period) one finds all of the clear and code cables (tens of thousands of items alone for the four year operation); details about the individuals who worked in the Congo in various capacities, such as Rajeshwar Dayal and Conor Cruise O'Brien who worked as Special Representatives; reports from the Investigating Commission on the death of Patrice Lumumba; military situation reports and memos; and a large set of files which, divided by individual countries, deals with United Nations Secretariat relations and contacts with some seventy-five different states, most of whom were involved, in one way or another, with the operation. There are also, of course, some very weighty correspondence files for this period and numerous other sections where information is available.

The United Nations Archives are a very straightforward, well organized collection of documents and their new home on Park Avenue makes research there quite tolerable (they moved from a dilapidated warehouse in Queens in 1979).[6] One does encounter the frustrations of a very general index system, meaning numerous hours spent working through what could ultimately be a useless series of cables or memos. However, work is made easier by the accuracy of the indexes and the researcher is unlikely to discover any major surprises in searching through the papers (though one or two supposedly nonexistent documents have been known to turn up unexpectedly). Probably the most valuable thing about the United Nations Archives for the scholar studying Hammarskjöld is that, together with Hammarskjöld's Papers in Stockholm, the two collections provide an almost total picture of the role that Hammarskjöld played as Secretary-General. The Hammarskjöld Papers in Stockholm are a collection with personality, reflecting a great deal about the man and his work, but things are missing and these have ultimately turned up in New York. The response to a letter or the original letter which led to a response, the official memoranda or notes of a meeting or the notes prepared by another official for the Secretary-General concerning a particular situation. It is these gaps in the Hammarskjöld Papers that the United Nations Archives are so often able to fill, though not always without hours or days of searching. Granted,

6. The other main research facility available to the public at the United Nations is the Dag Hammarskjöld Library, located in the southwest corner of the UN Headquarters site. While this library has little to offer in the way of primary source material on Hammarskjöld, it holds a praiseworthy collection of UN documents and publications, as well as other books, periodicals and material relating to the work of the organisation. It can also be noted that the UN Archives at the Palais des Nations in Geneva hold nothing of any significant value to the researcher working on Dag Hammarskjöld, though the Geneva Archives are a vital primary source for research on the League of Nations' Secretary-General.

there is a fair amount of duplication in these two collections (though it is far from all encompassing), but one also discovers that, in some cases two sets of supposedly similar documents are slightly different—there may be a few more cables in one collection than in another, and to assume that the Congo or UNEF Code labels in both collections are exactly the same is an almost certain guarantee that important communcations will be missed. It can also be noted that important and major gaps in the Bunche Papers are also filled by the United Nations Archives. In fact, all of the substantive material relating to Bunche's work is in the United Nations Archives and as noted above, the Office of Under-Secretary-General for Special Political Affairs produced an enormous amount of policy and directed numerous UN operations. This division of the Bunche Papers into the political and nonpolitical has essentially made it necessary for the UN scholar to work on the UN Archives first, turning to the Bunche Papers in California only as a last resort for filling gaps and adding "highlights."

The United Nations Archives are, for the most part, still in their original form, but the slow process of transferring each sheet of paper to microfilm is now underway and researchers may find certain portions of the Archives available on microfilm instead of paper. Some of the original paper documents dating back to the later 1940s and early 1950s have not withstood the test of time and are beginning to brown, and in some cases crumble at the touch. Using the original paper documents is always easier and many find, more enjoyable, but this will ultimately be impossible as the years go on and a microfilm archive will undoubtedly predominate.

No researcher or scholar who is studying the United Nations can afford not to attempt gaining acccess to the United Nations Archives, In fact, it is suggested that these archives be scheduled as a first step on any researcher's itinerary. Covering every aspect of UN history, from the establishment of the organisation itself to the creation of the Technical Assistance Board to the withdrawal of UNEF from the Sinai in 1967, they are an invaluable source of information. The papers of Trygve Lie are located here and the Archives have recently been very fortunate in obtaining the complete collection of papers belonging to former Secretary-General U Thant, papers that had been in the possession of his family since he left the United Nations. This large collection will add immeasurably to the value and esteem the UN Archives carry as a research tool on the activities of the United Nations.

Andrew Cordier Papers[7]

Viewed by many scholars as being slightly on the periphery of the main primary sources, the papers of Andrew Cordier, Executive Assistant to two

---

7. Chief Archivist, Rare Books and Manuscripts, Butler Library, Columbia University, New York, New York.

Secretaries-General are, nonetheless, a highly important resource for researchers of Dag Hammarskjöld and the United Nations. This collection is located at Columbia University, where Cordier was Dean of the School of International Affairs from 1962 to 1972 and President of the University from 1968 to 1970. The papers are housed in 346 document boxes and contain over two hundred thousand items. Columbia's cataloguers have made the researcher's work somewhat easier, as they have indexed the correspondence between Cordier and over one hundred "prominent" personalities. The collection as a whole is clearly listed in a three-volume finders' aid and it is obvious from looking at these volumes that a great deal of care went into the preparation of this collection. These volumes represent the three distinct periods of Cordier's life covered by the collection: his early life, as an undergraduate and graduate, as a professor at Manchester College in Indiana and in the US State Department; his United Nations period, as Executive Assistant to Trygve Lie and Dag Hammarskjöld and including his working files on his eight volume publication of *The Public Papers of the Secretaries-General of the United Nations;* and lastly, the period when Cordier was Dean and President at Columbia, including all of his personal and working files during this time.

Andrew Cordier was a United Nations figure whose contact with the world outside the UN was mimimal. His personal life remains rather obscure during the period he was with the UN and unlike his colleague, Ralph Bunche, he would appear to have avoided the bright lights and celebrations, in which Bunche so often took part and enjoyed. But his role at the United Nations consisted of far more than spokesman and Cordier was a pivotal, behind-the-scenes figure in the "Hammarskjöld Administration." As Executive Assistant to the Secretary-General and officer in charge of General Assembly affairs (which carried an Under-Secretary-General Rank), he was not only privy to almost everything emanating from the Secretary-General's office, but was also the originator of a great deal of policy himself. He took over control of the organisation when the Secretary-General went abroad and his office had penultimate responsibility for personnel matters and a large portion of the internal administration of the Secretariat. Cordier was a key figure in the planning of peacekeeping operations and worked closely with Bunche on the UNEF and ONUC and was also responsible for handling Secretariat action relating to the Hungarian invasion in 1956.

The Cordier Papers do have one unique feature in that the researcher interested solely in the United Nation's side of Cordier's life and his work with Hammarskjöld need not use the Cordier Papers at Columbia to undertake this research. When Andrew Cordier left the United Nations in late 1961, he took all of his papers with him, leaving something of a vacuum in the United Nations Archives. Upon his death, the United Nations was able to microfilm all of those papers in the Cordier collection

A Bibliographic Essay   165

which emanated from his office and were felt to be "archival material," therefore filling the gaps at the UN and making the Archives all the more complete. The researcher then has the choice of using either the original UN papers at Columbia University, found in Boxes 39 through 202, or the microfilm version at the UN Archives, printed on approximately forty rolls of film. The microfilm collection has a separate finders' aid of about fifty pages but like most of the other collections, does not go beyond a listing of the file title, leaving the contents of each file a mystery until individually examined.

As is the case with Bunche's Papers, and given the fact that the politically substantive material on Cordier's work is already in the United Nations Archives, it may be a disadvantage to many researchers to spend too much time on Cordier's Papers at Columbia. On the other hand, they represent a large collection of documents from a man who spent over sixteen years in the United Nations' service, and there is always something to be gained from examining the more personal side of such an individual's life.

Official Records of the United Nations

Early in his tenure as Secretary-General, Hammarskjöld came to realize that one of the best means of promoting a particular idea or project was to ensure that the item in question received the widest possible circulation among UN members. The Secretary-General was extremely aware of the importance of regular and detailed reports to the organization as well as the occasional, though usually well-timed statement before one of the principle organs or a committee. In this way, Hammarskjöld was able to present his own philosophies and ideas, and be certain that they would appear in the public record. Rarely, of course, were these ideas put forward as the Secretary-General's own, but rather, they were presented by him on behalf of the Secretariat. But few ever doubted that the views which were presented in a report or spoken by the Secretary-General had originated in any place other than in Hammarskjöld's own mind.

When undertaking primary source research on the United Nations one often takes for granted the Official Records of the Organization, mainly because of their sheer bulk (which can make them somewhat daunting), as well as the fact that they are so obvious. Clearly, they are unlikely to provide any new or original information of a substantive nature, but for the purpose of clarification and for verification of an issue, these records cannot be matched. More importantly and oft forgotten, the Official Records of the UN include much more than the records of debates in the Security Council or General Assembly. The Annexes and Supplements to the debates are a storehouse of documents, reports and speeches which add up to a highly valuable and extremely well organized source of information on for example, the development of the Secretary-General's thinking on a given issue. A brief survey of some of the more useful documents and records of the UN related to specific events and programmes during the Hammarskjöld era should illustrate the multi-faceted value of these records in primary source research on the Secretary-General.

Most notable of the multitude of documents emanating from the Secretary-General's Office are the "Annual Report[s] of the Secretary-General on the Work of the Organization" and the "Introduction[s] to the Annual Reports of the Secretary-General on the Work of the Organization." Hammarskjöld was responsible for nine of these Annual Reports between 1953 and 1961,[8] though his first,[9] was almost entirely based on Trygve Lie's final year in office. The "Introduction to the Annual Report" was written by the Secretary-General as a review of the United Nation's involvement in world affairs and up to 1955 (the 10th session of the General Assembly) it had been a part of the actual "Annual Report." But in 1956, Hammarskjöld released the "Introduction" as a separate document just prior to the opening of the 11th Assembly (1957) to give members an opportunity to read the summary and comment on it if desired during the plenary. It was a popular procedure and remained a part of the routine until approximately 1977, when the Secretary-General turned the "Introduction" into "The Report of the Secretary-General on the Work of the Organization," a document of the same short length as the earlier "Introduction." The actual "Annual Report" is now published as a United Nations sales item. Hammarskjöld was responsible for six "Introductions"[10] and in them one sees a great deal of the Secretary-General's own philosophies coming through. One reporter went so far as to dub Hammarskjöld's annual "Introductions" as his 'State of the UN Message,' to which Hammarskjöld replied that "he liked that very much."[11]

Of all the Secretary-General's "Introductions" though, none stands out as much as his last.[12] Prefaced "Two Differing Concepts of the United Nations Assayed" by the journal *International Organization*[13] it was Hammarskjöld's very personal attempt to analyze the state of the UN following the developments of 1960-61. Brian Urquhart notes that the "Introduc-

---

8. A/2404; A/2663; A/2911; & Corr. 1; A/3137; A/3594; A/3844; A/4132; A/4390; A/4800.

9. A/2404.

10. A/3137/Add. 1; A/3594/Add. 1; A/3844/Add. 1; A/4132/Add/1; A/4390/Add. 1; A/4800/Add.

11. Joseph Lash, "Dag Hammarskjöld's Conception of His Office," *International Organization*, Vol. 16, No. 3, Summer 1962, pp. 542-566.

12. A/4800/Add. 1.

13. Dag Hammarskjöld, "Two Differing Concepts of the United Nations Assayed: Introduction to the Annual Report of the Secretary-General on the Work of the Organization, 16 June 1950-15 June 1961" *International Organization*, Vol. 15, No. 4, Autumn 1961, pp. 549-563.

tion" had been dictated without notes and virtually without pause on a Sunday afternoon in August,"[14] and one is left with no doubt upon reading it, the depth of feeling and concern with which Hammarskjöld approached this task. But then looking back over much of the Secretary-General's writing, from the time he was first appointed, one has this impression from almost everything he produced.

The United Nations Security Council discussed Hammarskjöld's initial appointment in the course of private meetings held between 11 March and 31 March 1953,[15] with the issue moving into the General Assembly for consideration on 7 April 1953.[16] The Secretary-General took the oath of office on 10 April 1953[17] for the first time and was reappointed to a second term on 26 September 1957.[18] At his reappointment, he made an especially strong statement on the way in which he perceived of the Secretary-General's role in political matters and in particular, he noted that it was part of that role to "help in filling any vacuum that may appear."[19] Hammarskjöld's first major task, upon becoming Secretary-General, was to attempt a thorough re-organization of the UN Secretariat. He concentrated a large part of his energies in this area between 1953 and 1955, appearing on numerous occasions before the Fifth Committee of the General Assembly (Administrative and Budgetary Committee) to put forward his case for re-organization[20] as well as producing a yearly progress Report to the Organization on the re-organization process.[21] He was not unsuccessful in his attempts to create change in the Organization through the Committees of the Assembly, though it became apparent as time went on that the greatest catalyst for change was a crisis situation. His successful attempts in 1954-55 to secure the release of United States airmen held in China[22] only served to strengthen Hammarskjöld's hand in the re-organization process. But the greatest impact of all, up until 1960, was to be the Suez Crisis.

The Secretary-General's involvement in the Suez Crisis was both extensive and complex, and it would be impossible to note here every statement he made and every report he provided to the Organization on the matter. One can point to such highlights as his statement of 31 October 1956 before the Security Council[23] where he could only be said to have

14. Brian Urquhart, *Hammarskjöld* (London: Bodley Head, 1973), p. 541.
15. Official Records Security Council, Mtgs. 612-617 (hereafter S.C.O.R.).
16. Official Records General Assembly, Mtg. 423 (hereafter G.A.O.R.).
17. G.A.O.R., Mtg. 426.
18. G.A.O.R., Mtg. 690.
19. A/PV. 690, 26 September 1957.
20. A/C.5/580 & A/C.5/591 – 1954; and A/C.5/652 – 1955.
21. A/2554 (1953), A/2731 (1954), A/3041 (1955).
22. Report of the Secretary-General on attempts to secure the release of US airmen in China – 1955 – A/2891 & A/2954.
23. SG/515, 31 October 1956.

"thrown down the gauntlet" to the membership regarding the Secretary-General's role in conflict situations.

But it is in such documents as his regular reports to the Security Council and the General Assembly on the crisis that one finds the rapid development of not only the Secretary-General's role, but of areas such as peacekeeping. The following documents are of particular note with regards to the early stages of the crisis, the creation and functioning of UNEF and the Suez Canal Clearance:

Issued During the 1st Emergency Special Session (Mtgs. 561-563, 565-567, 572)

Reports of the Secretary-General on the Implementation of Resolutions 997 (ES-1) & 999 (ES-1)
–A/3267, A/3284, A/3287, A/3296

First Report of the Secretary-General on the plan for an emergency international United Nations force as requested in Resolution 998 (ES-1)
–A/3289

Second and Final Report of the Secretary-General on the plan for an emergency international United Nations force as requested in Res. 998 (ES-1)
– A/3302 and Add. 1-30 and Add. 4/Rev. 1.

Issued During the 11th Regular Session of the General Assembly (Mtgs. 574-576, 591-597, 624, 629-32, 644-646, 649-652, 659-662, 664-668)

Report of the Secretary-General on the basic points of the presence and functioning of UNEF in Egypt
–A/3375

Report of the Secretary-General of the administrative and financial arrangements for UNEF
–A/3256

Report of the Secretary-General on the arrangements concerning UNEF's status in Egypt
–A/3256

Reports of the Secretary-General on the withdrawal of British, French, and Israeli forces from Egypt
–A/3384, A/3512, A/3527, A/3568

Report of the Secretary-General on the arrangements for the Suez Canal Clearance
–A/3376

Second Report of the Secretary-General on the arrangements for the Suez Canal Clearance
–A/3492

Issued After the 11th Session of the General Assembly

Report of the Secretary-General on UNEF—1957
–A/3694 and Add. 1

Report of the Secretary-General on the completion of the Suez Canal Clearance, 1957

A Bibliographic Essay   169

–A/3719
  Report of the Secretary-General on UNEF—1958
–A/3899
  UNEF: Summary study of the experience derived from the establishment and operation of the force—Report of the Secretary-General, 1958
–A/3943
  Report of the Secretary-General on the manner of financing the force, 1959–A/4176 and Corr. 1,2 and Add. 1-2
  Report of the Secretary-General on UNEF—1959
–A/4120 and Add. 1 (Parts A & B)

At almost the exact moment that the Suez Crisis was breaking, the Soviets invaded Hungary, precipating another debate in the Security Council. These debates quickly fell victim to the Soviet veto, and the discussion was moved to an Emergency Special Session of the General Assembly (ESS-II). Hammarskjöld was less directly active in the Hungarian situation than in the Suez Crisis, but he did make a number of statements in the meetings of the Emergency Special Session[24] and he did issue four reports of some importance to the Organization.[25]

In June 1958 the crisis in the Lebanon was placed before the Security Council[26] and the Secretary-General was again called upon to establish a peacekeeping force in the Middle East. Hammarskjöld issued two major reports in the early stages of UNOGIL[27] and at the Council's 837th meeting, he made a strong statement regarding the Security Council's failure to act and the fact that it was entirely consistent with his role that he should attempt to fill any vacuums that might appear.[28] During the Lebanese crisis however, the majority of the substantive information being provided to the membership came not from Hammarskjöld, but from his three man Observer Group in Beirut, who filed five formal reports with the Security Council.[29]

In August of that year, the issue was moved into the General Assembly following the Security Council's inability to come to any decision and the Third Emergency Special Session of the General Assembly was convened.[30] The Secretary-General issued three major reports to the General Assembly on the Lebanese Crisis during the months of August and September, 1958[31] and made a major address to the Assembly at the opening of the Special

---

24. G.A.O.R. (ES-I), Mtgs. 564-568-571, 573.
25. A/3371 and Corr. 1 and Add. 1; A/3403; A/3485; A/3503.
26. S.C.O.R., Mtgs. 818, 822-825, 827-837, 840.
27. Report of the Secretary-General on the Implementation of Res. S/4023 – S/4029; and Further Report of the Secretary-General on the Implementation of Res. S/4023–S/4038 and Corr. I.
28. S.C.O.R., Mtg. 837, paras. 10-18; SG/708, 22 July 1958.
29. S/4051; S/4052; S/4069; S/4085; S/4100.
30. G.A.O.R. (ES-III), Mtgs. 732-746.
31. A/3934/Rev.1; A/3986; A/4056.

Session on 8 August, presenting some ideas he had previously worked out on the requirements for a lasting peace in the Middle East.[32] In late September Hammarskjöld reported to the General Assembly on the current and future state of affairs in the Middle East[33] and shortly afterwards, he presented his final report to the Security Council on the withdrawal of UNOGIL.[34]

The Congo Crisis, which began in July 1960, was the last major international conflict in which Hammarskjöld was involved before his tragic death in September 1961. But during the last fourteen months of his stewardship of the United Nations, the Secretary-General was personally responsible for more documents and reports than had ever before been produced in the Organization's history. Throughout the Crisis, from about late August 1960, most of the information being produced by Hammarskjöld for the membership on the status of the situation emanated from the Secretary-General's Special Representative in the Congo (in the form of Progress Reports). But Hammarskjöld himself remained closely atuned with the workings of the operation from its very inception; in fact, one must remember that Hammarskjöld brought the Crisis to the Security Council himself by formally invoking Article 99 for the first time.[35] During the period from July 1960 through February 1961, when the Security Council was formally seized with the matter,[36] Hammarskjöld filed four major reports with the Council[37] on the basis of three Security Council Resolutions[38] and made one of his most memorable statements ever with regard to the death of Patrice Lumumba.[39]

The Crisis was also dealt with through almost the whole of the General Assembly's 15th Plenary Session, which convened in the Autumn of 1960. It was during this session that the Soviets put forward their "Troika" proposals and here again, we see Hammarskjöld taking a strong stand to defend the Office of the Secretary-General. Hammarskjöld made a strong verbal attack on the proposals in the General Assembly in October of that year[40] and in the late spring of 1961, carried on this defense at a press conference in New York.[41] His most powerful statement on the subject came however, in a speech titled "The International Civil Servant in Law and in Fact" which he gave at Oxford in May 1961.[42]

32. G.A.O.R. (ES-III), Mtg. 732, paras. 34-45; SG/714, 8 August 1958.
33. A/3934/Rev. 1.
34. S/4116.
35. Letter from the Secretary-General to the President of the Security Council –S/4381.
36. S.C.O.R., Mtgs. 873, 877-879, 884-889, 896-906, 924, 942.
37. S/4389 and Add. 1-6; S/4417 and Annexes; S/4475 and Add. 1-3; & S/4482 and Add. 1-4.
38. S/4387; S/4405; S/4426.
39. S.C.O.R., Mtg. 935, paras. 3-37; SC/1008, 2 February 1961.
40. G.A.O.R., Mtg. 883, paras. 4-12; SG/966, 3 October 1960.
41. Note to Correspondents #2347, 12 June 1961.
42. SG/1035, 30 May 1981.

A Bibliographic Essay   171

The other major problem which came to the fore during the Congo Crisis was the long standing one of financing peacekeeping operations. The Secretary-General made numerous appearances before the Fifth Committee and issued two major reports on the subject,[43] though the problems still persist to some degree even today.

Hammarskjöld's death in September 1961 seemed to cut a strong path through all of the dissension and animosities that had developed in the Organization up to that time. The statements made in the General Assembly during the opening of the 16th Session[44] carried nothing but praise for the Secretary-General and his work and it was almost as if the events of the previous fourteen months had not even taken place. The Secretary-General was remembered not only for his work in establishing the Organization's role in international peace and security areas, but also for his work in other, oft forgotten but equally important aspects of the Organization's work. The following document references refer to only a few of Hammarskjöld's major contributions to some of the United Nations' other areas of concern.

Economic Cooperation and Development

Speech by the Secretary-General at the opening of ECOSOC—1955
–SG/430

Speech by the Secretary-General at the opening of ECOSOC—1956
–SG/493

Report of the Secretary-General on the International Flow of Private Capital —1958
–E/3128 and Corr. 1

Report of the Secretary-General on the United Nations Program of Technical Assistance—1959
–E/3236

Speech by the Secretary-General to ECOSOC on the importance of development
–SG/908

Report of the Secretary-General on the opportunities for international cooperation on behalf of former Trust Territories and newly independent countries —1960
–A/4584

Speech by the Secretary-General at the opening of ECOSOC—1961
–SG/1045

On the Problem of Equitable Geographic Distribution in the UN Secretariat

Report of the Secretary-General to the Fifth Committee—1960
–A/C.5/833 and Corr. 1 and Add. 1

43. Report of the Secretary-General to the Fifth Committee for the period July-December, 1960 – A/C.5/836; Report of the Secretary-General to the General-Assembly for the period from 1 January 1961 – A/4703.
44. G.A.O.R., Mtgs. 1007, 1009-1021, 1023-1039.

Statement by the Secretary-General to the Fifth Committee—1960
—A/C.5/843

Budget Defense with Special Reference to the Secretary-General's Use of Article 99
Statement by the Secretary-General to the Fifth Committee—1960
—A/C.5/828 and Corr. 1
Statement by the Secretary-General to the Fifth Committee—1960
—A/C.5/829

What has been presented in this section is not intended to be all inclusive, nor is it suggested that the documents noted are the most important. The Official Records of the United Nations are a vast collection of material and it would be presumptuous of any scholar to state that any one document has more significance than another. As in all primary source research, no single item has any real importance until placed into its proper context along side other documents and a valid framework of historical reference. One of the major advantages to using United Nations Official Records as a primary resource is that they are available all over the world. Almost every major city today has at least one library which has been designated as "United Nations Depository" and the researcher can therefore concentrate on primary source investigation utilising United Nations records from a home base, saving a great deal of time and expense. It should be made clear however, that the Official Records of the UN are no substitute for the other primary source material herein presented. They do complement this other material though and their value should not be overlooked in any research on the United Nations, especially that dealing with Secretary-General.

Other Primary Sources

If one hunts long enough, a multitude of additional documentation on Dag Hammarskjöld and the United Nations will eventually surface. Some of these potential sources are obvious, while others are more elusive.

The papers of former Swedish Foreign Minister, Östen Undén, found at the Royal Library in Stockholm, contain a substantial amount of correspondence between Hammarskjöld and Undén. The Foreign Minister was a close personal friend and confidant of the Secretary-General's and Hammarskjöld often "used" Undén and his office as a conduit for messages and contacts as well as a source of political intelligence, the vital machinery for which was lacking in the Secretariat. Many of these letters are revealing of Hammarskjöld's fears and concerns over his work and more generally, the state of the world. He also used this correspondence as a means of receiving feedback from a "neutral but sympathetic party" on ideas he had concerning the organisation of a particular operation or a key change in Secretariat policy or structure.

This correspondence between Hammarskjöld and Undén was apparently of a purely informal and personal basis, as none of it appears in the records of the Swedish Government Archives, a most comprehensive and detailed collection of Swedish state history. In fact, as far as can be determined, the Government Archives contain absolutely no record of any correspondence or business transacted with Hammarskjöld by any member of the Swedish Government during Hammarskjöld's tenure as Secretary-General. There are numerous records prior to this, of Hammarskjöld's work on the Economic Commission for Europe and in the Swedish Government, but all contacts from 1953 to 1961 would appear to have been on a personal, and highly unofficial, level. A most curious state of affairs and one which deserves further study.

One of the more interesting, and less likely sources of information on Dag Hammarskjöld can be found in the papers of Gunnar and Alva Myrdal. This collection, or actually two separate collections, are located in the Archives of the Arbetarrörelsens (freely translated as "Workers Movement") in Stockholm.[45] Gunnar and Alva Myrdal's papers are divided into two parts, one for each of them and researchers would be hard pressed to find a more detailed or better catalogued collection of personal papers. Every letter is indexed both by author and date so there is no difficulty in locating the correspondence between the Myrdals and Hammarskjöld.

Gunnar Myrdal was one of Hammarskjöld's professors at Uppsala University, and he was also Hammarskjöld's main "opponent" in his Ph.D. oral examination in 1934. This oral examination remains, many say, the longest to ever take place in the history of the University. The Myrdals and Hammarskjöld became friends in the 1930s and Hammarskjöld spent a great many evenings with the Myrdals in their home, discussing literature and economics. Almost all of their correspondence at this time was in Swedish, the first of which dates back to September 1927 (a letter from Hammarskjöld to Gunnar Myrdal). This correspondence with Gunnar Myrdal continued through 1945 and the latter period dealt heavily with the problems of European post-war economic planning. At about this time, English began to take over as the predominant medium of communication in this correspondence, and the largest portion of this correspondence between the two men began in 1947, when Myrdal was Secretary of the Economic Commission for Europe. It was a heavily one-sided exchange, especially after Hammarskjöld became Secretary-General, with Myrdal sending long, detailed accounts of the work of the ECE to Hammarskjöld and the Secretary-General often replying in only two or three lines. This correspondence ended on 3 July 1957 when, shortly after, Myrdal left the ECE to work on his book *Asian Drama*. This was the last recorded

---

45. Stellan Andersson, Arbetarrörelsens Arkiv, Uplandsgatan 5, S-111 81 Stockholm, Sweden.

correspondence, as an "ideological" rift had developed between the Myrdals and Hammarskjöld over the Secretary-General's straightforward, though often equivocal approach to the United Nations' assistance to developing countries.

The only correspondence of any significance between Alva Myrdal and Hammarskjöld occurred in March 1953, when, as Director of the Social Department of UNESCO, she arrived in New York only to be confronted by US Immigration and told her entrance to the country was liable to certain restrictions. As this was a violation of her status as a UN employee and the Headquarters Agreement with the US Government, the Secretary-General immediately took up the issue and through the intervention of Henry Cabot Lodge, he managed to work out a solution by July of that year. There are a few other letters in this collection, but the main correspondence is found in Gunnar's papers, as described above.

This is a collection which would be of limited use to the researcher undertaking detailed investigations of Dag Hammarskjöld, and then primarily for the period when he was involved in the Economic Commission for Europe and the Swedish Government. Its value in terms of Hammarskjöld's work as Secretary-General is highly limited and would not be worth the researcher's time unless already in Stockholm using the Hammarskjöld Papers. As a side note, it can be said that for the scholar looking into the work and background of Ralph Bunche, this collection is surprisingly full of resources, primarily from the period when Myrdal and Bunche worked together on Myrdal's *An American Dilemma*. Added to the material in Bunche's papers, a classic sociological study awaits writing on the work of these two men as they travelled through the United States searching for information on American attitudes about race.

There are numerous other collections of papers around the world; many of which contain material directly related to Hammarskjöld while others simply cover the Hammarskjöld era with the Secretary-General himself being of only peripheral interest. Notable among those which contain material on Hammarskjöld are the papers of John Foster Dulles and David Morse (both at Princeton University), Philip Noel-Baker (Churchill College, Cambridge) and Wellington Koo (Columbia University). In addition, one should always keep in mind the massive collections of Presidential papers found in the libraries named for the men in question. These can be an excellent source for de-classified documents and information relating to Hammarskjöld's tenure in office.

The Question of Access

In the course of time, other sources of information on Dag Hammarskjöld and the United Nations will emerge. Needless to say there is already a tremendous amount of material that has never been properly utilised and it remains to be seen to what extent use will made of it in the future. To date, only two serious researchers have utilised the Hammarskjöld Papers in Stockholm.

Part of this problem is, of course, access and the *how* of obtaining permission to use archival material has no easy answer. Each collection has its own "rules" and these vary depending on the individual applying—there is no comprehensive method. In all cases, however, a few standards do apply. It is essential one has a clear cut proposal, supported by strong references. In the case of the Bunche Papers, access is more or less open to anyone, though there are certain sections of the collection for which special permission of the UN is required, while other sections demand the permission of the Bunche family.

The Myrdal Papers require the permission of Gunnar and Alva Myrdal as the only pre-condition, but certain restrictions on using particular papers are also probable. It is also worth noting that the Myrdals will, in most cases, insist that people who use their papers also interview them. The tapes of these interviews are put into the Myrdal Collection and can be utilised by researchers using the papers. It is a novel and valuable idea and the growing oral history will ensure that the Myrdal's biographers will have a wealth of material at their disposal.

Access to the open portion of the Andrew Cordier Paper is, in the words of a Columbia University archivist, "open to qualified scholars engaged in legitimate research," though using the whole collection is generally tied to access to the United Nations Archives. While some sections of the Cordier Papers are immediately accessible to the "qualified scholar," over 160 boxes are closed, either under the United Nations' standard twenty-year restriction or by special order of the Secretary-General. In these latter cases, special clearance must be obtained from the Office of the Secretary-General.

The United Nations Archives themselves are subjected to no strict rules beyond the UN's own twenty-year rule (and those papers closed by the Secretary-General) and these restrictions are rather flexible. The researcher's project and background will weigh heavily in the extent to which access is granted to previously unused material. Permission to use restricted or closed material must be obtained, through the Chief Archivist, from the Office of the Secretary-General. Usage of much of the material in the Archives in highly dependent upon the global political scene at the time and the question of whether any individual state's political sensibilities will be offended.

The Dag Hammarskjöld Papers present, at least potentially, the most difficult collection for the researcher to gain entry to. The papers are under the control of the head of the Manuscript Department at the Royal Library in Stockholm and a board of trustees who must all give their approval before the papers can be used. There are only two members of this board of trustees today, as the third member, Uno Willers, has recently died. It was Willers who, as an old and close friend of Hammarskjöld's and Director of the Royal Library, managed to secure the Papers for the Library's collection. As of this writing, there are no plans to secure a third member to replace Willers. It is advisable that before researchers attempt access to these papers that they have some track record of work on other related collections, especially the United Nations Archives.[46]

The general rule for access to most archives and primary sources is that mentioned above by the Columbia archivist. The "qualified scholar" who is undertaking "legitimate research" should not have any serious problems, as long as requests are realistic and sensible. This is not to imply that access will always be granted and researchers should never assume that a particular project will be readily acceptable to those who control the use of these papers. Patience and determination are two qualities which are an obvious necessity when undertaking primary source research. The first access though, will probably provide the "ticket" for successful application to subsequent collections. The researcher who hopes to dig up gossip or scandal will only damage the opportunity for others in the future to use these collections and those people who already have a reputation for such tactics can be advised that those responsible for these collections will always lock carefully at every applicant for use of those papers under their care.

One final point should be made with regard to the question of restrictions on the use of material gathered in these collections. It is a requisite courtesy that the researcher, upon completion of writing based on research in a particular collection or group of collections, offers a draft to the individual responsible for the papers. In some instances, the collection's "trustees" can make this a condition of access to these papers. One can expect that if the collection has been misused or if items in the collection have been used in a manner deemed to be unacceptable to the "trustees," the researcher will be asked to either make certain changes or to remove the offending item completely. It is vitally important that the researcher clarify his position on this matter prior to beginning work, as well as any restrictions on using material in a thesis as opposed to a book or article. This will help to avoid disputes over use of papers and ease the way for future researchers who wish to use the same papers.

The information which has been presented in this chapter should be of value to those people who wish to undertake research on Dag Hammarskjöld, some of his colleagues and the United Nations in general. It may however, also raise numerous questions in the minds of the reader of a more philosophical nature, not the least of which might be, why UN officials are permitted to remove their papers upon leaving the Organisation (through

---

46. In a document discovered at the Royal Library in early 1981, it would appear that Bo Hammarskjöld had placed an embargo on the use of the second part of the collection (that considered the private papers) until 1986. While the current trustees cannot lift this embargo, they do appear to be willing to make exceptions in certain cases concerning the use of this part of the papers.

retirement or death). It is something one will obviously ruminate over while travelling across the globe, at considerable expense, conducting research on the various collections herein described. How much easier it would have been simply to keep all of these papers at the United Nations. The problem is a universal one though and people who have conducted research on presidential papers in the United States will surely have experienced similar thoughts, even though the distance between Independence, Missouri and Hyde Park, New York is small compared with that between Los Angeles and Stockholm. It is a problem, regretfully, for which no solution is likely in the foreseeable future. Senior executive staff of large organisations or governments will continue to remove their "personal papers" to places far removed from the original decision-making arena and researchers will continue to clamber after them in the endless pursuit of some idea or vision. The thing to remember though is that no one forces us to pursue this knowledge. We do it because it is enjoyable and it has rewards, be they intrinsic or material. The discovery of something new or the re-interpretation of something old is a pursuit as ancient as humankind. It is this pursuit which has provided us with what little knowledge we have about the world today and hopefully, it is a quest which will continue to bring forth new insights into the way the world functions. The work of the United Nations plays a major role in the development of the international system since 1945 and one hopes that it will continue to do so. The more intensely we study its work, both past and present, the better able we will be to correct the errors which have been made and hence, give the UN a brighter future. This was Dag Hammarskjöld's goal as Secretary-General and he knew that the UN was the main hope for human survival in the future. It is significant that in his final message to the Organisation, in his Sixteenth Annual Report, he put it to the membership that they had but two choices for the UN's future—a "static conference machinery" or a "dynamic instrument" which would evolve into a more effective instrument of global cooperation. The UN would still appear to be wavering between these two choices almost twenty years later, but with continued research and study of the Organisation, perhaps the academic scholar can help push it in the direction Hammarskjöld felt so strongly it should go.

Bibliography

Books

Amery, Rt. Hon. L. S., C. H. *My Political Life, VII: War and Peace 1914-1929* (London: Hutchinson, 1953).
Aulén, Gustaf. *Dag Hammarskjöld's White Book: An Analysis of "Markings"* (Philadelphia: Fortress Press, 1969).
Bailey, Sidney D. *The Secretariat of the United Nations*, rev. ed. (New York: Praeger, 1964.)
Barnett, A. Doak. *Communist China and Asia. A Challenge to American Policy* (New York: Vintage Books, 1961).
Barros, James. *Betrayal from Within: Joseph Avenol, Secretary-General of the League of Nations, 1933-1940* (New Haven: Yale University Press, 1969)
 Office Without Power: Secretary-General Sir Eric Drummond, 1919-1933 (New York: Oxford University Press, 1979).
 The Cold War's Secretary-General: Trygve Lie, 1946-1953 (forthcoming).
 ed. *The United Nations: Past, Present, and Future* (New York: The Free Press, 1972).
Bartels, Eyvind, et. al. *Dag Hammarskjöld og Hans Gud* (*Dag Hammarskjöld and His God*) (Copenhagen: Kristeligt Dagblad, 1964).
Bechhoefer, Bernard C. *Postwar Negotiations for Arms Control* (Washington, D.C.: Brookings Institution, 1961).
Behanon, Kavoor T. *Realities and Make-Believe: Personnel Policy in the United Nations Secretariat* (New York: William-Frederick, 1952).
Bengs, Bengt-Åke. *The Ndola Accident* (Stockholm: Bengt-Åke Bengs, 1966).
Beskow, Bo. *Dag Hammarskjöld: Strictly Personal—A Portrait* (Garden City, N.Y.: Doubleday, 1969).
Bloomfield, Lincoln. *The United Nations at Twenty and After* (New York: Foreign Policy Association, 1965).
Boen, S. E. *The Leadership Role of the Secretary-General in Times of International Crisis* (Ann Arbor, Mich.: University Microfilms, 1965) Ph.D. Dissertation.
Bowett, D. W. *United Nations Forces: A Legal Study* (New York: Frederick A. Praeger, 1964).
Boyd, Andrew. *United Nations: Piety, Myth and Truth* (London: Penguin, 1962).

Brandon, H. *Conversations with Henry Brandon* (London: Deutsch 1966).
Burns, Arthur Lee, and Nina Heathcoate. *Peace-keeping by U. N. Forces: From Suez to the Congo.* (New York: Frederick A. Praeger, 1963).
Burns, E. L. M. *Between Arab and Israeli* (New York: I. Oblensky, 1962).
Calvocoressi, Peter. *World Order and the New States.* (New York: Frederick A. Praeger, 1962).
Campbell, John C. *Defense of the Middle East*, rev. ed. (New York: Frederick A. Praeger, 1960).
Carnegie Endowment for International Peace, *Proceedings of Conference on Experience in International Administration* (Washington: Carnegie Endowment for International Peace, 1943).
Proceedings of Exploratory Conference on the League of Nations Secretariat. The United Nations Secretariat U. N. Study No. 4 (New York: Carnegie Endowment for International Peace, 1950).
Claude, Inis. *The Changing United Nations* (New York: Random House, 1967).
Clifford, J. M. *The Thirty-Eighth Floor* (New York: McGraw-Hill, 1965).
Cohen, Benjamin V. *The United Nations: Constitutional Developments, Growth and Possibilities* (Cambridge, Mass.: Harvard University Press, 1961).
Commission to Study the Organization of Peace. *The Secretary-General and the Secretariat.* (New York: Commission to Study the Organization of Peace, 1962).
The United Nations Secretary-General: His Role in World Politics (New York: Commission to Study the Organization of Peace, 1962).
Copp, Dewitt and Marshall Peck. *Betrayal at the UN: The Story of Paul Bang-Jensen* (New York: Devin-Adair Co., 1961).
Cordier, Andrew and Wilder Foote, eds. *Public Papers of the Secretaries-General of The United Nations:* Vol. 2, Dag Hammarskjöld, 1953-1956; Vol. 3, Dag Hammarskjöld, 1956-1957; Vol. 4, Dag Hammarskjöld, 1958-1960; Vol. 5, Dag Hammarskjöld, 1960-1961 (New York: Columbia University Press, 1972-1975).
The Quest for Peace: The Dag Hammarskjöld Memorial Lectures (New York: Columbia University Press, 1965).
Cordier, Andrew and Kenneth Maxwell, eds. *Paths to World Order* (New York: Columbia University Press, 1967).
Dallin, Alexander. *The Soviet Union at the United Nations* (New York: Frederick A. Praeger, 1962).
Dayal, Rajeshwar. *Mission for Hammarskjöld: The Congo Crisis* (Princeton: Princeton University Press, 1976).
Eden, Anthony. *The Memoirs of Anthony Eden, Full Circle* (Boston: Houghton Mifflin Co., 1960).
Eichelberger, Clark M. *The United Nations: The First Twenty-Five Years* (New York: Harper & Row, 1970).
Organizing for Peace: A Personal History of the Founding of the United Nations (New York: Harper & Row, 1977).
Elaraby, Nabil A. *The Legal Framework of the Secretary-General's Diplomatic Role in the Settlement of Disputes* (New York: New York University Press, 1970).
Elder, Neil C. M. *Government in Sweden* (Oxford: Pergamon Press, 1970).

Erlander, Tage, et al. *Arvet fran Hammarskjöld (The Legacy from Dag Hammarskjöld)* (Stockholm: Gummessons Bokforlag, 1961).
Falk, Richard & Saul Mendlovitz, eds. *The Strategy of World Order: The United Nations,* Vol. 3 (New York: World Law Fund, 1966).
Fifield, Russel H. *The Diplomacy of Southeast Asia, 1945-1958.* (New York: Harper and Brothers, 1958).
Finer, Herman, *Dulles Over Suez* (Chicago: Quadrangle Books, 1964).
Foote, Wilder, ed. *Servant of Peace: A Selection of the Speeches and Statements of Dag Hammarskjöld, Secretary-General of the United Nations, 1953-1961* (New York: Harper & Row, 1962).
Fosdick, Raymond, *The League and the United Nations after 50 Years: The Six Secretaries-General* (Newtown, Conn.: R. B. Fosdick, 1972).
Frydenberg, Per. *Peace-keeping Experience and Evaluation-The Oslo Papers.* (Oslo: Norwegian Institute of International Affairs, 1964).
Frye, William R. *A United Nations Peace Force.* (Dobbs Ferry, N.Y.: Oceana Publications, 1957).
Gardiner, Richard N. *The Future of the UN Secretariat* (Rensselaervile, N.Y.: Institute on Man & Science, 1972).
Gavshon, Arthur L. *The Mysterious Death of Dag Hammarskjöld* (New York: Walker, 1962).
Gillet, Nicholas, *Dag Hammarskjöld* (London: Heron Books, 1970).
Goodrich, Leland M. *The United Nations in a Changing World* (New York: Columbia University Press, 1974).
Goodspeed, Stephen S. *The Nature and Function of International Organization* (New York: Oxford University Press, 1969, 2nd ed.).
Gordenker, Leon, ed. *The International Executive,* World Order Studies Program Occasional Paper No. 6 (Princeton: Center of International Studies, 1978).
The United Nations in International Politics (Princeton: Princeton University Press, 1971).
The UN Secretary-General and the Maintenance of Peace (New York: Columbia University Press, 1967).
Gordon, King. *United Nations in the Congo. A Quest for Peace* (New York: Carnegie Endowment for International Peace. 1962).
Graham, Norman and Robert Jordan, eds. *The International Civil Service: Changing Role and Concepts* (New York: Pergamon, 1980).
Gross, Ernest A. *The United Nations Structures for Peace* (New York: Harper and Brothers, 1962).
Haas, E. *Beyond the Nation-State* (Stanford, Cal.: Stanford University Press, 1964).
Hammarskjöld, Dag. *Markings,* translated by W. H. Auden & L. Sjöberg (New York: Alfred Knopf, 1964).
Hazzard, Shirley. *Defeat of an Ideal: The Self-Destruction of the United Nations* (London: Macmillan, 1973).
Heilprin, Marilyn. *The Evolution of the United Nations Presence under Dag Hammarskjöld* (Washington, D.C.: The American University, 1963) M. A. Thesis.
Henderson, James L. *Hammarskjöld: Servant of a World Unborn* (London: Methuen Educational, 1969).
Hershey, Burnett. *Soldier of Peace: Dag Hammarskjöld* (Chicago: Britannica Books, 1961).

Higgins, Rosalyn. *United Nations Peace-keeping, 1946-67: Volume I, The Middle East* (London: Oxford University Press, 1969).
Howard-Ellis, C. *The Origin, Structure & Working of the League of Nations* (London: George Allen & Unwin, 1928).
Huss, P. J. and C. J. Carpozi, Jr. *Red Spies in the UN* (New York: Coward McCann, 1965).
Iklé, Fred Charles. *How Nations Negotiate* (New York: Frederick A. Praeger, 1964).
Jackson, R. *A Study of the Capacity of the UN Development System* (UN: 1969).
James, Robert Rhodes. *Staffing the United Nations Secretariat*, Institute for the Study of International Organisations, Monograph No. 2 (Brighton: University of Sussex, 1970).
Jenks. W. *The Common Law of Mankind* (New York: Praeger, 1958).
Johnson, Franklyn A. *Defence by Committee: The British Committee of Imperial Defence, 1885-1959* (London: Oxford University Press, 1960).
Jordan, Robert S. *The NATO International Staff/Secretariat, 1952-1957, A Study in International Administration* (London: Oxford University Press, 1967).
—— ed. *Multinational Cooperation: Economic, Social and Scientific Development* (New York: Oxford Univerity Press, 1972).
—— *Political Leadership in Nato: A Study in Multinational Diplomacy* (Boulder, Colorado: Westview Press, 1979).
Kelen, Emery. *Dag Hammarskjöld: A Biography* (New York: Meredith Press, 1969).
—— *Hammarskjöld* (New York: Putnam, 1966).
Kelen, Emery, ed. *Hammarskjöld—The Political Man* (New York: Funk & Wagnalls, 1968).
Lall, Arthur. *The UN and the Middle East Crisis, 1967* (New York: Columbia University Press, 1968).
Langrod, Georges. *The International Civil Service: Its Origins, Its Nature, Its Evolution* (Dobbs Ferry, N.Y.: Oceana, 1963).
Laqueur, Walter Z. *The Soviet Union and the Middle East* (New York: Frederick A. Praeger, 1959).
Larus, Joel, ed. *From Collective Security to Preventive Diplomacy: Readings in International Organization and the Maintenance of Peace* (New York: Wiley, 1965).
Lash, Joseph P. *Dag Hammarskjöld* (London: Cassel, 1962).
—— *Dag Hammarskjöld: Custodian of the Brushfire Peace* (New York: Doubleday, 1961).
Laves, W. and C. Thomson. *UNESCO* (Bloomington, Ind.: Indiana University Press, 1957).
Lefever, Ernest W. *Crisis in the Congo: A UN Force in Action* (Washington, D.C., Brookings Institution, 1965).
Legum, Colin. *Congo Disaster* (Baltimore: Penguin Books, 1961).
Lentner, Howard H. *The Political Role of the United Nations Secretariat* (Ann Arbor, Mich.: University Microfilms, 1964) Ph.D. Dissertation.
Levine, Israel. *Dag Hammarskjöld: Champion of World Peace* (New York: Messner, 1962).

Lie, Trygve. *In the Cause of Peace: Seven Years with the UN* (New York: Macmillan, 1954).
Lord Gladwyn, *The Memoirs of Lord Gladwyn* (London: Weidenfeld and Nicolson, 1972).
Lord Hankey, *Diplomacy by Conference, Studies in Public Affairs* 1920-1946 (London: Ernest Benn, 1946).
  The Supreme Command 1914-1918, *Vol. I* (London: George Allen and Unwin, 1961).
Lord Riddell. *Lord Riddell's Intimate Diary of the Peace Conference and After, 1918-1923* (New York: Reynal and Hitchcock, 1934).
Loveday, Alexander. *Reflections on International Administration* (Oxford: Clarendon Press, 1956).
Mackintosh, John P. *The British Cabinet* (London: Stevens and Sons, 1962).
McDougal, Myres S., and Florentino P. Feliciano. *Law and Minimum World Public Order* (New Haven: Yale University Press, 1961).
McLaren, Robert. *Civil Servants and Public Policy* (Waterloo, Ont.: Wilfred Laurier University Press, 1980.
Mayer, Ann M. *Dag Hammarskjöld: The Peacemaker* (Monkato, Minn.: Creative Education, 1974).
Meigs, Cornelia. *The Great Design: Men and Events in the United Nations from 1945-1963* (Boston: Little Brown, 1964).
Meron, Theodor. *The United Nations Secretariat: The Rules and the Practice* (Lexington, Mass.: D.C. Health, 1977).
Mezerik, A. G., ed. *Congo and the United Nations,* Vol. I (New York: International Review Service, 1960).
Michaels, David. *Privileges and Immunities of the International Civil Servant* (Falls Church, Va., 1970).
Miller, Richard. *Dag Hammarskjöld and Crisis Diplomacy* (Dobbs Ferry, N.Y.: Oceana, 1962).
Montgomery, Elizabeth. *Dag Hammarskjöld: Peacemaker for the United Nations* (Champaign, Ill.: Garrard, 1973).
Morley, Felix. *The Society of Nations* (Washington: The Brookings Institution 1922).
Mortimer, Raymond A., *The Third World Coalition in International Politics* (New York: Praeger, 1980).
Munro, Sir Leslie. *United Nations: Hope for a Divided World* (New York: Henry Holt and Co., 1960).
Nicholas, H. G. *The United Nations as a Political Institution.* 5th ed. (New York: Oxford University Press, 1975).
Nicol, Davidson, ed. *Paths to Peace: The UN Security Council and Its Presidency* (New York: Pergamon Press, 1981).
Nicolson, Harold. *Peacemaking 1919* (New York: Grosset and Dunlap, 1965).
O'Brien, Conor Cruise. *Murderous Angels: A Political Tragedy and Comedy in Black and White* (Boston: Little Brown, 1968).
  To Katanga and Back: A UN Case History (New York: Simon and Schuster, 1962).
O'Brien, Conor Cruise & Topolski, Felix. *United Nations Sacred Drama* (New York:

Simon & Schuster, 1968).
Ogley, Roderick. *The United Nations, 1945-1965: Its Political Role* (London: United Nations Association, 1965).
Padelford, Norman and Leland Goodrich, eds. *The United Nations in the Balance: Accomplishments and Prospects* (New York: F. A. Praeger, 1965).
Pak, Chi Young. *The Political Role of the Secretary-General of the United Nations in Theory and Practice* (Ann Arbor, Mich.: Michigan University Press, 1963).
Pechota, Vratislav. *The Quiet Approach: A Study of the Good Offices Exercised by the United Nations Secretary-General in the Cause of Peace* (New York: UNITAR, 1972).
Purves, Chester. *The Internal Administration of an International Secretariat* (London: The Royal Institute of International Affairs, 1945).
Qubain, Fahim Issa. *Crisis in Lebanon* (Washington, D.C.: Middle East Institute, 1961).
Ranshofen-Wertheimer, Egon F. *The International Secretariat: A Great Experiment in International Administration* (New York: Carnegie Endowment for International Peace, 1945).
Reuter, Paul. *International Institutions* (London: Allen & Unwin, 1958).
Rhodesia and Nyasaland, Federation of. Commission on the Accident involving Aircraft SE-BDY: *A Report of the Commission on the Accident involving SE-BDY (carrying Dag Hammarskjöld, Secretary-General of the UN)* (Salisbury, Assembly Papers—C. Fed. 202., 1962).
Rikhye, Indar Jit. *The Sinai Blunder* (London: Frank Cass, 1980).
Robertson, Terence. *Crisis. The Inside Story of the Suez Conspiracy.* (New York: Atheneum, 1965).
Rosner, Gabriella. *The United Nations Emergency Force* (New York: Columbia University Press, 1963).
Rovine, Arthur W. *The First Fifty Years: The Secretary-General in World Politics, 1920-1970* (Leyden: A. W. Sijthoff. 1970).
The Royal Institute of International Affairs, *The International Secretariat of the Future* (London: Oxford University Press, 1944).
Russell, Ruth B. *A History of the United Nations Charter* (Washington, D.C.: The Brookings Institution, 1958).
United Nations Experience with Military Force: Political and Legal Aspects. Research Paper P-27 (Washington, D.C.: Institute for Defense Analyses, International Studies Division, 1963).
Rustow, Dankwart A. *The Politics of Compromise. A Study of Cabinet Government in Sweden.* (Princeton: Princeton University Press, 1955).
Sanchez, Eva de. *Dag Hammarskjöld* (Stockholm, 1961).
Schachter, O. *Sharing the World's Resources* (New York: Columbia University Press, 1977).
Schelling, Thomas C. *The Strategy of Conflict* (New York: Oxford University Press, 1963).
Schiffer, Walter. *The Legal Community of Mankind: A Critical Analysis of the Modern Concept of World Organization* (New York: Columbia University Press, 1954).
Schwebel, Stephen M. *The Secretary-General of the United Nations: His Political Powers and Practice* (Cambridge, Mass.: Harvard University Press, 1952).

Settel, T. S., ed. *The Light and the Rock: The Vision of Dag Hammarskjöld* (New York: Dutton, 1966).
Simon, Charlie M. *Dag Hammarskjöld* (New York: Dutton, 1967).
Siotis, Jean. *Essai sur le Secrétariat International* (Geneva: Droz, 1963).
Soderberg, Sten. *Hammarskjöld: A Pictorial Biography* (New York: Viking Press, 1962).
Stolpe, Sven J. *Dag Hammarskjöld: A Spiritual Portrait* (New York: Scribners, 1966).
Story, Tekla W. *Dag Hammarskjöld: Spokesman for Internationalism* (Carbondale, Ill.: Southern Illinois University, 1968) Ph.D. Dissertation.
Tavares de Sa, Hernane. *The Play Within the Play: The Inside Story of the United Nations* (New York: Alfred Knopf, 1966).
Taylor, P. G. & A. J. R. Groom, eds. *International Organisation: A Conceptual Approach* (New York: Nichols, 1978).
Teltsch, Kathleen. *Crosscurrents at Turtle Bay: A Quarter Century of the United Nations* (Chicago: Quadrangle Books, 1970).
Tetlow, Edwin. *The United Nations: The First Twenty-Five Years* (London: Peter Owen, 1970).
Thant, U. *View from the UN* (Garden City, N.Y.: Doubleday, 1978).
Portfolio for Peace: excerpts from the writings and speeches of U Thant, Secretary-General of the United Nations, on major world issues, 1961-1970 (New York: United Nations, 1970).
Thorpe, Deryck. *Hammarskjöld—Man of Peace* (Devon: Stockwell, 1969).
Townley, Ralph. *The United Nations: A View from Within* (New York: Scribner, 1968).
Torre, Mottram, ed. *The Selection of Personnel for International Service* (Geneva: World Federation for Mental Health, 1964).
Twitchett, Kenneth J. *The Evolving United Nations: A Prospect for Peace?* (London: Europa, 1971).
United States Department of State, *Foreign Relations of the United States 1952-1954* (Washington, D.C.: Government Printing Office, 1979).
United States Policy in the Middle East. September 1956-1957. Documents. Department of State Publications 6505. Near and Middle Eastern Series 25, August 1957.
Urquhart, Brian. *Hammarskjöld* (New York: Alfred Knopf, 1972).
Van Dusen, Henry. *Dag Hammarskjöld: The Statesman and his Faith* (New York: Harper & Row, 1967).
Dag Hammarskjöld: A Biographical Interpretation of "Markings" (London: Faber & Faber, 1967).
Van Langenhove, Fernand. *Le Role Prominent du Secrétaire Général dans L'Opération des Nations Unies au Congo* (The Hague: Martinus Nijhoff, 1964).
Virally, Michel. *L'O.N.U. d'Hier a Demain.* (Paris: Editions du Seuil, 1961).
Towards a Reform of the UN Secretariat? (Geneva: M. Virally, 1961).
Von Horn, Carl. *Soldiering for Peace* (New York: David McKay Company, 1967).
Waldheim, Kurt. *Building the Future Order: The Search for Peace in An Interdependent World*, ed. by Robert L. Schiffer (New York: The Free Press, 1980).
The Challenge of Peace (New York: Rawson, Wade, 1980).

Walters, Frank P. *Administrative Problems of International Organization*, Barnett House Papers, No. 24 (London: Oxford University Press, 1941).
A History of the League of Nations, 2 vols. (New York: Oxford University Press, 1952).
Waters, Maurice, ed. *The United Nations: International Organization and Administration* (New York: Macmillan, 1967).
Weiss, Thomas G. *International Bureaucracy: An Analysis of the Operation of Functional and Global International Secretariats* (Lexington, Mass.: D.C. Heath, 1975).
Wigforss, Ernst, *Minnen*. Vol. III (Stockholm: Tidens Forlag, 1954).
Wriggins, Howard. *The Status of the United Nations Secretariat* (New York: Woodrow Wilson Foundation, 1954).
Young, Oran. *The Intermediaries: Third Parties in International Crises* (Princeton: Princeton University Press, 1967).
Young, Tien-Cheng. *International Civil Service: Principles and Problems* (Brussels: International Institute of Administrative Sciences, 1958).
Zacher, Mark W. *Dag Hammarskjöld's United Nations* (New York: Columbia University Press, 1970).
International Conflicts and Collective Security, 1946-1977: The United Nations, Organization of American States, Organization of African Unity, and Arab League (New York: Praeger, 1979).
Zagoria, Donald S. *The Sino-Soviet Conflict, 1956-1961.* (Princeton: Princeton University Press, 1962).

Articles and Monographs

Aghnides, Thanassis. "The standards of conduct of the international civil servant," *International Review of Administrative Science* (1953).
Ahman, Seven. "Dag Hammarskjöld," in American Swedish Historical Foundation, *Yearbook*-1962.
"Mr. Hammarskjöld's Not-So-Quiet Diplomacy", *The Reporter*, (4 September 1958).
Alexandrowicz, Charles H. "'The Secretary-General of the United Nations", *International and Comparative Law Quarterly*, Vol. II, Part 4, October 1962.
Anglin, Douglas G. "Lester Pearson and the Office of Secretary-General", *International Journal*, Vol. 17, (Spring 1962).
Armstrong, Hamilton Fish. "U.N. Experience in Gaza," *Foreign Affairs* XXXV (July 1957).
"U.N. on Trial," *Foreign Affairs*, XXXIX (April 1961).
Ascoli, Max. "The Future of the U.N.—An Editorial," *The Reporter*, XXV (October 26, 1961).
"On Reading Hammarskjöld," *The Reporter*, Vol. 32, No. 10, (20 May 1965).
"The Price of Peacemongering," *The Reporter*, XV (29 November 1956).
Astrachan, Anthony. "Waldheim: Learning the Uses of Limited Power," *Saturday Review*, Vol. 1, (23 March 1974).
Bailey, Sydney. "The Troika and the Future of the UN," *International Conciliation*, No. 538, (May 1962).

Barros, James. "A More Powerful Secretary-General for the United Nations?" *American Journal of International Law (Proceedings of the American Society of International Law)*, Vol. 66, No. 4 (September 1972).

"Pearson or Lie: The Politics of the Secretary-General's Selection, 1946" *Canadian Journal of Political Science*, X, No. 1 (March 1977).

"Trygve Lie: De Mortuis nil nisi bonum," *International Journal*, XXV, No. 2 (Spring 1970)

Beigbeder, Yves. "Current Staff Problems in United Nations Secretariats," *International Review of Administrative Sciences*, 46, 2 (1980).

Bess, Demaree. "The Most Impossible Job in the World," *Saturday Evening Post*, (7 January 1956).

Bokhari, Ahmed S. "Parliaments, Priests and Prophets," *Foreign Affairs*, XXXV (April 1957).

Bolintineanu, A. "Preventive Multilateral Diplomacy of the United Nations," *Rev. Roumaine d'Etudes Int.* (Rumania), Vol. 25, No. 9, (1975).

Boyd, Andrew. "The Unknown United Nations," *International Journal*, XIX (Spring 1964).

Chamberlin, Waldo. "Administrative Matters," *Annual Review of UN Affairs:* 1955-1956, New York: New York University Press, 1957.

Claude, Inis L. "The UN and the Use of Force," *International Conciliation*, No. 532 (March 1961).

"United Nations Use of Military Force," *Journal of Conflict Resolution*, VII (June 1963).

Cohen, Maxwell. "The United Nations Secretariat-Some Constitutional and Administrative Developments," 49 *American Journal of International Law* (1955).

Connery, Donald S. "The Making of a Secretary-General," *Vista*, (March-April 1972).

Cordier, Andrew W. "Hammarskjöld's Legacy to the UN," *New York Times Magazine*, (16 September 1962).

"Motivations and Methods of Dag Hammarskjöld," in *Paths to World Order*, Andrew W. Cordier and Kenneth Maxwell, eds. (New York: Columbia University Press, 1967).

"The Role of the Secretary-General," *Annual Review of U.N. Affairs*, 1960-61.

Cox, Robert W. "The Executive Head: An Essay on Leadership in International Organization," *International Organization*, Vol. 23, No. 4, (Spring 1969).

Crocker, W. R. "Some Notes on the United Nations Secretariat," *International Organization* IV (1950).

Curtis, Gerald L. "The United Nations Observation Group in Lebanon," *International Organization*, XVIII (Autumn 1964).

"Dag Hammarskjöld," *The New Yorker*, (30 September 1961).

Davies, Jack, G. W. "The Work of the Secretariat," *Annual Review of UN Affairs:* 1952 (New York: New York University Press, 1953).

Draper, Theodore. "Ordeal of the U.N.: Khrushchev, Hammarskjöld and the Congo," *The New Leader*, Section 2 (7 November 1960).
Dworkis, Martin B. "Administrative Matters," *Annual Review of UN Affairs 1954*. (New York: New York University Press, 1955).
Egger, Rowland. "Road to Gethsemane," 6 *Public Administration Review* (Winter 1946).
Ennis, Thomas E. "Laos: Pawn in Power Politics," *Current History* XXXVIII (February 1960).
Erven, L. "The question of the Secretary-General," *Review of International Affairs* (Yugoslav), (20 October 1961).
Finger, Seymour M. & John F. Mungo. "The Politics of Staffing the United Nations Secretariat," *Orbis*, Vol. 19, No. 1, (Spring 1975).
Finkelstein, Lawrence S. "The United Nations and Organizations for the Control of Armaments," *International Organization*, XVI (Winter 1962).
"Five Powers Present Plan for General Disarmament as Ten-Nations Disarmament Conference Convenes," *The Department of State Bulletin*, XLII (4 April 1960).
Franck, Thomas, and John Garey. "The Role of the United Nations in the Congo—A Retrospective Perspective," *The Hammarskjöld Forums* (New York: The Association of the Bar of the City of New York, (30 April 1962).
Friedmann, W. "The United Nations and National Loyalties," *International Journal* 8 (1952-1953).
Gaskill, Gordon. "Timetable of a Failure," *The Virginia Quarterly Review*, XXXIV (Spring 1958).
Good, Robert C. "Congo Crisis: The Role of the New States," *Neutralism* (Washington, D.C.: The Washington Center of Foreign Policy Research, 1961).
Goodrich, Leland. "Hammarskjöld, the UN and the Office of the Secretary-General," *International Organization*, Vol. 16, No. 4, (Autumn 1962).
Gordenker, Leon. "Conor Cruise O'Brien and the Truth about the United Nations," *International Organization*, Vol. 23, No. 4, (Autumn 1969).
Hammarskjöld, Dag. *Castle Hill* (Uppsala, Sweden: The Dag Hammarskjöld Foundation, 1977).
"Education's Stake in World Peace and Progress," *United Nations Bulletin*, XVI (1 February 1954).
"For a New Approach to International Aid and Technical Assistance," *United Nations Review*, III (July 1956).
"In 'Age of Responsibility' All Can Wield Influence," *United Nations Bulletin*, XVI (13 February 1954).
"Politik och ideologi," *Tiden*, XLIV (1952).
"Private Investment and International Aid," *United Nations Review* (May 1960).
"Stratstjanstemannen och samhallet," *Tiden*, XLIII (1951).
"The Element of Privacy in Peacekeeping," *United Nations Review*, IV (March 1958).

The International Civil Servant in Law and in Fact (Oxford: Clarendon Press, 1961).

"Two Differing Concepts of the United Nations Assayed: Introduction to the Annual Report of the Secretary-General on the Work of the Organization, 16 June 1960-15 June 1961," *International Organization*, Vol. 15, No. 4 (Autumn 1961).

"United Nations Only Coming of Age but Confidence Already 'Voted'," *United Nations Bulletin*, XVI (1 June 1954).

"United Nations—The Way Ahead," *United Nations Bulletin*, XVI (1 January 1954).

"Why the United Nations?," *United Nations Review*, V (July 1958).

Hazzard, Shirley. "The League of Frightened Men," *The New Republic*, (19 January 1980).

Hershey, Burnet. "Dag Hammarskjöld: A Personal Portrait", *Look*, Vol. 25, (24 October 1961).

Hoffman, Stanley. "In Search of a Thread: the U.N. in the Congo Labyrinth," *International Organization*, XVI (Spring 1962).

"Sisyphus and the Avalanche: The United Nations, Egypt and Hungary," *International Organization*, XI (Summer 1957).

Honig, F. "The International Civil Service: Basic Problems and Contemporary Difficulties", *International Affairs* (April 1954).

Jackobson, Max. "Detente Nourishes a New UN," *Saturday Review*, Vol. 1, (23 March 1974).

Jackson, Elmore. "Constitutional Developments of the United Nations: The Growth of Executive Capacity," *Proceedings of the American Society of International Law*, LV (1961).

"The Developing Role of the Secretary-General," *International Organization*, XI (Summer 1957).

Jackson, William D. "The Political Role of the Secretary-General under U Thant and Kurt Waldheim: Development or Decline?" *World Affairs*, Vol. 140, No. 3 (1978).

Jacobson, Harold Karan. "ONUC's Civilian Operations: State-Preserving and State-Building," *World Politics*, XVII (October 1964).

James, Alan M. "The Role of the Secretary-General of the United Nations in International Relations," *International Relations*, (October 1959).

Jarring, Gunnar. "Dag Hammarskjöld: In Memoriam," *Swedish Pioneer Historical Quarterly*, (January 1962).

Jenks, Wilfred. "Some Problems of an International Civil Service III *Public Administration Review* (1943).

Jessup, P. H. "The International Civil Servant and his Loyalties," *Journal of International Affairs* IX (1955).

Jordan, Robert S. "What Has Happened to Our International Civil Service? The Case of the United Nations," *Public Administration Review*, (March/April 1981).

Jordan, Robert S. and John P. Renninger. "The New Environment of Nation-Building," *The Journal of Modern African Studies,* 13, 2, (1975).

Jordan, William M. "Concepts and Realties in International Political Organization," *International Organization,* XI (Autumn 1957).

Kaladhar, M. G. "Dag Hammarskjöld & U Thant—The Evolution of their Office," *Case Western Reserve Journal of International Law,* Vol. 7, No. 1, (1974).

Knight, Jonathan. "On the Influence of the Secretary-General: Can we Know What It Is?" *International Organization,* Vol. 24, No. 3, (Summer 1970).

Kraft, Joseph. "The Untold Story of the UN's Congo Army," *Harper's Magazine* CCXXI (November 1960).

Kuntz, Josef L. "United Nations Secretary-General on the Role of the United Nations," *American Journal of International Law,* Vol. 52, No. 2, (April 1958).

Lash, Joseph P. "Dag Hammarskjöld's Conception of His Office," *International Organization,* Vol. 16, No. 3, (Summer 1962).

"The Man on the 38th Floor," *Harpers* (October 1959).

"The UN's Hammarskjöld," *The Progressive,* (January 1957).

Laves, Walter H. and Donald C. Stone. "The United Nations Secretariat," *Foreign Policy Reports* XXII, No. 15 (15 October 1956).

Lengyel, Peter. "Some Trends in the International Civil Service," *International Organization,* Vol. 13, No. 4, (Fall 1959).

Lippman, Walter. "Dag Hammarskjöld: United Nations Pioneer," *International Organization,* Vol. 15, No. 4 (Autumn 1961).

Lodge, Henry Cabot. "A Colleague's Salute," *Life,* Vol. 51, (29 September 1961).

Malkin, Lawrence. "Battle for the Independence of the UN Secretariat," *Reporter* (27 September 1962).

Masland, John W. "The Secretariat of the United Nations," *Public Administration Review,* Vol. 5 (Autumn 1945).

McPherson, Myra. "Waldheim," *Washington Post,* (18 January 1980).

Miller, E. M. "Legal Aspects of the United Nations Action in the Congo," *American Journal of International Law,* LV (January 1961).

Moore, Bernard. "The Secretariat: Role and Functions," *Annual Review of UN Affairs* 1949 (New York: New York University Press, 1950).

Morgenthau, Hans J. "The New Secretary-General," *Commentary* (January 1963).

"The U.N. of Dag Hammarskjöld Is Dead," *The New York Times,* (14 March 1965).

Narasimhan, C. V. "Administrative Changes in the Secretariat," *Annual Review of United Nations Affairs,* (1961-1962).

Pearson, F. S., J. M. Reynolds, and K. E. Meyer. "The Carter Foreign Policy and the Use of International Organization: The Limits of Policy Innovation," *World Affairs,* Vol. 142, No. 2 (Fall 1979).

Pearson, Lester F. "Force for U.N.," *Foreign Affairs,* XXV (April 1957).

Pyman, T. A. "The United Nations Secretary-Generalship: A Review of Its Status,

Functions and Role," *Australian Outlook,* XV (1961).
Reymond, Henri. "The Staffing of the United Nations Secretariat: A Continuing Discussion," *International Organization* XXI (1967).
Rosenthal, A. M. "Dag Hammarskjöld Sizes up his UN Job," *The New York Times Magazine* (10 August 1953).
Rovine, Arthur W. "A More Powerful Secretary-General for the United Nations?" *American Society of International Law (Proceedings),* Vol. 66 (1972).
Rusk, Dean. "Parliamentary Diplomacy: Debate Vs. Negotiation," *World Affairs Interpreted,* Vol. 26 (1955).
Sabosan, Jeffrey G. "Politics and Spirituality: A Study of Dag Hammarskjöld," *Cithara,* Vol. 14, No. 1, (1974).
Saksena, K. P. "Hammarskjöld and the Congo Crisis: A Review," *India Quarterly,* Vol. 34, No. 2, (1978).
"Secretary-General U Thant," *India Quarterly,* Vol. 31, No. 4 (1975).
Schachter, Oscar. "Dag Hammarskjöld and the Relation of Law to Poltics," *American Journal of International Law,* Vol. 56, (January 1962).
"Some Reflections on International Officialdom," in Fawcett and Higgins (eds.), *International Organization: Law in Movement, Essays in Honour of John McMahon* (Oxford University Press 1974).
"The Uses of Law in International Peace-keeping," 50 *Virginia Law Review* 1096 (1964).
"The Relation of Law, Politics and Action in the United Nations," 109 *Hague Academy Recueil des Cours* 171 (1963).
Schiffer, Walter. "The League as a Universal Quasi-Government," in *The Legal Community of Mankind: A Critical Analysis of the Modern Concept of World Organization,* (New York: Columbia University Press, 1954).
Schwebel, Stephen M. "The International Character of the Secretariat of the UN," *British Yearbook of International Law* (1953).
"Origins and Development of Article 99 of the Charter: Powers of the Secretary-General of the United Nations," 28 *British Yearbook of International Law* (1951).
"The Choice of a New U.N. Secretary-General," *The Washington Post,* (23 December 1971).
"Selecting a New Secretary-General for the U.N.," *The Washington Post,* (13 September 1971).
Scott, F. R. "The World's Civil Service," *International Conciliation,* No. 496, (January 1954).
Sharp, Walter R. "Trends in United Nations Administration," *International Organization,* Vol. 15, No. 3 (Summer 1961).
Simmonds, K. R. "'Good Offices' and the Secretary-General," *Nordisk Tidsskrift for International Ret,* Vol. 29 (1959).
Stanton, Edwin F. "A 'Presence' in Laos," *Current History,* XXXVIII (June 1960).
Stark, Andrew A. "The Secretariat—Twenty-Five Years After," *UN Monthly Chronicle,* Vol. 7, No. 8 (August-September 1970).
Stein, Eric. "Mr. Hammarskjöld, the Charter Law and Future Role of the United

Nations Secretary-General," *American Journal of International Law* LVI (January 1962).
Stone, Donald C. "Organizing the United Nations," *Public Administration Review* (Spring 1946).
Swift, Richard N. "Personnel Problems in the United Nations Secretariat," *International Organization,* Vol. 11, No. 2, (Spring 1957).
Tandon, Yashpal. "UNEF, The Secretary-General and International Diplomacy in the Third Arab-Israeli War," *International Organization* XXII (1968).
Tead, Ordway. "The Importance of Administration in International Action," *International Conciliation,* No. 407, (January 1945).
Thant, U. "The Role of the Secretary-General," *UN Monthly Chronicle,* Vol. 8, No. 9 (October 1971).
Turner, Bruce. "The Secretariat," *Annual Review of UN Affairs:* 1950 (New York: New York University Press, 1951).
Urquhart, Brian. "Point of Rest," *The New Yorker,* 1964.
  "International Peace and Security" *Foreign Affairs,* Vol. 60, No. 1, (Fall 1981).
  "Problems of the Secretariat," *Annual Review of United Nations Affairs,* (1963-1964).
  "United Nations Peace Forces and the Changing United Nations: An Institutional Perspective," *International Organization,* XVII (Spring 1963).
Van Bilsen, A. A. J. "Some Aspects of the Congo Problem," *International Affairs,* XXXVIII (January 1962).
Virally, Michel. "Le Role Politique de Secrétaire Général des Nations-Unies," *Annuaire Francais de Droit International,* IV (1958).
Winchmore, Charles. "The Secretariat: Retrospect and Prospect," *International Organization,* Vol. 19, No. 3, (Summer 1965).
"World Community 'Epitomized': Henry Pitney Van Dusen on John Foster Dulles and Dag Hammarskjöld," *Journal of Presbyterian History,* Vol. 48, No. 4, (1970).
"Wreath-laying marks Anniversary of Death of Dag Hammarskjöld," *UN Chronicle,* Vol. 15 (October 1978).
Zacher, Mark. "The Secretary-General: Some Comments on Current Research," *International Organization,* Vol. 23, No. 4 (Autumn 1969).
  "The Secretary-General and the United Nations Functions of Peaceful Settlement," *International Organization,* Vol. 20, No. 4 (Autumn 1966).

Documents*

United Nations: General Assembly. *Official Records.*
United Nations: Security Council. *Official Records.*
United Nations: Office of Public Information, Press Services, Press Releases.
United Nations: Office of Public Information, Press Services, Notes.

Compiled Papers*

The Ralph Bunche Papers. (Los Angeles; University of California, Department of Special Collections, University Research Library).

* For clarification, see the Trachtenberg chapter contained in this book.

The Andrew Cordier Papers. (New York: Columbia University, Butler Library, Rare Books and Manuscripts).

The Dag Hammarskjöld Papers. (Stockholm, Sweden: The Royal Library, Manuscript Department).

The Gunnar and Alva Myrdal Papers. (Stockholm, Sweden: Archives of the Arbetarrorelsens).

The Osten Unden Papers. (Stockholm, Sweden: The Royal Library).

United Nations Archives. (New York: United Nations, Archives Section).

Index

Acheson, Dean - 28; 33.
Administrative Committee on Coordination (ACC) (UN) - 70.
Adoula, Cyril - 102; 104.
Agrippa, Menenius - 57.
Alexander, H. T. (Maj. Gen.) - 97.
Amachree, Godfrey - 97.
Arab League - 93.
Auden, W. H. - 81.
Avenol, Joseph - 28; 29; 31.

Belgium-
and Congo crisis - 93ff.
Ben-Gurion, David - 15; 90; 143; 156.
Berlin - 114; 119.
Bizerte crisis - 73; 120.
Black, Joseph E. - v.
Bloch, Henry - 73.
Blum, Léon - 28.
Bomboko, Justin - 82; 99.
Boris, Georges - 67.
Bourguiba, Habib - 73.
Britain-
and Suez crisis - 82; 86.
British Committee of Imperial Defence (CID) - 4.
Bull, Odd (Gen.) - 90.
Bunche, Joan - 157.
Bunche, Ralph - 83; 94ff; 108; 156; 157ff; 162; 163; 174; 175.
Bunche, Ralph, Jr. - 160.
Burns, E. L. M. (Maj. Gen.) - 83; 84; 86; 98; 105.
Byrnes, James F. - xi.

Campbell, Roy - 57.
Canada - 85.
Cecil, Robert (Lord) - 27.
Central Treaty Organization (CENTO) -89.

Charter (U.N.) - 7; 9; 15; 16-17; 20; 21; 26; 31; 34; 48; 50; 74; 123; 124.
Art. 1 - 48; Art. 2 - 48; Art. 51 - 91; Art. 98 - 16-17; Art. 99 - 16-17; 32; 94; Art. 100 - 41; 42; 44; Chapt. VI -85; Chapt. VII - 79.
Chamoun, Camille - 89; 90; 92; 156.
Chehab (General) - 92; 93.
China, People's Republic of - 7; 17; 78; 116; 121; 141; 167.
Chisholm, Brock - 60; 61.
Chou En-Lai - 7; 15; 139; 141.
Congo crisis - 10-11; 32; 35-36; 40; 43; 48; 49; 52; 73; 78ff; 93ff; 115ff; 121; 122; 126; 158; 160; 170.
Cordier, Andrew - 83; 96; 100; 101; 106; 128; 163ff; 175.
Cutler, John B. (Gen.) - 84.
Cyprus - 19; 20; 122.

Dayal, Rajeshwar - 90; 104; 107; 162.
de Gaulle, Charles - 15; 73; 143.
de Seynes, Philippe - 65; 67; 70; 74.
Department of Economic and Social Affairs (U.N.) - 67; 70; 72.
Drummond, Eric (Sir) - 4; 5; 7; 8; 28; 35; 37.
Dulles, John Foster - 89; 174.

Economic and Social Council (ECOSOC) (U.N.) - 68; 71.
Economic Commission for Latin America (ECLA) (U.N.) - 59.
Eden, Anthony (Sir) - 15.
Egypt -
and Lebanon crisis - 89ff.
and Suez crisis - 82ff; 108; 118; 128.
Eisenhower, Dwight D. - 15; 137.
Engen, Hans - 83.
Entezam, Ambassador - 72.

es-Said, Nuri - 91.
es-Sol, Samy - 90.
Evatt, Herbert V. - 31.

Fawzi, Mahmoud - 143; 156.
Faisal, Prince - 89.
France (see also Bizerte crisis) -
and peacekeeping - 125.
and Suez crisis - 82; 86.

Galo Plaza, President - 90.
Gardiner, Robert - 97.
General Assembly (U.N.) - xi; 5, 7; 8; 9;
  10; 12; 43; 48; 66; 71; 77; 84; 85ff;
  101; 108; 121; 124; 165; 169.
Gizenga, Antone - 101.
Group of 77 - 112.
Guatemala - 139.

Haas, Ernst (Prof.) - 60.
Hammarskjöld, Bo - 153.
Hammarskjöld, Dag - ii; xi; xii
  and chief administrative officer - 26;
    40; 43; 46; 53; 70; 78; 95; 123; 138;
    165; 170.
  and the cold war - 113ff.
  and concept of law - 48; 51; 124; 129.
  and death - xv; 11; 20; 93; 104; 118.
  and dialectical view of U.N. principles
    - 49.
  and early training - 11; 35; 44; 65-66;
    74; 78; 135-136.
  and exercise of his office - 6; 7; 8; 9;
    13; 15-16; 19; 25; 34-35; 50-51; 74;
    124; 128; 129; 133ff; 140-144.
  and Oxford lecture - 39-41; 45.
  and peacekeeping - 78ff; 84; 95; 103;
    104ff; 112ff; 120; 121; 125ff.
  and preventive diplomacy - 8; 15; 49;
    52; 80; 90; 115.
  and relationship to the General As-
    sembly - 81; 127-128.
  and relationship to the Security Coun-
    cil - 20-21; 50; 79-80; 90; 94-95; 97;
    98; 102; 124; 127-128.
  and sense of religion - 134ff; 143-145.
  and Third World development -
    11-12; 20; 67ff; 107; 112; 115; 145.
  and troika - 3; 10; 27; 45; 101; 105.
Hammarskjöld, Hjalmar - 135.
Herriot, Édouard - 28.
Holderman, James B. - ix; xiii.
Hungarian crisis - 114; 119; 128.
Hussein, King - 91.
Huxley, Julian - 60.

Indo-China - 17; 19; 36; 116; 158.

International Court of Justice (ICJ) - 42.
International Monetary Fund (IMF) - 72;
  75.
Iran - 19.
Iraq - 89ff.
Israel - 128.
  and Lebanon crisis - 93.
  and Suez crisis - 82ff.

Jackson, Robert (Sir) - 56.
Jebb, Gladwyn (Sir) - 29.
Jenks, Wilfred (Sir) - 60.
Johnson, Lyndon - 23.
Jordan - 89ff.
Jordan, Robert S. - xv; xvi; 3.
Julien, Harry (Sgt.) - 104.

Kalonji, Albert - 101.
Kassavubu, Joseph - 9; 100ff.
Kashmir - 18; 78.
Kassem, Abdul (Brig.) - 89; 91.
Kennedy, John (Pres.) - 101.
Khiary, Mahomoud - 103; 104; 107.
Koo, Wellington - 174.
Korean crisis - 5; 29; 32; 36; 37; 78ff;
  137.
Krushchev, Nikita - 3; 10; 15; 27; 42;
  45; 101; 105; 117; 143.

Lall, Arthur - 83.
Lash, Joseph - 127-128.
Laval, Pierre - 28.
League of Nations - 16; 25; 27; 28-29;
  37; 53; 71; 162.
Lebanese crisis - 17; 19; 89ff; 116; 122;
  154-155.
Lester, Sean - 37.
Lewis, Arthur (Sir) - 68.
Lie, Trygve - 5; 6; 28-29; 31; 32; 36; 79;
  137; 164; 166.
Linner, Sture - 95; 103; 107.
Lippmann, Walter - 27; 39; 49-50.
Litvinov, Maxim - 42.
Lloyd, Selwyn - 143.
Lodge, Henry Cabot - 91; 139; 143; 174.
Lumumba, Patrice - 9; 34; 73; 82; 93;
  98ff; 106; 107; 143; 162; 170.

MacFarquhar, Alexander (Sir) - 96.
Martola, I.A.E. (Gen.) - 85.
McCarthy, Joseph (Sen.) - 137; 139.
McCloy, John - 33.
McKeon, Sean (Gen.) - 104; 107-108.
Mendes-France, Pierre - 67.
Mobutu, Joseph - 9; 100ff; 106.
Mollet, Guy - 72.
Morse, David - 60; 154.
Myrdal, Alva - 173-174; 175.

Index   197

Myrdal, Gunnar - 31; 60; 68; 159; 173-174; 175.

Narasimhan, C. V. - 96.
Nasser, Gamal Abdul - 15; 86; 89; 90; 109; 155-156.
Nehru, J. - 15.
Nkrumah, Kwame - 15; 72; 94.
Noel-Baker, Philip - 28; 174.
Nwokedi, Francis - 97.

O'Brien, Conor Cruise - 103; 104; 107-108; 127-129; 162.
Organization of American States (OAS) - 120.
Organization of Petroleum Exporting Countries (OPEC) - 12.
Organization for Economic Cooperation and Development (OECD) - 65; 67.
Organization for European Economic Cooperation (OEEC) - 11; 65; 137.
Orr, John Boyd (Sir) - 60.

Paris Peace Talks (League of Nations) - 4.
Peacekeeping (U.N.) - xii; 9; 16; 53; 77ff.
Pearson, Lester - 78; 82; 142; 143.
Perse, St. John (Alexis Saint-Léger Léger) - 143; 153.
Prebisch, Raoul - 59-60; 68.

Raja, Brigadier - 107-108.
Rikhye, Indar Jit (Maj. Gen.) - 77.
Rusk, Dean - 31.

Sahbani, Tare - 97.
Sandstrom, Emil (Judge) - 153.
Saud, King - 89.
Schachter, Oscar - 39.
Scheyven, Raymond - 73.
Secretariat (U.N.) - 4; 10; 12-13; 39ff; 53ff; 69-70.
 and concepts of - 60-62; 74; 123; 126; 128; 170.
Secretary-General (U.N.)
 and functions of - 17-18; 19; 25-27; 35-37; 128; 141.
 and multilateral diplomacy - 47ff.
 and office of - xi; xii; xv; 8; 9; 10; 15; 21-22; 47; 126; 137; 156; 161; 162; 170.
 and powers of - 5; 6; 8; 10; 15.
 and troika - 3; 10; 45.
Security Council (U.N.) - 5; 6; 8; 9; 10; 12; 15; 17; 19; 20; 28; 29; 36; 43; 48; 66; 79; 80; 86; 89; 91; 94; 97; 98; 121; 124; 125; 165.
Special United Nations Fund for Economic Development (SUNFED) - 112.

Singer, Hans - 68.
Siotis, Jean - 127-128.
Soviet Union - 10; 40; 45; 72; 80; 89; 100; 105; 114; 116-117; 125; 137.
Spaak, Paul-Henri - 102.
Stalin, Joseph - 137.
Stavropoulos, Constantin - 88.
Steinbeck, John -
Steiner, Peter - vi.
Stevenson, Adlai - 33; 101; 126.
Suez crisis - 17; 82ff; 116ff; 128; 167-169.
Syria - 89ff.

Talleyrand - 28.
Tourë, Sekou - 143.
Trachtenberg, Larry - 147.
Trusteeship Council (U.N.) - 160.
Tshombe, Moise - 73; 93; 94; 98; 100ff; 107.

U Thant - 9; 12; 20; 29; 32; 108; 109.
U-2 Incident - 114.
Undén, Östen - 172-173.
United Nations Conference on Trade and Development (UNCTAD) - 71; 112.
United Nations Congo Force (ONUC) - 9; 10; 78ff; 97ff; 117; 162.
United Nations Emergency Force (UNEF) - 8; 9; 48; 8ff; 92; 97; 117; 163; 169.
United Nations Observation Group in Lebanon (UNOGIL) - 9; 82; 89ff; 154-155; 169-170.
United Nations Truce Supervision Organization (UNTSO) - 83; 95.
United States
 and cold war - 112ff; 139.
 and Congo crisis - 93ff.
 and Lebanese crisis - 90ff.
Uniting for Peace Resolution - 5; 10.
Urquhart, Brian - 79; 80; 133; 166.

Verwoerd, Hendrik - 142.
von Horn, Carl (Gen.) - 95; 97; 105.
Venizelos, Eleftherios - 27-28.

Waldheim, Kurt - xi; xii; xiii; 12; 15; 29.
Walker, Richard L. - ix; xvi.
Ward, Barbara (Lady Jackson) - 130.
Weber, Max - 54.
Webster, Charles K. - 28.
Wieschoff, Heinz - 96; 147.
Willers, Uno - 175-176.
Wilson, Woodrow - 28.
World Bank (IBRD) - 72; 75.

Zacher, Mark W. - 111.
Zaire (see Congo)